SPIRITUAL THERAPEUTICS;

OR,

DIVINE SCIENCE.

APPLIED TO

MORAL, MENTAL AND PHYSICAL HARMONY.

TWELVE LECTURES.

SPIRITUAL THERAPEUTICS;

OR,

DIVINE SCIENCE.

APPLIED TO

MORAL, MENTAL AND PHYSICAL HARMONY.

TWELVE LECTURES.

BY

W. J. COLVILLE,

Author of "The Spiritual Science of Health and Healing." Etc. Etc.

ALSO A LECTURE ON

"UNSCIENTIFIC SCIENCE"

BY

Dr. ANNA KINGSFORD

Author of "The Perfect Way," Etc. Etc.

GYAN

Published by

Gyan Publishing House
5, Ansari Road
Daryaganj, New Delhi-110002
Phone: 011-47034999, 9811692060
E-mail: books@gyanbooks.com

Distribution Network
gyanbooks.com
India, USA, Canada, UK, Australia, France

ISBN : 978-81-212-6302-3 (PB)
First Published, 1888

2nd Impression 2022

Printed at: Gyan Press, Delhi.

SPIRITUAL THERAPEUTICS; OR, DIVINE SCIENCE.
APPLIED TO MORAL, MENTAL AND PHYSICAL HARMONY.
TWELVE LECTURES.
Author: W. J. COLVILLE

SPIRITUAL THERAPEUTICS;

OR,

DIVINE SCIENCE.

APPLIED TO

MORAL, MENTAL AND PHYSICAL HARMONY.

TWELVE LECTURES.

BY

W. J. COLVILLE,

AUTHOR OF "THE SPIRITUAL SCIENCE OF HEALTH AND HEALING," ETC., ETC.

ALSO A LECTURE ON

"UNSCIENTIFIC SCIENCE"

BY

DR. ANNA KINGSFORD

AUTHOR OF "THE PERFECT WAY," ETC., ETC.

1888.

PREFACE.

THIS work is issued to meet a long-felt want for a compendious statement of the essential principles of Spiritual Science as presented in harmony with the advanced thought of the present day. No endeavor has been made to accomplish the impossible, therefore the claim is not put forward that any subject is treated finally or exhaustively. The Spiritual Science of Health and Healing, published in 1887, first in Boston and then in Chicago, has met with so large a circulation all over the world that the author has consented to pnblish this new work for the purpose of answering many questions, and more fully elucidating many problems raised in the minds of readers of Spiritual Science of Health and Healing. The original intention of this work was to put in the hands of enquirers into Spiritual Science everywhere a handy text-book, portable in form and procurable at nominal expense, designed expressly as an aid to study both in the class-room, the home circle and the private study. In addition it has been found highly desirable to append a considerable number of thoroughly authenticated cases of healing without the use of medicine or any physical contact whatsoever.

The questions and answers have been carefully selected from those asked and answered in classes and also from a great number forwarded to the author in response to public invitation through the press. The directions for treatment have received special attention, and it is confidently believed by the projectors of this volume that every man, woman and child of average intelligence, who will study this subject carefully and give it the serious attention it so richly deserves, will find him or herself able to demonstrate the truth of much, at least, of what is expounded in the following pages. With the earnest hope and fervent prayer that a perusal of these pages may be fraught with blessing to all who study them, the reader is referred to the body of the volume.

N. B.—The following synopses of twelve class lessons are intended as skeleton hints for persons desirous of pursuing a systematic course of thoughtful study in the privacy of their own homes. They are also suggested as fruitful for consideration in assemblies of inquirers, where the custom is to have something read by a president, and then talked over by the members of the fraternity or club. They will, also, perhaps, be found of some slight assistance to young teachers in preparing themselves to meet their classes.

CONTENTS.

LESSON IV.

LESSON V.

LESSON VI.

LESSON VII.

LESSON VIII.

LESSON IX.

LESSON X.

LESSON XI.

LESSON XII.

MISCELLANEOUS

TEACHINGS

UNSCIENTIFIC SCIENCE.

A FORM OF TREATMENT.

LEAVES FROM STUDENT'S NOTE BOOK.

APPENDIX.

LESSON I.

GOD—THE RELATION OF MAN TO THE INFINITE—DIFFERENCE BETWEEN REASON AND INTUITION.

SEEKERS after truth, whoever you may be, wherever you may dwell, the topic we are now about o discuss appeals vitally to every one of you. As the subject is infinite and eternal in its bearings, neither we who address you nor you who are addressed can rightfully be expected to fully comprehend the subject of this lesson; but it is not to your intellectual comprehension so much as to your spiritual perception we address ourselves. Consider first how man has grown into a belief in Deity. Whence did this belief spring? How did it originate? These are questions we must look boldly in the face. The mind of man is a mirror, a reflector, but not a creator. The thoughts of the human mind never transcend, but invariably and inevitably fall very far short of the realities of Absolute Being, therefore, all human errors are limitations of truth, negations of fact, but never in a solitary instance has an erroneous human opinion been found to transcend reality. Man perceives God, *i. e.*, he realizes intuitively his relation to an Infinite Power, Energy or Force which permeates the Universe, and is the Life of the Universe. This Infinite Life we call God, which is an Anglo-Saxon word meaning All Good, or the Good One.

Agnostics admit the eternity and infinity of Power Energy or Force, but they pronounce its nature and attributes unknowable, and perhaps to the unassisted intellect they are so. We do not disparage or trample upon human reason in any sense when we proclaim the infinite superiority of intuitive perception of truth no intellectual realization of external facts. Intuition is super-rational, but never does it urge upon us the acceptance of anything irrational or sub-rational. Reason infers, intuition proves the being of God, thus we have two witnesses instead of one, ready to testify to the reality of the Divine Being. We wish you at once, before we proceed any further in this lesson, to notice how studiously we avoid speaking of the divine *existence*, which we consider a word misapplied whenever used in connection with the Infinite. Being alone is eternal, existence is temporal. God *is*, the external universe *exists*. God is the source of all being, is indeed Being itself, consequently cannot be limited or personified. God then is super-personal Spirit, not impersonal but super-personal. Impersonal means less than personal, while super-personal means superior to personality. There are three words we shall often introduce into these lessons:

1st. Identity.

2d. Individuality.

3d. Personality.

These refer respectively to Spirit, to Mind and to Matter, which constitute the three-fold expression of the absolute Life. The circle has always been chosen as the symbol of infinity and eternity, but any circle we can describe is finite, and therefore resembles man who is in the image of God, but cannot resemble God in so far as it has limitations, for God is necessarily limitless. You have all heard often enough of macrocosm and the microcosm, the former, you know, means the infinite whole, the latter signifies the finite likeness of the whole. God is the macrocosm. Man is the microcosm. The difference, then, between God and Man is quantitative and not qualitative. What God is, that is Man, for Man is in the image and likeness of the Eternal One. The best instructed minds in spiritual truth are by no means invariably such as have profited most by the methods of scholasticism, for scholarship is purely intellectual, while spiritual discernment is altogether independent of the bookworm and pertains entirely to the culture of the psychic faculty. There is in man a psychic element which defies external investigation, and baffles intellectual research, because it invariably transcends the reason, which it, however, never contradicts. Our first lesson, of necessity, brings us to a point where we are under the necessity of discriminating between reason and intuition, as intuition only can unlock the door of the inner temple of our being which remains forever barred against the persistent knocking of any lower power. God is *known* only to intuition. Reason is a faculty whereby mankind is able to decide with reference to all questions which can be submitted to the human mind for judgment. It is a purely intellectual and analytical faculty, the possession of which enables one to rise to the loftiest heights of purely mental glory, but reason is soulless. We do not say it is in opposition to man's highest spiritual nature. It simply fails to apprehend it.

It is agnostic in its attitude toward all purely spiritual revelation or discovery. It can, of course, be employed to prove the reality of spirit and the good of the affections, but it can also be used to deny the very being of Deity and can argue against as readily as for the immortality of man. Reason is unable to cope with spiritual truth; it can neither prove nor disprove what intuition affirms. Intuition is perception. It is a purely spiritual faculty, and is no more intended to change places with reason than eyes are to do duty in the stead of ears. Reason looks to the earth; it is a naturalist, a geologist, by natural bent, while intuition looks to the heavens and discovers stars while reason delves amid fossils. We do not for a single instant decry reason, nor would we underrate its power for good in the world, but, like all the physical faculties possessed by man, it is a two edged sword. It can be used either for good or evil. It will defend right or wrong as the case may be. In the hands of a criminal lawyer the closest reasoning, severest logic is often used to justify the wrong doer and thereby to defeat justice and defraud the innocent. The greatest reasoners are by no means always the greatest saints neither are they proverbially the greatest sinners, but we fail to see where unaided reason contributes much to the highest welfare or greatest happiness of the race. The steam engine, the telephone, various electrical appliances, the deadliest weapons of warfare, the cruelest devices for torturing men and criminals, are all alike products of human reason, it depends upon the use to which secular information is put as to whether or no it really benefits mankind in the sense of moral elevation.

We cannot be too rational, too inventive, or too analytical, provided always we are first moral and spiritual. Intuition, as we understand it, signifies clear moral perception, genuine spiritual discernment. Intuition is always loving, kind and just. It is divine reason, and therefore lies beyond the realm in which what is ordinarily known as reason finds its field of operation. Intuition is certain and infallible. It deals with spiritual truth by exact methods just as the multiplication table deals with figures—twice 2 must always be 4. We can arrive at certitude in numeration, Mathematical demonstrations are absolute. Are there then no means of arriving at exact spiritual truth? We believe there is a royal way through the gateway of spiritual perception, which discerns spiritual realities with demonstrable exactitude. The question is continually asked us, How do you stand with regard to the matter of education? Do you consider a person need be literary in order to excel as a spiritual healer? We always reply in the decided negative, for many of the best healers we have ever met were, from a scholastic point of view, the most illiterate.

Let us see if we cannot decide why this is so. All information is of some value to its possessor. We can, none of us, know too much, but Pope, perhaps, was right, when he sang, "A little learning is a dangerous thing," but wherein consists the danger, probably the poet would have answered in the language of the great philosopher, Francis Bacon, "A little learning inclineth man to atheism." But why should it? What is there in learning, any way, to shake man's faith in God? Does not everything testify to the being of an Infinite

Intelligence? Is not the argument for design unanswerable. Verily, still the mind, when first steeped in the pleasure of intellectual acquisition, becomes so infatuated and intoxicated with the charms of outer things, and withal so vain of its petty achievements that a frame or mood is too often excited, which correctly expresses itself in the dominant conviction, "what I don't know, is not worth knowing." If there are any such mental states in the way of your accepting a new truth, new to you, though to others old as the universe, you must be converted and become as little children in all teachableness of disposition, before you can possibly perceive the truth of Spirit. Blessed are the clean or pure of heart, for they shall see God, is no idle dreamer's romance.

Purity of affection, cleanliness of desire, is as necessary to enable one to arrive at spiritual knowledge as ever eyes can be to see with or windows in houses to admit the light of day. Strive to forget at the threshold of these instructions that you know anything; let every proposition come before you with the charm and weight of novelty; give your memory a rest and come prepared to fully consider in all candor and sincerity whatever may be advanced. In this temper alone can you be prepared to give, to what may seem to you as a new science, the attention it deserves and rightfully demands at the hands of intelligent lovers of and seekers after truth. Let us for a moment try to discriminate carefully and clearly between memory and consciousness. Memory is invariably treacherous at best, in our present stage of development, while consciousness is persistently, invariably the same. I am at this instant conscious that I am. That I am what? This question I may be unable to answer satisfactorily even to myself; I may have to fall back upon words attributed by Bible writers to Jehovah, "I am that I am." What I am I may not realize. I know that I am, *i. e.*, I am conscious of having being and I feel moreover that however nearly I may be connected or however intimately associated with others, I am not another and another is not I. What, then, am I who am not another? and what, then, is another who is not I? The mystery of individual identity is displayed and illustrated in all nature from the greatest to the smallest. The identity of the unit is most sacredly preserved. This is never sacrificed to the mass.

Absorption into the Deity is a foolish expression. Many persons in their struggles to modernize and occidentalize oriental writings, have labored hard in the course of fatiguing disquisitions concerning *Nirvana* to persuade the world that the extinction of individual consciousness is the blissful summit of human attainment. Such, however, is not the highest Eastern thought. Edwin Arnold, at the conclusion of his *Light of Asia*, takes far nobler ground than this, and in his *India Revisited* he tells us of the grateful thanks and cordial welcomes he received from Buddhist priests, both in Hindoostan and Ceylon, as tribute to the faithfulness with which he had portrayed the tenets of Buddhism in his story of the "great renunciation." We allude to this, not because we turn to Asia for that spiritual light which can come only from within, but to show how misleading it is for any one to think that all of truth is concentrated in a single system of religion. Universal Theosophy or Spiritual Science is the friend of Truth wherever found, but its main object is to call it out from within the depths of every individual. A knowledge or perception of the logos, divine word, or essential Christ, which is indeed the Way, the Truth and the Life, is the Universal Enlightener and the only absolute source of divine guidance for the individual.

LESSON II.

THE HUMAN MIND; ITS ORIGIN AND DESTINY—AT WHAT PERIOD DID IT BEGIN IN TIME?—WHAT ROOM DOES IT OCCUPY IN SPACE?—IS IT SUBSTANCE OR FORCE?—IS IT A CAUSE OR AN EFFECT?—WHAT SPECIFICALLY IS ITS SHAPE, SIZE AND SUBSTANCE?—UPON WHAT PRINCIPLES OR BY WHAT PROPERTIES CAN IT RESIST DESTRUCTION? (A SUBJECT GIVEN TO MRS. CORA L. V. RICHMOND BY A PHILOSOPHICAL SOCIETY IN CHICAGO, AND TREATED UPON BY THE AUTHOR OF THIS VOLUME BY PARTICULAR REQUEST.)

SUCH a subject as this can only be satisfactorily dealt with in a series of discourses, there is so much included in these questions concerning the mind of man. The question in such a form as it here assumes would never be asked by enlightened Theosophists acquainted with the spiritual side of man's nature, but is constantly propounded by realistic philosophers, who maintain that everything must be material in order to be real; must have size and shape, gravity and ponderability evident to external sense in order to be in the realm of real existence.

Now the human mind must be conceived of as distinct from the human soul. Therefore, as our present subject is the human mind we shall deal only with mind as we understand it, leaving the question of the divine soul—which is beyond the mind—which is considered in our first lesson, or only touching upon it when necessary to explain the nature of mind as derived from the soul.

Now Mind Cure is a popular term, but spiritual healing is a far more appropriate one and covers a great deal more ground than mental healing, because the spirit is superior to the mind, even as intuition or moral perception is superior to the intellectual We may be intellectual, rational, very learned; we may be paragons of perfection in an intellectual sense, through acquaintance with arts, physical sciences and philosophy and yet be miserably devoid of soul culture, and if devoid of soul culture, if the divine breath is not made manifest in us, if we are not unfolded on the spiritual side of our nature, all our intellectual development will not avail to save us from sickness and suffering.

The mind of man must be subordinate to the divine soul. Intellectual progress must be made subordinate to spiritual culture. Reason must be subordinated to conscience or the moral sense. If nothing higher than the mind of man be recognized, if nothing beyond intellect or reason be cultivated, a man, though a prodigy of valor, or an encyclopedia of information, concerning worldly knowledge, will lack the only wisdom that can guide him safely over the tempestuous waters of earthly discipline.

The human mind, its origin and destiny, must signify the origin and destiny of a servant of the soul. There is a power within you beyond the mind, which causes you to often build wiser than you know. You declare that your mind changes, and it does. Your mind is only the accumulated mass of your thoughts. All your thoughts together constitute your mental state; but the thinking principle, the power that gives you your mind (the mind being only an organ or perhaps only a function of the spirit) is the spirit (*atma*).

The individual mind of man originates in the soul of man. We will express our idea in this wise: The soul of man we regard as the ultimate spiritual atom, the essential primary. Those of you who are familiar with scientific analyses and with the terms used by the schools, know well that a distinction is made in the scientific world, and that a very broad one, between the atom or primal, the monad and the molecule. The atom or primal it is inferred is self existent, and being self existent it was of course never created and can, therefore, never be destroyed. The molocule or monad is only an expression of life, a manifestation; therefore scientific inference, granting that substance is eternal (as science invariably declares), concludes that an atom always has existed and always will.

There may have been periods when the molecule or monad was not. Molecules or monads having come into existence during time and being results of the movements of atoms, may pass away in time, but the atoms themselves, whose movements have made the existence of molecules or monads possible, can never pass away.

It strikes us as extremely singular that learned bodies of men, such as the Presbyterian assembly, for example, should ever have fallen into the error of supposing that, according to a true rendering of Genesis, the human body must have been created by a direct act of God's sovereignty out of nothing. Such a ridiculous hypothesis is equivalent to saying God is nothing; because, according to Gensis, everything is the result of God's activity. The spirit of God is said to have moved upon the waters, moved through the vast expanse filled by what is called—for want of a better term—chaos, without form and void, and this directing intelligence organized the original cosmic fluid into organic forms. Such a definition of creation is certainly not to the effect that anything was made out of nothing, but that everything was made from and by the action of the spirit of God.

The spirit of God is not "nothing," but according to the Rosicrucian definition, it may be spoken of as No Thing, which signifies the Eternal and Infinite cause of everything. The spirit of God, the divine life, is the one Eternal, Primordial Being which defies all analysis and cannot be discovered by any mortal method of research, because it is altogether impalpable, immaterial and wholly spiritual, and if apprehended at all, must be apprehended by the soul which is in the image and likeness of Eternal Spirit.

Now this theory gives you a logical basis for existence. Out of nothing, nothing comes, but every manifested thing proceeds from something greater than itself. Every effect proceeds necessarily from a cause adequate to produce it. The cause may be greater than the effect, but cannot possibly be less than the effect. As a cause must be equal to or greater than the effect which it produces, and as "nothing" is an unmeaning term, for you can have no idea of "nothing" in your mind (an idea being something), it is absurd to infer that anything was ever made out of nothing, it is also a *reductio ad absurdum* of sciolistic ignorance that mind is a creature of matter, because mind is demonstrably the rightful lord over matter.

If every thing proceeds from what is infinitely greater than itself — every manifestation of life being only an expression of the intelligence of All Pervading Deity — if the life of the entire universe, primordially and elementally is God's life, then we can understand that there is no creation other than organization, and no destruction other than disintegra tion. There can be no annihilation, for annihilation means the destruction of being, but there can be disorganization. Spiritualists affirm that in materializing circles forms are built up, apparontly, out of invisible atmosphere; that they stand palpably in the presence of the sitters for a while and then vanish from sight. The New Testament declares that Jesus after His crucifixion appeared to His disciples, manifesting to them in palpable form, and then vanished out of their sight. Chemistry declares that all substances can be volatilized, *i. e.*, converted into impalpable ether; solids and fluids change into gases; the hardest substances float away into invisible and intangible realms.

The researches and knowledge of the scientific world abundantly prove that the realm of potentiality is a realm of invisibility. Electricity, that wondrous motor power now coming into universal use, is strictly invisible; the wind which as it blows manifests such terrible and mighty force in tornado or hurricane is invisible; the steam that propels gigantic vessels across the ocean is invisible, and so with all the forces of which man knows anything. According to scientific statements there are many millions of sounds and colors that are neither heard nor seen, because the vibrations which cause them and which indeed, they are, make no impression upon your optic or auditory nerves. Now as the great and mysterious realm of causation, which materialists admit is superior to gross matter, is absolutely unknown to external sense; when we declare life to be invisible, the immortal soul to be real though invisible we simply conclude that everthing logically that everything destined to outlive the mortal body is invisible and spiritual we accord with science. The fleshly body is only an aggregation of molecules, which are ever being displaced to make room for others. Attraction and repulsion change outward forms incessantly. While consciousness abides, we can reasonably declare that the immortality of the soul, yea, and the pre-existence of the soul also is an inference of science.

Epes Sargent, one of the most eloquent and scientific writers upon modern spiritualism, in his work entitled, "The Scientific Basis of Spiritualism," proves conclusively by the soundest argument and clearest logic that immortality is inferred by physical as well as mental science.

Rev. M. J. Savage, a popular Unitarian minister of Boston, has taken the ground that immortality may be conjectured from analogical evidences supplied by nature. Many lights in the Unitarian church, and in other liberal denominations, many luminaries in the scientific world, and many philosophers outside all creeds and denominations take a similar position. The question of questions to-day is, "Are we matter or spirit?"

Now, the primal source of being must be unitary. There can not be two Eternals, two Infinites, two Almighties, and we maintain that the fact of the human mind being totally invisible to sense, and the fact of the soul being entirely beyond the reach of the scalpel or dissecting knife (neither vivisection nor any other cruel practice invented by the barbarism of materialism to account for the origin of life having discovered its source in anywise), the fact that soul and mind can not be materially discovered furnishes abundant proof that all that is real abides forever in the realm of the All Powerful, which is Spirit. Our senses never apprehend one hundredth part of what our souls recognize, this experience alone sufficiently demonstrates to the unprejudiced thinker that the invisible realm of intelligence is the seat of causation.

In art everything is conceived by the painter mentally before there can be any outward expression. The inventor has his model and machine in working order in his mind before he can take the first step toward preparing a model for public exhibition or setting any one at work to construct the external body of his invention.

You may pronounce transcendentalism folly, you may demand something practical, but you could never have any practical object or external knowledge unless some one had first beheld a design in mind. Even in the matter of dress the fashion plate is the result of some new thought in some one's mind; before there can be any outward garment made it must be planned in mind. So with every material comfort, with every external thing you enjoy, mind first operates and matter proves its servant.

As mind first produces plans and models and sets hands to work afterward constructing apparatus to apply motor power externally, it is invariably the case that the nearer you approach the realm of absolute mentality, the more wonderful are discoveries, the mightier and more matchless the exhibitions of man's consummate skill. This is instanced by the fact of no outward effort, however superb, fully satisfying the designer.

The mind of man is the handiwork of the soul, which is an embodiment of the divine creative energy displayed in universal nature. Materialists or Atheists looking no further than man, often declare that while they find no God in the universe to worship, they are willing to worship great men. So great, so marvelous are the achievements of the human mind guided by the soul that infidelity may almost be excused for putting man upon the throne of the universe and worshiping man, who is in the image of God, as God. In every school that disallows the existence of an Infinite Divine Spirit as the cause of the universe we behold, man is made to take the place of God (*vide* the school of Auguste Comté). At this we do not wonder, as the highest manifestation of God is through the divine in man. We do not wonder that glorious intellects are bowed down to, or that human reason is deified; but we must not forget that at the close of the last century, when churches were closed and religious worship proscribed, when all religious teaching was under the ban of popular anathema, and reason was set up publicly as a goddess, men were shot down and stabbed in the streets of Paris and elsewhere, and this was because reason alone, intellect, apart from spirituality, is not capable of saving or redeeming a nation. No one is capable of governing wisely and well unless his reason is married to intuition. Conscience, the moral sense, the divine affection of the spirit, must be the dominating force, or an age of reason is an age without heart.

Do not think for a moment that we underrate the power of reason, or that we decry the glorious human intellect, or that we undervalue the advantages of mental training in colleges and seminaries. But history certainly proves that Greece and Rome fell in spite of their intellect and their wonderfully beautiful art, and they fell solely because the people lacked spirituality. Phœnicia, Babylonia, and many another land once bright and glorious, but now desolate heaps of ruin, fell into decay because reason, esoterically speaking — man without woman, intellect without soul, brain without conscience — held sway and was idolized. All deep thinkers agree that in the present generation if there be no recognition found for something beyond human reason, if nothing above intellect is acknowledged, men will become cultured tyrants.

Mind of man, thou art no ruler save of the physical body. Reason of man, thou art not the supreme interpreter of Deity, still thou hast a mission appointed thee to govern the senses. Mind of man, wonderful intellect, glorious reason, thou art a captain appointed over all the bodily functions and carnal appetites and thou must reign supreme over these; but thou hast a Commander, a General, a higher Officer of the army in which thou art stationed, whom thou must acknowledge as thy Ruler, for with all thy vaunted strength and boasted superiority, thou art the servant of a loftier power, even the power of the soul divine which is the source even of thy existence.

It is the power of soul, of religion pure and undefiled, of genuine spirituality, of the divine life in man that can alone save and uplift a nation or an individual.

We care not how distinguished may be halls of learning, how great the dignity of professors of art and literature, or how profound the teachings of the schools, if there be lacking the power of the living spirit, beyond the finite reason, man will not and cannot be perfected, neither can the earth complete the cycle of its changes and arrive at the golden age so long foretold when sickness, sin and sorrow will be utterly unknown.

The mind of man is not the supreme or primal cause; it is a secondary cause, beyond which we trace the divine soul which is the primal or ultimate atom of life, related to eternity, the one absolute individuality which is your real self and with which you can never part, no matter what lies before you in the way of experience, either in this or any other world. The soul of man has made itself known to the intellect in some measure, but is quite beyond the perception of bodily sense. Scientists are ever searching for the atom which their microscopes have ever failed to find. Intellect, however, is already somewhat conscious of spiritual existence. It dimly apprehends spiritual entities which are immortal, even souls which can never cease to be, for they never began to be.

The question is often asked, "Were souls always individual? Did man always know himself as an individual spark of divine life?" This question is unanswerable unless we deal with it problematically; as one of the profoundest questions ever submitted to the intelligence of man, philosophy has often answered it in this manner, *i. e.* through processes of deduction.

According to the Greek philosophers the soul is eternal. But though the soul has always existed, it may not always have reflected upon its existence as we now reflect. It may have existed as a seed exists before it is sown. It contains, within itself, unexpressed, all the potentialities of manifested life. What is earthly discipline but the evolution of the mind's reasoning, intellectual and reflective powers? The soul produces a material form in the act of unfolding the attributes always within it.

Agriculturists know that it is impossible to really create anything, still by planting a certain kind of seed, a certain unfoldment will follow. The germ of a rose will never produce a geranium. Every potentiality or possibility of fruition must inhere in the planted seed, for what is not within, can not be produced by any outward effort. So with our earthly discipline. We see what growth can do for the seed and how that can be made manifest which is already contained in the primal germ.

Here we take decided issue with materialists, and challenge all who declare that mind is the product of matter, and human intelligence the result of physical organization. But another view of the statement shows us that if mind is the result of physical organization the declaration is proved true that all is mind and there is no matter. If materialism is logical it is only logical on the basis of the most extreme metaphysics, which declare that everything is mind and therefore there is no matter; if so called matter evidences mind, it is not matter but mind in another phase of existence.

Now we all know that we can not apprehend anything except by the use of our mental faculties. You talk about seeing with the eye; but let an eye be taken out of your head, will the eye see anything? After the spirit has left the body, what can eyes behold? They see nothing, for they are only mediums of communication between two objects both of which exist in mind. If there were no intelligence behind the eye looking through it, or no intelligence beyond the brain, or no connection between that intelligence and the brain, or no connection between the brain and the retina of the eye, or between the retina of the eye and something external to the eye, could there be any perception through an organ of vision? But, you argue, "we cannot see without eyes." We beg to differ from you, for we have known many persons physically blind who have seen clearly without bodily eyes; such we appropriately call clairaudients, meaning persons who see with unusual clearness. If you refer to the experiments of Mesmer and others upon the subject of clairvoyance and clairaudience, and also pay heed to what is constantly transpiring at the present time, you will find there are many people who see without a bodily eye, and clairvoyance does not enable persons to come in contact with ideas exclusively, but it also enables them to describe distinctly the color, form and texture of material objects; and clairaudients when physically deaf or with their ears completely stopped up, can hear sounds both near at hand and far away when there can be no action upon the physical ear, they will often describe sounds perfectly which are occurring in very distant places and that with perfect accuracy.

Psychometric experiments prove conclusively that an object placed in the hand, or for that matter upon the back of the neck of a blindfolded person, can be accurately described as to its texture, color, form, dimensions and everything else you term material. There is evidence in the scientific world, among many who have not investigated spiritualism, but who have investigated clairvoyance and clairaudience, and have encountered persons gifted with psychometric power, that people constantly hear independently of bodily ears, taste without material palates, smell independent of nostrils, and detect a difference between velvet and stone, without coming into any physical contact with either the velvet or the stone. If you investigate psychometry you can abundantly prove that there is in man a (power that works independently) "soul-measuring" of his material body, a power that far transcends it and proves that the spiritual or psychic body is not an unreality, a mere phantasm, but far more real than the fleshly body of man. We declare that the real body of man is spiritual, man's whole nature is spiritual. But when we endeavor to apply the principle of metaphysics to healing mental and bodily infirmities we do not adopt the phraseology of those teachers who say you can see as well without an eye as with one. We prefer to say you can see perfectly with your spiritual eye if you have no bodily eye, you can hear perfectly with your spiritual ear if you have no physical ear; therefore if you lose your physical sight or your whole material body, remember you have a spiritual body, or you may call it, if you chose, an astral body, which is a body that has form, size and dimensions, and which exists in the realm of mind, and is the cause of your material body, and being its predecessor, outlasts it.

If size appears in outward expression, there is prior size in invisible realms. If there are external dimensions there are dimensions in the realm of their causation, which is the realm of mind. If there are colors in outward expression there are colors in spirit. Shut your eyes and you can think of colors and sounds. Anything you can think about has an existence in the realm of thought. If it did not exist in the realm of thought you could not think about it. As everything produced in the material world is the result of thought, mind must necessarily be the power that produces it. That which you term matter is only a result of vibrations in lower octaves of the vibrations which cause what Swedenborg terms spiritual substance.

If the soul of man had not an eternal past, it cannot have an eternal future. But if, as we affirm, the soul has always existed in the bosom of the Infinite, if the soul has always been an individual atom in the eternal life, your immortal individuality is secure. Your reflection upon your individuality may have been brought about in time; in time you may have made discoveries, through your intellect, of something you always perceived in your soul. When the figurative books shall be opened and the soul fully testifies of itself, then will the great mystery of dual consciousness be explained; then will you understand how you are fully conscious in spirit when quite unconscious of outward things; then will your dream life no longer remain to you a mystery; then will all spiritual experiences glow with the light of complete interpretation, and you will be all aflame with a knowledge of your relation to the Eternal. You will then no more bow down before idols of material belief than you would pray to the images of wood and stone worshiped by poor Pagans who know not of life in spirit.

Materialism says life springs from protoplasm. If everything comes from protoplasm, if it be primal, then it is spiritual, but if protoplasm is only another word for spirit, it is improper to employ it because it is misleading. Is it not affirmed in the scientific world that the discovery has been made by Darwin, Spencer and others of a primordial cell from which all life arises, and that this cell is the same for the monad as for man, the same for the jelly fish or the tadpole as for the philosopher? If this be true, we simply exclaim that this primordial cell, representing the absolute primary in the material world, is the primal manifestation of intelligence in the realm of effect. All that Darwin or any evolutionist can accomplish is to trace effects to their seeming cause, from the circumference inward toward the center. Involution starts at the center. The soul is the center. Protoplasm is toward the circumference. Materialism starts near the circumference and endeavors to find the soul in dust. When you have found the soul you will comprehend protoplasm, which is a product, a creation by the soul. When you only know protoplasm you can know nothing of the soul, and thus you endeavor to argue that unconscious dust has evolved spirit, that material atoms have evolved intelligence, and that consequently, on the breaking up of the physical organism, the intelligence vanishes, as brightness from a polished shield when dampness approaches it. It goes nowhere, you say, whereas, from the standpoint of spirit, there is found an adequate and satisfactory solution for every material phenomena, while from the standpoint of materialism consciousness is an utterly miraculous phenomenon.

In the realm of spirit the soul is the acknowledged creator of its expressions. The source and center of all is the divine life. In the divine life there is perfect rest, for it is absolute being. Divine life is the only center of the wheel of life. All revolutions are around that center, and no matter how rapidly the wheel may rotate, the center is always calm. From the inmost center, which is the divine cause, to the outermost effect, or circumference of the wheel, life is made manifest through the descent of spirit (involution) and the ascent of matter (evolution).

We believe in the gradual development of species, in the ascent of the body of man; but this is a result of the descent of spirit. When spiritual descent and material ascent are understood by being studied together; when spiritually minded professors of involution enlighten professors of evolution, light from the realm of causation—which is spiritual—will make comprehensible the realm of effect, which is termed material. Then instead of supposing that you are mere creatures of dust, or that a handful of dust has evolved an immortal soul; instead of dreaming that matter has been refining itself age after age until from unconscious dust a conscious soul has been at length produced; instead of imagining that everlasting life may be the result of an evolution from unconscious molecules, you will understand that from eternal life, wherein ever exists the soul, has every outward expression proceeded. Man, then, instead of claiming relationship to dust will claim relationship to Deity.

It is manifestly absurd to argue that effects are greater than causes, and works greater than their maker. If you are superior to every other form of life on the planet then your soul may have been a world builder, as in ages gone by the triumphant souls called in the Hebrew Scriptures "*Elohim*," the angels who shouted for joy at the completion of the external world, may have lived on earths long since depopulated and outgrown. Those angels must have been souls who had for ages been ascending the ladder of progress, who, from their glorious homes in spirit, may have caused their thoughts to have assumed form upon earth, creation may have therefore been—as one of the Hebrew accounts declares—the work of the "*Elohim.*"

The soul is the creator of all material things. In spiritual life you may change your spiritual bodies as you change your material forms on earth; you will graduate to higher and ever higher forms of expression; you will accrete to you thought essences from the spiritual atmosphere, and finally, expression in all its outward forms having been fulfilled, the soul will know itself as conqueror over all.

A period will arrive when you will be able to produce any form you please; when upon the wings of thought you will pass from planet to planet as easily as birds navigate the air or fish swim in water. As rapidly as your thought can move from one country to another, and from one star to another, does your soul pass from point to point in the boundless universe.

When your eyes are opened to the sublimities of eternity there will appear to you no longer any vacuum or void, no interstellar spaces in the universe. Where now you imagine there is no life, you will find orders upon orders of intelligences, homes and habitations of spirit, all the universe being filled with thought and its expressions. Then when you have attained to the glorious states which hold sway over all planetary bodies, you will know the material center of gravity on any earth is but the outermost expression of angelic thought, what you now term most real is only the fleeting shadow—the world of outward sense being phantasmagoric, while the world of soul is alone real and eternal.

Spencer says the origin of life is unknowable, and therefore he would not dare to call it material. Matthew Arnold speaks of an eternal energy; the greatest astronomers, geologists and chemists that have ever lived have bowed reverently before the Divine Over soul and have acknowledged matter as only an expression of infinite intelligence.

Behind all phenomena is God. Man can never be educated out of his intuitive belief in spirit. When you are prepared for the teachings angels are ready to give, when minds on earth are prepared to receive such instructions, you will listen to glowing words of truth vibrating from celestial homes through this earth's atmosphere, filling your minds with truth eternal, giving you perfect knowledge of spirit. Spiritual involution will completely account for earthly evolution. Darwin may yet descend from the realm of spirit to write another "Origin of Species" in which you will find stated the descent of spirit as the all sufficient cause of the ascent of life through material form.

LESSON III.

THE DIVINITY OF CHRIST, THE ONLY BEGOTTEN SON OF GOD—THE ESSENTIAL AND THE HISTORICAL CHRIST CONTRASTED.

IF OUR conceptions of the Christ do not harmonize with the theological opinions of any persons who peruse this volume, they will please to remember that we do not consider the holding of our views upon the divinity of Christ as necessary to anyone's salvation, and therefore if you entertain views different from ours, according to the spiritual philosophy we are endeavoring to inculcate, you stand as good a chance of salvation, both in this world and in that which is to come, as though your views were precisely the same as ours. Now, belief rests upon evidence; no intelligent person can believe anything without sufficient evidence. If you believe in the presence of any material object it is because you rely upon the evidence of your bodily senses; and before you believe in the truth of any doctrine, it must be submitted to your intellect for consideration. Spiritual truth appeals to your conscience or moral sense and thus summons as its witness the divinest element of your being. When conclusions are arrived at by any speaker, writer, philosopher, or school of thought which are at variance with truth as it appeals to your individual mind, you are not only not bound to agree with such teaching, but you are bound in duty, reason, and justice to disagree; we may, however, agree to disagree, or, more properly, to differ. Now, we regard all phases of human thought and feeling as natural expressions of human intelligence, and as doctrines concerning Deity, the divinity of Christ, the personality of the Holy Spirit, trinity in unity and unity in trinity, besides other kindred theological themes, too numerous to mention, may be justly catalogued among the most difficult problems which can be presented to the human mind for solution, the wonder is rather that there are comparatively so few differences in the world, than that there are so many; the wonder is that there are so few sects in Christendom rather than that there are so many; for though there are perhaps three hundred distinct Christian sects, the majority of the sects are, broadly speaking, orthodox, as they agree to accept the divinity of Jesus, and the Trinity or tri-personality of God, even though all contend also for the divine unity.

Universalists, and particularly Unitarians, have departed from the orthodox standard of Christendom by positively affirming that Jesus, though possibly superior to all other men, was still only a man, and though the son of God, in the sense of being peculiarly divine through the nobility and purity of his nature, is not God the Son. If you are acquainted with church history you are well aware that Servetus was put to death at the instigation of Calvin, because he would not acknowledge the incarnation of God in Jesus and persisted that Jesus was only the son of God while Calvin insisted that Jesus was God the Son; when preparation was complete for the burning of that noble martyr, Calvin stood ready to doom his soul and body to everlasting flames because of this difference in theological opinion. The friends who gathered around Servetus urged him to confess that Jesus was God the Son, but he consistently prayed, "Jesus, thou son of the living God, have mercy upon me." That prayer. he knew, would not suffice, to save him from a terrible martyrdom; he must say "Jesus, thou Son of the living God," no longer, but "Jesus, the living God," or there could be no salvation for him, either in this world or any other. He expired refusing to comply, and thus allowed himself to be offered as a holocaust to theological intolerance.

Now, as the doctrine of the absolute deity of Jesus is entirely distinct from the simple doctrine of his divinity, many people declare their belief in the divinity of mankind, in the divinity of natural law, and yet do not mean that they believe in the deity of man or of natural law; the word divine does not necessarily mean deific, "deific," being a very much higher word in theological parlance than "divine." The divine soul in man is shared by all humanity, almost all philosophers believe in a divine human soul. Esoteric Buddhists call it *Atma*, and designate it the seventh principle. The divine soul is superior to the spiritual soul, and again the human soul is superior to the animal soul, in Buddhistic theosophy. In the first chapter of the fourth Gospel, we are introduced to a learned dissertation upon the *Logos* or divine Word; the Gnostics of the early Christian Church declared the Logos to be the indwelling word, revealing the will or law of God in every human heart. Now it is quite possible to interpret the divine sonship of Jesus in such a light as to include the divine sonship of all humanity. And while departing from the ordinary theological standards and rejecting the canons of interpretation which are regarded as alone sound in the orthodox Christian world, we may profitably interpret the Gospel of John as a spiritual disquisition concerning the spiritual nature of the universe and man, rather than as a historical narrative. Let us remove this subject entirely out of that petty, arbitrary and quarrelsome realm, to which, unfortunately, it is so often degraded, and from the noble height of spiritual contemplation see Jesus standing before us not as a mythical personage, or a solar myth, nor as a man mysteriously endowed with a nature foreign to that of all other human beings, but as one who has run the race which we are now engaged in running, won the prize for which we are now fighting, already wearing the crown which shall forever rest upon the brow of each of you when you have accomplished your spiritual warfare as he long ago accomplished his.

Jesus in history represents whoever has overcome the world; he says to his disciples, "Be of good cheer, I have overcome the world." If he has overcome the world you also will overcome, because he has overcome it; because he lives you will live also; because he has entered into the heavens you will also enter into them; because he has ascended to his Father, who is also your Father, therefore you will also ascend.

Thus in the true light in which the New Testament story presents Jesus to mankind, he does not stand to us in the relation of an incarnate deity, a super angelic personage, or one belonging to a divine order of beings altogether separated from humanity, but he appears simply in the light of one who has graduated with the highest honors from the school of earthly discipline, one who has learned every lesson that can be learned on this planet, one who has completed the circle of embodiments on this orb, one who has passed beyond the need of further discipline, and has therefore entered that realm of absolute spiritual being which is the true home of every soul.

Now, many say, is it not strange that out of the records of past history you should be able to gather sufficient materials for an ideal character? Is not our ideal in the future rather than in the past? Is not the glorious Eden-time in advance instead of in the rear? Is it not true that to-morrow will surpass to-day in spiritual advancement? Is not to-day in advance of yesterday? In affirming that one who lived 1,800 or 1,900 years ago had already attained to spiritual perfection, are you not denying evolution, which demonstrates an incessant improvement of species and progress of mankind?

We answer, we are not denying advancement in any sense; but the progress of universal mankind has certainly been indicated or outlined by the special attainments of exceptional Messiahs or Avatars who have blessed the world in ancient days, souls who have periodically visited like spiritual comets different nations of earth, wandering like spiritual stars over the spiritual firmament of many climes, in many ages, prophesying of universal human attainment.

Occasionally upon the tree of human life a fruit has

appeared fully ripened; that thoroughly ripened specimen has been gathered into the celestial kingdom; the remainder of the fruit is yet green. Here and there in life's harvest field a golden sheaf has fully ripened, and that sheaf has been gathered in. These ripened sheaves are first fruits, which have already been waved in the temple as an earnest of the abundant harvests which are to follow.

Jesus attained to perfection; he expired physically upon the cross with the words upon his lips, "It is finished;" and you realize that the majority of human beings pass away with the thought in their minds, "my work is unfinished," they feeling almost invariably that there is much work for them still to do, and if they could only live their life over they could improve that life in every respect. A great deal of the fear of death, of reluctance or unwillingness to take the step into the unseen state is occasioned by a feeling that earthly tasks are not finished, duties appear unfulfilled, conquests yet need to be won, many talents have not been utilized. In contrast to all this, can you not imagine something of the glory of a soul that can pass from earth exclaiming, "My work is finished?" Not finished for eternity, but finished for time; not finished with regard to all the blazing worlds in space, but finished with regard to this planet; not finished in regard to my total spiritual mission, which will occupy me throughout eternity, but perfectly finished with regard to this planet. Jesus is reported to have said, "For a certain cause came I into the world." He declared he could not leave the world until this work was done. He stands before us all in history as a perfect representation of human perfection,

You who have studied "The Light of Asia" as interpreted to Englishspeaking readers by Edwin Arnold in his charming poem bearing this title, or "the Great Renunciation," will remember that Buddha attained to Nirvana, or the state of absolute spiritual blessedness (perfect oneness with Deity) before he quitted the material form. This leads us to ask, Is it not possible in this earthly school that once in a while a scholar should graduate with highest possible honors? That once in a while we should behold a foregleam of the utmost possibilities of humanity? Is it not possible that here and there some great and regal spirit should appear before you and willingly take upon himself all material discipline in order that humanity may be uplifted, and then discover at last that there is no vicarious atonement in the orthodox sense of the term, but that every one who willingly lays down his life for another's good lays it down for himself as well as for others? The greatest difficulty which has ever beset theological controversialists is the difficulty of vicarious suffering. Now we all see that there is much vicarious suffering in the world. Many suffer for the good of others. Martyrs have been put to death and many future generations have been benefited by their martyrdom. Warriors and soldiers have willingly shed the last drop of their life blood for their countrymen, and their patriotism has been rewarded in the salvation of the nation for which they died. But if you follow such into spiritual life you will find that no deed of heroism, no act of patriotism, no willingness to suffer for the sake of humanity has ever left the sufferers unrewarded. Each soul has suffered for its own advancement, even though unacknowledged, as well as for others; and in enduring suffering with no thought of self, heroes have reached the sublimest heights of unselfishness and are thereby placed above all need for further encounter with difficulty for the last demon you have to conquer is selfishness; the last enemy you must put under your feet is the devil of personal pride and human ambition; the last sin that is finally dislodged from the human breast is the love of one's self more than one's neighbor. When divine love for humanity is fully manifest in any individual, when any are willing to lay down their life for the world regardless of consequences to themselves, not looking for happiness hereafter or thinking anything about reward, but only desiring to work for humanity, demanding no recompense, doing good for the love of it—when any soul reaches such a point in its advancement, we care not whether the man or woman is an avowed atheist or theist, whether the mind is spiritualistic or materialistic in its external proclivities, we care not whether such are members of any church or advocates of any religious system they may worship in a cathedral or in the open air, or they may not recognize that there is any need for outward worship in the universe; we care not whether such individuals sat on thrones on earth or begged bread from door to door, in such do we behold a true manifestation of divine life.

True spirituality is not a question of head, brain or intellect, neither is it one of theology, or of belief in a life to come. It is altogether a question of being so truly imbued with divine life that you love a million of your neighbors a million times better than you love yourself.

If you love each of your neighbors as well as you love yourself, you must love two neighbors twice as well as yourself, and the great bulk of humanity as many times better than you love yourself, as the mass contains more units than one.

As the bulk of humanity is composed of units, each one must be as valuable as yourself in the sight of the Eternal and you are not established fully in truth till you look at humanity from the divine standpoint.

There is certainly in history an ideal life, and we do not hesitate to affirm that no one could ever have written the life of a nobler man than ever lived, for had there been no materials to furnish the story there could have been no record. You can not portray a character nobler than your own conception of it. You can not paint a picture beyond your highest conception of art. You can not compose music transcending your highest genius. If there is a lack anywhere it is always in the outward form, for this can not surpass what is in the author's mind. The author's mind is, however, frequently above the book he writes. Therefore if an author presents you with a hero who dazzles you by the splendor of his soul, that hero whose life is written is not so great a hero as the hero who was an actual reality to the author. If anyone sings a song ever so divinely, that song is not so divine in its rendition as it is in the spirit that is beyond all outward interpretation.

So, when, after reading a life of Buddha or of Jesus the Christ, you have asked, "But did such a man as Buddha ever exist? Was there ever anyone on earth so good as he? Anyone who voluntarily gave up all the splendors of an empire to identify himself with suffering humanity? Was there ever anyone so pure as Jesus of Nazareth?"

The answer is emphatically yes. The theory that Jesus is a solar myth and the twelve apostles twelve signs of the zodiac, is utterly inadequate to account for the moral and spiritual side of the narrative as all reasonable people must be well aware. We admit that in ancient days the sun was the chosen symbol of divine life and light; but when the Egyptians paid adoration to the god of day they did not according to esoteric teachings, bow before the material orb we call the sun, but before the mighty angel Osiris, who dwelt in the sun. And when they turned their eyes in worship to Alcyone the center of the Pleiades they declared that central orb in the universe to be the abode of the highest intelligence which could be made manifest to human comprehension.

Solar worship was not idolatry, not materialism, but sprang from recognition of every world in space being the result of spiritual laws and operations. When you turn your eyes to the spheres above you, contemplate the stars, and strive to number the constellated worlds shining in the midnight heavens, each star a sun blazing forth in glory with planets and satellites revolving around it in the depths of space, remember that this is not the only inhabited world; we are not the only conscious intelligent beings looking out upon the glorious night. Every star and every sun is, was, or will be inhabited, every satellite bears some form of life, and according to the grandeur of the sun, the majesty of the planet, or the development of the satellite is the developed life thereon.

When the old system of solar worship, which a large number of people are to-day bringing forward as proof that there was no personal Christ, no personal Buddha, no personal Osiris, no living Messiahs and Avatars in ancient days is understood and interpreted in the light of the spirit, it will be found to mean next to nothing of what it is supposed to mean by the school of Dupuis and others who declare it to be nothing beyond external worship of celestial orbs. Every world is a manifestation of mind. In a higher stage of the world's development men will be able to navigate the air, and eventually on wings of spirit to pass from planet to planet. Observatories will some day be erected upon earth's hilltops, and there, by means of powerful instruments of observation, entirely unknown to you and impossible in your present state of development, you will behold the condition of other worlds and know absolutely of this earth's relation to other realms in space; you will at length perceive those who at the close of any cycle have passed on (numbering 144,000, in mystical Apocalyptic numeration), have passed from the earth to the next planet. It is to the planet Mars that you must turn to-day for illumination from those who have graduated from the earth and have passed to comparatively celestial states.

We introduce these remarks into this lesson because of the opportunity they afford for reconciling what a great many people imagine to be irreconcilable statements concerning the rise and fall of nations. We tell you the very ground upon which you now tread was once occupied by intellectual giants in comparison to which you are pigmies; that the civilization of pre-historic California was far beyond its civilization to-day, and that when through natural changes wrought by upheavals on the Pacific Slope, ancient centers of civilization were entombed, the immortalized inhabitants having developed out of material conditions passed on to the next planet, and now shine down upon you from the sphere of Mars.

Whenever one cycle of advancement is completed anywhere a new era commences. The future of this world will witness the absolute spiritualization of the entire earth. The future golden age will include in its blessings every human being. The culminations of the most exalted prophesy, will be seen in the perfection of the entire planet and all upon it. In the past, here and there, there have been seen expressions of what the world and humanity will at length attain to, and these expressions have been the essential Christ within humanity revealing itself externally. Many persons constantly use the word God in reading the Bible as though there were only one original equivalent for God, whereas every one who can interpret Scripture with the light thrown upon it by an accurate knowledge of Hebrew, understands that the word God is used in three if not more senses. You are told that no man hath seen God at any time. God in this place means the Eternal One, the Infinite Being who is utterly invisible and beyond all outward recognition. You are told in the first and second commandments of the decalogue that there is no form known to man which may be termed the form of God, you conclude then, God is not in human form, because if God were in human form then the form of God would be known. God the

Eternal, self-existent Being has never been seen by man, the form of God is not known. Madam Blavatsky in her "Isis Unveiled" comes much nearer to a correct interpretation of the highest thought concerning Deity than do those whose theology is protrayed by Gustave Doré in his celebrated picture of the Trinity, which represents God as an older man, a younger man and a dove. The older man is called the Father, the younger man the Son, and the dove the Holy Spirit. In an eternal trinity there *can* be no senior and junior persons, but there *can* be an older and a newer *manifestation* of God; thus in a secondary sense a conception of God in human form is not inaccurate as the Infinite Being is revealed to man through humanity and can be revealed in no other manner.

In an inferior sense the word God has been used to signify a mighty angel, the ruler of the planet. Therefore though God the Eternal has never been seen by man, the representative or messenger of Deity, the special angel who reveals God to the world has been seen. In a third and yet lower sense of the word God, you read in the New Testament that they were called gods upon whom the spirit of God came; in ancient days they were also called sons of God and sons of God were often called gods. In early chapters of the Bible you are told that sons of God inter-married with daughters of men. Who were these sons of God? They were members of those ancient orders at the head of which stood the order of Melchisidec, sons of light, or sons of the sun, they were called in ancient Egypt. Now if those peculiarly endowed and highly privileged persons inter-married with earthly women, not for the purpose of spiritually refining them but for purposes of material gratification, those who belonged to the higher orders in spirit degraded themselves without elevating those with whom they became united. The fallen angels of theology are only those who were appointed to a higher mission, but fell through false ambition, while the unfallen are those commissioned with a divine and glorious authority who have been faithful to their trust and never diverged in the slightest degree from that high and holy mission appointed them.

Two Adams appear in the Bible—a first Adam and a second Adam. One Adam is of the earth earthy, the Adam who fell is called the first Adam, while the Adam who restored the loss caused by the fall of the first is called in the New Testament the second Adam. Christ is called the second Adam, but Christ esoterically means the higher principle in man which redeems the lower. Now the Adam of early days interpreted spiritually signifies the human soul in its primal innocence, but the soul in a condition of ignorance, not yet having encountered the trials and temptations of earth. This state may be termed celestial infancy, spiritual babyhood ; and is like to a child reclining upon the mother's breast, pure and spotless. You call it an immaculate little darling, not knowing the difference between right and wrong, or good and evil, but while you cannot attribute sin to the child, still do you wish your child to remain a child forever? The child must grow up to man's or woman's estate, must go out into the world and encounter every form of temptation, for it is temptation that tries the power of the spirit. Therefore when upon the heights of Calvary, Jesus with triumph exclaims, "It is finished," and he is identified with the second Adam, he represents the soul that has finished its earthly course, having put matter with all its temptations forever beneath his feet. The soul which has vanquished every earthly trial and arisen victorious on the wings of spiritual effort and self sacrifice is above the need of painful discipline forever after.

The Christ of history and theology is more than the personal Jesus, being the representative of idealized and glorified humanity. What Jesus has already become you will all in future ages attain unto.

The divine Logos or Word is "The light that enlighteneth every man that cometh into the world," and is therefore not a person but the spiritual principle in humanity which personality must at length make manifest.

Now, if the divine Word were confined to the personal Jesus, how could it illumine every man that cometh into the world? If salvation depended upon knowledge of a personal Christ, since Jesus was on earth but thirty-three years at one period in the world's history, it would be utterly impossible for hundreds of millions of human beings to be saved, because they could have no opportunity of knowing that such a person as Jesus ever lived. Bishop Thomas, an eminent Methodist, has declared that he does not believe in the necessary damnation of the heathen, and says he could not carry any Christianity to the heathen if he felt that Christianity compelled him to teach such an infamous doctrine as the damnation of the heathen, who had no opportunity to be saved. This view may be regarded as representative of all enlightened Christian teaching, which is to the effect that only willful rejection of truth is an unpardonable offense.

But if belief in an individual Christ is not necessary to the redemption of the world, if heathens and Jews can be saved as well as Christians, if Mohamedans and Buddhists can go into the Kingdom of Heaven together, then what is essential to salvation?

The essential Christ is the divine life within you, your own divine soul, which is the candle of the Lord burning upon the candlestick of your moral nature; and, as salvation does not depend upon belief in historical records, neither upon trust in a person, it does depend upon following this divine light. And, as salvation depends entirely upon following the divine light, you can readily understand how Jesus taught a gospel totally distinct from that gospel in which his name has been disfigured instead of glorified by popular Christianity. Jesus said, Many shall say to him at the judgment, "*Lord, Lord,*" who will not enter into the kingdom of heaven.

The only passport into the Kingdom of Heaven is the passport of charity, morality and justice expressed by ministering to one's fellow beings. Surely an Atheist can feed the hungry, clothe the naked, give consolation to the sick and distressed and visit those in prison. Does not Jesus say those who have done these things shall be upon the right hand, those who have not shall be upon the left.

The way of salvation laid down by the gospel proves that a true following of Christ signifies becoming imbued with the spirit of truth in love. It is utterly apart from theological controversy, and depends solely on following the divine voice within the soul.

We declare there is no one upon earth who has not the divine candle within; no one who has not heard the voice of the true Christ; no one who has not been appealed to by the angel side of his own nature; no one who is not invited to become a member of the body of Christ. When Paul said there are many members but one body, and even so is the Christ, did he not say that the Christ was the compact body, the spiritual organization of true, tried and faithful souls?

Jesus may have represented the head to Paul, Buddha representing the head to many Asiatics; Osiris may have represented the head to the ancient Egyptians in some older dispensation scarcely known to history; other lights whose names are unrecorded may have represented the Christ to those who lived in pre-historic antiquity; still the Christ ever represents the sphere of perfected souls, and the light shines down from the celestial heavens pulsing ever earthward until it reaches to the outermost boundaries of human perception. The Christ of antiquity, the spiritually endowed, the truth-bringer, the truth-teller is not confined to person or age but is the one divine life made manifest to all humanity.

We do not urge upon any one to accept a historical manifestation of Christ if they have difficulty in doing so on account of the paucity of evidence. No one should be required to accept anything as spiritual truth which his own soul is not capable of discovering for itself. External authority must be displaced in favor of interior conviction.

We are often asked concerning the position of Jesus in the spiritual world. We state that it has been given to earth on the testimony of the most exalted intelligences who have ever communicated with man, that Jesus occupies, as an individual soul, a place of peculiar exaltation in the spiritual heavens overshadowing the earth. If many do not know of Jesus in spirit life, they are simply in ignorance concerning him. But we would urge upon you all when dealing with communications of a negative character, no matter where they come from, to remember that negative testimony is not accepted in any court of law, only affirmative testimony is considered of value. If one honorable, upright person whose word need not be doubted, goes into court and states that he knows such and such a thing to be true, the testimony of that one person is considered of infinitely more value than the negative utterance of a million persons, who know nothing whatever of the matter under consideration. If one person, whose veracity is unquestioned positively affirms anything, his testimony is accepted and from it jury and judge alike consider and decide. So it is ever with regard to spiritual truth and the higher aspects of spiritual teaching; not what the majority do not know, but what the minority know and are able to impart intelligently is the measure of spiritual truth favorably considered by an intelligent community.

We have encountered many — yes, we say "many" advisedly — who have absolute knowledge that Jesus now exists in the spiritual world and that he is an exalted being. We can not then be so foolish as to say that he does not exist, which would be equivalent to putting out our own spiritual eyes because somebody else can not see, or destroying our own spiritual ears because somebody else can not hear.

True charity demands no false compromises. We cannot depend for evidence upon what is not known or not revealed; but all should be ever on the alert at all times and everywhere to receive the very utmost that can be received from the spiritual heavens within and without man on earth.

The gospel of Jesus stands, however, without reference to his personality as the very highest truth ever embodied in literature. We can surely all maintain that if we live in accordance with that gospel, obey those precepts, and conduct commercial transactions in harmony with the Golden Rule, the world will soon become a paradise. We would rejoice to see merchants put it to the test, and then give an opinion. The trouble between labor and capital is all because the Golden Rule is not obeyed. There can be no settlement in case of strikes and other labor agitation favorable to both sides and to all humanity until the Golden Rule solves the problem of labor and its relation to capital.

The deepest significance of the Golden Rule is, that you feel toward others as you would have others feel toward you, but there are unfortunately a large number of people who are willing to let their religion lie in the realm of sentiment without putting it into practice such people will readily say, "Oh, yes, you should feel kindly toward eveyone," but while they accept truth, theoretically, they are not willing to translate it into action. Jesus found this condition among the people whom he distinctly taught that sentiment was not sufficient, religion must be taken out of the realm of sentiment and become a part of every-day life, the highest spiritual convictions are useless until practiced. Jesus practically interpreted convictions in this life, and thus earned immortal qualities.

Because Jesus is the son of God is no proof that others are not sons of God. Because light shone in Palestine 2,000 years ago is no proof that there can not be a spiritual revelation in this day or in future times.

We maintain that the teachings attributed to Jesus are intrinsically valuable. We do not care whether they were uttered by him in Palestine 2,000 years ago or in an ante-deluvian country 20,000 years ago. If the teachings now on record are put in practice the world will be saved and redeemed, and if those teachings are not practiced all the belief in the world, all the baptism in the world, all the reception of sacraments, all the preaching possible will fail to redeem humanity. You must eat and drink spiritual truth. You must eat the flesh and drink the blood—that is, your daily life must become one with that spirit of truth which was made specially manifest in the higher teachers of humanity.

Jesus as an historical personage we decidely believe in as one who lived in harmony with the highest law; and the same highest law is now in existence—the law of love. The highest teachings now given to the world, are in response to human needs. Let there be no hostility between Jew and gentile; no dispute as to whether Moses or Jesus are personages, the teaching is true in principle, in spirit it is now here and can stand upon its merit. Whatever has demerit must fall, because of inherent inperfection and from no other cause. Carping critics who can not interpret the beauty and sublimity of the gospel would pick flaws in the character of an angel far more quickly than in an ordinary mortal, because angelical dispositions are not so much in harmony with their affections. Every one admires most whatever is most in accord with his own standard of excellence; and as every one has a standard of his own you must perceive the highest standard in order to truly admire the highest teachings. Therefore it is a compliment to Jesus, to the gospel and to all highest expressions of spiritual truth when sensual people throw dust and discredit upon them. Was there ever a martyr or reformer, man or woman, who stood above the age, who was not persecuted by those who could not comprehend them? They who have lived in advance of their time have ever been termed in league with Satan. Because Jesus proclaimed the higher truth he was said to be under the influence of Beelzebub, the prince of Devils. Later on Galileo and Copernicus were called fools and fanatics, so with all great reformers and inventors; until the world has grown up to their plane of thought it reviles them. Spiritual truths are often under a ban, but truth must conquer, and that perfect light which is in each one, the ideal life will eventually include in its embrace the entire family of man. Then will the great body of the Christ be revealed. Then will all be one in spirit and at length visibly constitute one great united family.

Personalities will no longer be objects of worship, but the perfection of spirit made manifest through all mankind will constitute the perfect coming of the Christ in the ultimation of God's kingdom upon earth,

LESSON IV.

EVIL AND ITS REMEDY.

THE following discourse is in answer to numerous questions concerning the Devil, evil spirits, demoniacal possession, obsession, causes of insanity and many subjects of like nature concerning which we have been literally deluged with inquiries. We trust the reader will find in the next few pages a reasonable exposition of our view of evil and its remedy.

That belief in an outside devil or in some evil spirits exterior to man, is widespread none will deny, and that there is, in a certain sense, valid ground for supposing the existence of extraneous diabolical agencies scarcely needs arguing; at the same time we can not see how any theory of a personal devil can help to solve the great problem of the ages, the mystery of seeming evil. The very watchword of metaphysicians is, "All is good; there is no evil," and so startling is this affirmation to the ears of many, that, having heard it proclaimed, they turn away in resentment from the only system of thought which can possibly explain the riddle of existence in harmony with the idea of infinite love and wisdom as supreme in the universe.

Now, very many orthodox or semi-orthodox persons who can not endorse Calvinism with its frightful doctrine of election and reprobation, endeavor to explain the existence of evil in man by reference to an outside prince of darkness, who injects evil and irreverent thoughts into the human mind. They consider it fearful to contemplate evil as inherent in man. Their view of human nature is too bright and lenient to permit of their attributing evil to man directly. They therefore indulge in the subterfuge of a scape-goat, and argue from Scripture, poetry and philosophy to prove the existence of a veritable personal devil, whose manœuvers are so incessant and effectual that man is constrained against himself, and contrary to his own desires, to eschew good and practice evil.

Such a theory is at once illogical, nonsensical and pernicious, as we will now endeavor, as briefly as possible, to prove, and, as believers in the sacredness of the Bible are frequently inclined to favor such a ridiculous conclusion, before directing our gaze elsewhere, we will take up *seriatim*, the scriptural narrative on which the devil theory is usually based.

The second chapter of Genesis is ordinarily appealed to, to sustain the theory of the personality of the source of evil in the world, the metaphorical serpent being usually considered as his Satanic Majesty in the guise of a talking snake. This narrative, when intelligently interpreted, however, gives no sanction at all to such a theory; on the contrary, it completely refutes it. Four characters are introduced to us by whoever was the author of this very ancient allegory, which the Jews probably derived partly from Egyptian and partly from Persian sources. We are told of God and His divine voice, of a male

Adam, a female Eve, and a representative of a sub-human kingdom, who, in the form of a reptile, undertook to dissuade Eve and Adam from obeying the divine counsel, promising them knowledge and bliss as the fruit of disobedience.

Now, a careful analysis of the four characters already referred to will prove to our satisfaction that these four actors are ever present on the stage of human life. God is revealed to us through our interior nature, through the moral sense or conscience, of which none are wholly destitute, though it is quite conceivable that primitive or barbaric races have little if any conception of this light. Eve, an interior principle, though not the innermost of all, stands for human affections; while Adam, the external man, represents the intellect. The serpent is none other than the animal or lower self-hood.

Now all these elements are intrinsically good. Evil is inverted good, and besides inverted good, there is no evil. Evil then, has no real existence; it has no fundamental principle; it is not, but simply appears to be.

Inversion occurs only when the affections are led downward and outward, instead of upward and inward, at the solicitation of the animal proclivities, and thus the only devil (old Saxon *de evil*) there is, is inordinate self-love, which means a disregard of the monitions of the higher nature in order to satisfy the lower.

This view of the serpent of temptation is at once reconcilable with anthropology and common sense. Who is there who has not felt the promptings of a higher and lower nature? Who has not felt the counter influence of good and evil genii? Paul, in the seventh chapter of his Epistle to the Romans, sets forth the inner conflict with amazing accuracy. After 1,800 years the world still feels that what that wonderfully gifted Roman lawyer, Saul of Tarsus, experienced, every one experiences now, unless it be that some are so blunt, so dead to all higher impulses, that, living wholly in the senses, they know nothing of the conflict, which can not be said to rage where no contrast of the opposites is presented to the understanding.

We venture to declare that there is not a child in any school or family who can not be brought up to rightly interpret the story of the fall and subsequent elevation of man, for just what every little one undergoes physically exactly corresponds to what he must pass through mentally and morally. Conflict is essential to growth; without it there could be no growth, no development of moral character. Intellectual greatness is inconceivable apart from effort, and so is moral growth.

Now the symbol of the serpent is a singularly expressive and appropriate symbol of man's lower nature, as being the most subtle of all earthly creatures, and yet a creeping thing. It suggests immediately a something at once attractive and repellent; a something good enough in its own way, and in its own place, but exceedingly dangerous when permitted to usurp the throne of the affections, and thence domineer over human intellect, using it as a servant of sense, when it should ever be the faithful follower of spirit.

Serpents are mentioned in the first chapter of Genesis, in which earliest account of creation we are informed that God created creeping things and blessed them. Reptiles were included in the work of the Almighty, which He blessed. The Eternal, we are told, looked with complacent delight upon primitive man, in whom were all the lower kingdoms, and the lower kingdoms themselves were pleasant in the divine eyes. Evil is in man, but what afterward appears as evil is originally good, and only becomes evil after a conscious act of inversion on the part of man.

All temptation to error comes through the affections, therefore, it is said, the woman tempted man, and caused him to eat the fruit of the forbidden tree. The woman Eve stands for the affectional impulses, which are the desires and wishes of our nature. Our will is not in intellect, but in affection; therefore, the old word "heart" is used instead of mind when temptation is alluded to in Scripture: "Keep thy heart with all diligence, for out of it are the issues of life," signifies, be especially careful as to the bent of your affections, while "out of the abundance of the heart the mouth speaketh," means that all our conversation and conduct proceeds not from our intellectual convictions or beliefs, but from our loves.

Our loves make us what we are. While, in a sense, it is strictly true that as a man *thinketh*, so he is, it is plainer and deeper truth that as a man loveth, and therefore willeth or desireth, so he is.

To deny the freedom of the human will *in toto* is to advocate a barbarous fatalism, so subversive of human weal as to conduce to the justification of every possible crime and misdemeanor, and surely the intent of all would-be reformers is to purge the world of wickedness, to rescue the evil-doer from the clutches of iniquity, reform the sinner, and thus effectually protect and elevate society.

Those who say that reverence is natural to man, while the devil is always irreverent, and make like assertions, prove themselves ignorant of the entire nature of man as expressed on earth. The spiritual or interior nature is the good genius of our human intellect, and is forever urging us to a higher and nobler state. Reverence is our love for a superior state, and manifests the attraction which the heavens within have for the thinking and reflecting mind; while irreverence is occasioned by the seductions of the lower nature, which is always leading us to the hells or inferior states of our animal existence.

When Paul advised the Corinthians to be on their guard lest the serpent which beguiled Eve also beguile them, he did not refer to a talking snake, which would be a curiosity to-day in any menagerie, nor to a snake which walked uprightly, and was afterward condemned to crawl, nor to a fallen angel who, in the similitude of an enticing reptile, parleyed with our first parents in a terrestrial paradise. He simply warned them against being led away from higher things by the seducing charms of external nature; and thus he told them to ever be sober and vigilant, lest the inward adversary should lead them, when off their guard, into the flowery but dangerous paths of sensuous enjoyment, when duty or moral obligation called upon them to heed a higher call and follow a diviner lead.

We deny that the sensual nature is an evil nature; it is a lower nature, good after its kind, but good in a lesser degree than the intellectual, as the intellectual in its turn is good in a lesser degree than the moral or spiritual nature; it is a good and useful servant, but an atrocious and tyrannical master. Rightful subordination of the lower to the higher instincts makes man an angel, while inordinate development makes him a devil, and the only devil there is, no better definition of which has ever been given than the old Latin sentence, *Demon est Deus inversus.* We see then at once how in the absolute sense there is no evil, evil being a condition, a state, but not the inherent nature of anything.

Infinite Good is the sole creator, and man makes evil out of good, by turning good upside down. It is then in his power to repent and be converted, and his conversion is his act which turns the good he has inverted right side up again. This spiritual truth is also a truth of reason, and can be amply sustained and aptly illustrated by phrenology, physiognomy, and all kindred external sciences, which, like thermometers and barometers, reveal the condition of the mind whose emotions they portray. A student of phrenology places before him a chart of the human head upon which he sees delineated the various organs of the brain. In the frontal or coronal regions he beholds such words as benevolence, conscientiousness, etc., indicating the noblest propensities, but toward the base of the brain, and at the back of the head, he reads destructiveness, secretiveness, amativeness, etc. Now, if he be ignorant, he will at first assume that the utter suppression of the lower faculties, even to the point of their annihilation, is necessary to the development of a lovely character, and following this mistaken trend of thought, multitudes of self-immolating fanatics have sought in vain to attain the highest heaven here on earth, as well as after the body's dissolution, by torturing their lower propensities out of existence.

Science and reason interpose to say *subordinate, do not destroy*, for the hells in man must ever be rendered subject to the heavens in man, that divine order and harmony may prevail. To rein in the lower instincts, to make them utterly submissive to higher loves, is the only way to round out a graceful and delightful character. What we call evil then is lower good, and is therefore not evil, evil in actual sense being only possible when a perverse inclination disposes one to subordinate conviction to appetite, thereby reversing the divine order which is that appetite should be subdued by reason, and intellect become the servant and exponent of the divine innermost in man, which is called sometimes the essential *ego*, and sometimes the *atma* in theosophical and other explanatory treatises.

Now, having thus far very briefly given a glance at the serpent, who generally is regarded as the devil in orthodox circles, let us turn to the satan in the Book of Job, and see whether we can not account for that mysterious personage without having recourse to any mythical object of mediæval superstition, such as many theologians offer for our acceptance.

In the Hebrew rendering of the Massoretic text (we mean that translation which is commonly used when the Scriptures are read in English, or referred to in that tongue in Jewish synagogues), the word Satan is missing, its place being occupied by the word accuser, a word, which, in its original sense, has undoubtedly reference to the ancient idea of an accusing angel whose mission it was to arraign evil doers before the bar of divine justice. There can be but little doubt that in Egyptian and other ancient allegories the accuser was nothing other than what we are accustomed to call accusing conscience, conscience offended, which, when it raises its protesting voice, to use Shakespeare's immortal phrase, "makes cowards of us all." This same conscience, when it speaks approvingly, makes heroes of us all.

Now, the two personages who appear in ancient allegories as recording angels are probably in their deepest ethical significance two aspects of conscience. In the first case conscience, as the approving angel, smiles on all well-doers; in the other instance this same conscience, as the accusing angel, frowns upon evil doers and evil doings. Everybody loves the approval, and hates the disapproval of conscience. Whatever conscience is, it is invariably beloved, courted, encouraged when it smiles, while all possible measures are resorted to, to deaden and silence it when it utters a protesting word.

Now, in fighting against this accuser or adversary within, man is fighting against his best and truest friend, as he eventually discovers often to his own most bitter cost. Just as it is with inward conscience, or the moral sense we endeavor to stifle, should it upbraid, so it is with all extraneous influences which bear upon us and pronounce judgment on our acts. Many a man has been reduced to ignominy and disgrace by the flatteries of mistaken friends, while the bitter though wholesome tonic of adverse criticism has made giants of many who, had they been left entirely to the tender mercies of particular admirers would have been dwarfs.

To learn from an enemy, to appreciate hostile criticism, to regard an opponent as a friend, is to learn a hard though much needed lesson. We may many of us pray, if we pray wisely, to be delivered from our flatterers far more than from our censors, and not only is insincere or stupid flattery detrimental to our highest interests, but too much unqualified honest admiration is apt to be injurious, as it leads us into self-complacent modes of thought and by making us thoroughly contented with present attainments, offers no spur, and holds out no inducement to future victory.

Job's adversary, Satan, proved his best and most helpful friend. The character of Satan is not altogether charming, we must admit. The best elements in the character are undoubtedly sublime from ancient writers' recognition of the important part, all seemingly adverse influences play in human evolution, but the darker shades are no doubt taken from those unlovely attributes of character so often displayed by those who take delight in hostile criticisms of others. Satan is not, however, despicable or unjust. There is nothing mean or contemptible about him. He evidently wants to put Job severely to the test, and after proving him at every point, shows himself incapable of hurting him, while, on the contrary, he proves himself at length Job's greatest benefactor.

There is ample room for considerable divergence of opinion with regard to Satan's motives and intents. A discussion could easily be carried on with considerable vigor on both sides, were one to undertake to defend the character as royal and noble, while another undertook to prove it harsh and unlovely in the extreme. It stands probably for justice devoid of mercy, for a stern, uncompromising, unmarried justice, and whenever justice, appears without its consort, mercy, it is repellant and severe. We may even go far enough to say that Satan is a personification of one divine attribute, while the Lord, with whom Satan converses, is another attribute. These attributes of Deity, Justice and Mercy, are often represented as separate and distinct persons holding converse with each other. Indeed the orthodox Christian trinity has originated in many theological schools with this very highly personified description of the attributes of Deity to be met with in ancient Scriptures. God the Father is Justice, God the Son is Mercy, and the two are one. We can not, of course, accept the doctrine of three persons in one God in the sense in which the word person is commonly employed, but we can readily see how the divine justice has given the world a conception of a severe and implacable Sovereign, while the divine mercy has given the idea of an infinitely gentle and loving Savior. A broader view reconciles these attributes to each other in human thought, and a genuine atonement or reconciliation is effected between the divine attributes, so far as we are concerned, when we see them for the first time in their true relation.

The whole difficulty in theological controversy has been that men will persist in arguing about oppositions and changes in the divine character and attitude, while every seeming change in God is only a reflection we behold of a change in ourselves.

When Job is subjected to Satan's buffetings, he is as much in the hands of infinite beneficence as he was before the commencement of those dire catastrophes depriving him of all his possessions, calamities apparently utterly unmerited, and therefore most difficult to understand and most hard to be reconciled to. Job shows his wisdom truly when he raises the cry, Shall we receive good at the hands of God, and shall we not also receive evil from the same divine source?

A flippant critic will point to such passages as these in proof of his rabid and hasty theory of Biblical contradictions, but the careful and cautious student, the deliberate thinker, who, perusing ancient records, strives to discover how men thought about the darkest and most perplexing phases of human experience in days of old, will see in it a faithful and penetrative admission that much, if not all, that appears evil is good in disguise.

It was a thought of olden days widely spread that six months in every year were under the dominion of good, and the other six under the control of evil genii. Anyone acquainted with Egyptian beliefs must be aware that the vulgar thought among the unenlightened was that out of the twelve constellations through which the earth annually passes, six were good and six were evil. The reign of the good began in March and ended in September, while the reign of the evil began with the autumnal and ended with the vernal equinox.

In Persia, Ormuzd, the power of light, is represented as creating six gods. Ahriman, the power of darkness, is said to have created six also. But in Egypt, every year on the 25th of December, the victory of light over darkness was celebrated. And, the builders of that miracle in stone, the great pyramid of Gizeh, so constructed it that twice every year it should be fully bathed in the glorious light of the sun, the befitting symbol of the eternal and ineffable Deity, whose light never grows dim, and whose goodness is meted out to man as truly in the dark winter of adversity, when man's mortal mind, symbolized by earth, turns away from its illuminator, as in the bright summer of prosperity, when that same mortal thought is in perihelion with the divine.

In the Christian calendar, Michaelmas day, September 29th, is a festival of rejoicing in honor of an archangel's victory over the dragon, and it is a very impressive circumstance, deserving of far more than passing notice that such a festival occurs at the very season when the earth passes into Draco, or Scorpio, the first of the six evil signs. The intent of such a festival, when traced to its origin, is to show that in religious thought God is as much the author of what we call evil as of what we call good; that evil is only some obstacle or impediment in our way, which we needs must overcome; and, while trials need to be surmounted, passions to be subdued, and all lower affections to be brought into subjection to the higher, the mystical Michael in us, our higher nature, must subdue the mystical dragon, our lower nature. And this lower nature is a blessing, when rightly subordinated, as it affords a substantial base on which the temple of genuine character can stand erect.

The oft-rendered solo from the "Messiah," "I Know

That my Redeemer Liveth," is one of the most exquisite portrayals of confidence in the absolute and certain demonstration of real good out of apparent evil ever written. Remember Job, to whom the words are attributed, is in the lowest depths of misery and suffering when he utters them, and the trumpet of his voice gives forth no uncertain sound. He declares that he has knowledge that all is working for the best. Were the word *hope* or *believe* instead of *know*, it would be inadequate. That word *know* is a note of triumph. The word "Redeemer" can be translated "vindicator," if one prefers that rendering, which is equally correct; while the controverted portion of the passage, "Though worms destroy this body, yet in (or out of) my flesh shall I see God," is really so rich in meaning, that the two seemingly opposite translations are susceptible of a perfect harmonization. Sometimes it is *in the flesh*, whilst we yet remain on earth; sometimes it is not till we are *out of the flesh*, or have cast aside the mortal robe, that we clearly see the divine hand in all our afflictions; but, whether in or out of the flesh, the perfect issue is not to be doubted.

The common orthodox interpretation which makes this passage allude to a physical resurrection is an utter falsification of the entire spirit of the prophecy, and if those who have any doubts on this score will read the last chapter in the book of Job, they will encounter an unanswerable objection to their material idea of a bodily resurrection in a fleshly sense, as Job, after his trials were over, it is said, exclaimed, prior to physical dissolution, when addressing Deity in strains of jubilant thanksgiving, "I had heard of Thee with the hearing of the ear, but now mine eye seeth Thee." Second Adventism is here robbed completely of one of its chief supports. Its very choicest proof text is seen at once by any enlightened commentator to favor Swedenborg, entirely at the expense of Christadelphus, who relied on it for so much support.

We must now proceed to consider very briefly the New Testament doctrine of demons which needed casting out of minds and bodies afflicted and insane. We need scarcely remind you that demon and demonology, in their strictly philosophic sense, are not words of evil import. Socrates called his highest counselor a demon, which, correctly translated, means only an influence operating otherwise than through the medium of a corporeal structure. Now every student of oriental beliefs must be well aware that the Palestinian Jews in the days of Jesus shared the common oriental belief in evil spirits, and looked upon sick people in general, and insane persons in particular, as subjects of an infernal kingdom, of which Beelzebub was ruler.

Without entering upon a dissertation concerning Bel, Belus, Baal, Belial, and all the various names given to the false god whom the Israelites were perpetually encountering in some one of its many forms as an object of idolatrous worship, we may safely conclude that as Aaron's golden calf must have stood for mammon worship, or inordinate greed of gold and other material possessions, this infamous idol, called the prince of infernal dominions, was sensuality. The worship of this hideous monster was the disgusting desire and practice of sensuality in all its hybrid forms of degradation. When infamous idolaters sacrificed their sons and daughters unto devils, they delivered them up to the curse which follows upon depraved and depraving sensuality.

If all who are striving to strengthen the moral convictions of society, and who take an interest in the young, would tell the young men and women of the present day that their sensual appetites are the devil, that the source of temptation is in their own lower nature, that they must subdue their carnal appetites by turning their thoughts and affections in spiritual, moral and intellectual directions; if they would but assure them that the only tempter to be dreaded is the one acknowledged by James when he says, "Every man is tempted when he is drawn away by his own lust and enticed," they would do infinitely more to strengthen morality than by seeking to prove the existence of an altogether too convenient scapegoat.

Devils are to be cast out, and how can they be cast out if they are not in us? They are our own impure thoughts of every kind and name, and until we engage in the work of exorcism, in the right spirit and according to the true method, we shall never be able to relieve the insane, or elevate the moral tendency of society. Sensuality in thought is the cause of demoniacal possession or obsession. Lunatic asylums are filled with inmates driven thither either through inordinate gratification, or unwilling repression of sensual appetites; and we should never forget, when discoursing on psychic influence, that we draw to us from the unseen states which are all about us whatever our desires attract.

Do we believe that persons on earth are ever under control of outside devils? We believe they become so related to the psychic emanations of the impure minded, that they come under the dominion of error from whatever source it may emanate. Do we believe that sensitives are peculiarly liable to come under such malign influence? That depends entirely, not simply upon their surroundings, but upon their thoughts and dispositions. We attract and submit to whatever we fear or love. We can not resist what we fear or what we love. Resistance only comes with brave and determinate opposition toward what we neither fear nor love. A weak, yielding, altogether too negative and forceless habit of mind leads to insanity. Victims of mental aberration are frequently those who lack mental and moral stamina. They reflect whatever conditions are thrown around them. Indecision and weakness of will lead to insanity; while fear, as well as love of base things, brings us under the dominion of the insidious powers of darkness, which prevade the air.

No moral education is worthy the name unless it promotes vigorous activity of the higher promptings. Children need to be taught the great importance of correct thinking, and should never be left without employment and then scolded for being naughty because they have no proper occupation for brain or hands.

Swept and garnished houses are no safeguards against the approach of evil, for unless we are constantly occupied with good, we fall easy prey to the seductions of any tempter who may chance to come our way. Saloons, gaming hells, and other villianous haunts, will exert no attraction over the mind of youth, if, before exposing young men and maidens to the perils and dangers of a city, parents, guardians and teachers wisely direct their thoughts into channels of usefulness and purity. No disease can invade an organism not receptive to the animalcules in the atmosphere, which are repelled when the body is in a healthy, and invited when it is in an unhealthy state.

Pure thought can not but eventuate itself in purity of word and act, and no influence from without can gain an entrance, unless invited from within either by morbid desires or mental vacuity. To resist the tempter is not possible unless our minds are attuned to celestial forces, and then, with the actual, positive force of active, operative good, we can overcome all evil.

Talmage and other sensational pulpit mountebanks, in their insane tirades against Spiritualism, are practically denying God and giving omnipotent power to the devil. Many of the Roman Catholic clergy, including the far-famed Monsignor Capel, are no wiser than Talmage, when treating a similar subject. Concerning the influence of the departed upon those yet upon earth, we have always stoutly maintained that the old proverb, "Birds of a feather flock together," is literally true, and that close mental associations are impossible of continuance apart from kinship of thought and affection.

If persons believe they have a work to do in elevating those in darkness, and allow mental contact for the benefit of those whom they seek to uplift, we can not conscientiously discountenance their work; but we do maintain that no error is more pernicious than that which teaches that man is a creature of uncontrollable circumstances, and therefore must perforce submit to any and every influence which may seek to gain ascendancy over him. Look for the source of evil within and not without. Fortify yourselves by noble pursuits, wise companionship, and elevating trains of thought, at those points where now you experience weakness; and when you feel some dark influence approaching you, and seeking to allure you to destruction, realize that your strength is in perfect trust and absolute confidence in Infinite Good, coupled with sincere and active effort to translate your highest sentiments into noble acts and words.

When Goethe represents Faust in the clutches of Mephistopheles, he shows throughout the play or opera how deftly the seducing tempter plays upon the weakness of the student who seeks to win the earthly love of Marguerita, by any wile or artifice an adroit temptation may suggest. As a person, Mephistopheles is anyone who is desirous of rendering a service to another, no matter how unscrupulous the work in hand, if by so doing he can command a greater service from that other on his own behalf. Mephistopheles is not at all outside of humanity so far as his personality is concerned. He is to be found in clubs and drawing-rooms, at fashionable fêtes and banquets; but instead of wearing a grotesque costume and protruding horns and tail, his dress is of the latest fashion, his broadcloth garments are of superfine material and of latest cut, his linen is immaculate, while a choice and fragrant flower, symbolical of innocence and grace, adorns his buttonhole; his manners are suave as suave can be, his diction most polite, his avowed morals irreproachable;

he often takes a class in a Sunday-school, and sometimes mounts the pulpit stairs and there delivers an address of unctious sanctity. He can be all things to all men, in order that he may entrap some, and thereby further his own selfish and nefarious designs.

Utterly unscrupulous, he seeks his prey wherever he may find it. He is the worst type of a man about town — a polished swindler, an attractive dancer, an educated liar, a polite villain. He finds himself smiled upon everywhere, and often laughs among his boon companions at the stupidity of his admirers, who are shallow enough to promise him their earthly all in a moment of intoxication induced by himself, after he has carefully studied their weak points and flattered their vanity.

Mephistopheles, subjectively regarded, is that element of selfishness, vanity, or sensuality within our breasts that gives the adventurous libertine in society his opportunity. Mothers with marriageable daughters, you may be seeking Mephistopheles as a son-in-law when you are desirous of seeing your daughters marry well, in a worldly sense. Young men of business, you are courting Mephistopheles whenever you sacrifice principle to policy, and barter your honor for money or the world's applause. The love of money is the root of all evil. The devil is the god of gold; and he or she who loves material things inordinately is a devil worshiper.

How shall we kill this devil? We can not annihilate a single particle of dust, nor can we destroy one iota of the force which pulsates in the forms of men and women, but we can transform, we can transmute what we can not and should not endeavor to destroy. Transmutation leads to glory. We may take all our lower impulses, and mastering them by the might of spirit, so overcome them in their lower sense, so transform their downward tendency, that while in their perverted state they are the occasions of our stumbling, in their transfigured form they are the faithful servants of the soul divine within us. Asceticism is a mistake. All endeavors to eradicate aught that inheres in the constitution of man must prove disastrous in its consequences, while to find the true philosopher's stone which is capable of converting all inferior metals into gold is to find the soul within us, and so subdue our *appetites* to reason and our intellects to moral principle, that the devil in us, which is but inverted goodness, will be at length transformed into a glorious angel of light.

Let us all accept our earthly discipline as a means of noblest conquest, and in the understanding of what is meant by the words, "He that overcometh shall inherit all things," we can thank God for His goodness in giving us a lower nature to subdue.

LESSON V.

RESURRECTION.

AS we have received a great number of questions all bearing on the subject of Resurrection, we have deemed it desirable to reply to a number of them in the following address which will be found to contain answers to a number of leading inquiries continually recurring in the minds of all who devote much thought to this intensely interesting theme.

The resurrection of Jesus from the dead is the corner-stone of Christianity; without it the whole system falls to pieces. By Christianity in this sense we of course mean that great religious system which prevails throughout that part of the world commonly called Christendom, not that excellence of character and ami ability of disposition which many people are accustomed to indiscriminately designate "Christian."

Now, so intensely important a doctrine as that of the resurrection can not be supported in any literal or external sense in the face of modern criticism. In its letter the doctrine is most surely doomed. It has long been dying, and is now almost if not entirely dead among earnest and liberal thinkers on the subject; but while in its letter it is rapidly becoming obsolete, and will soon have to be regarded as an effete dogma, a product of ancient ignorance and mediæval superstition, in its spirit it is revealing itself in a light always perceived by a few intuitive and clearly reasoning minds, but never until very recently beheld by the masses of mankind, unless it be in some remote period lost in the dim haze of legendary narrative which antedates the so-called "historic period."

As an introduction to what we have to say concerning the resurrection of Jesus in particular, let us glance at a few of the numerous instances of resurrection from the tomb, or from death, recorded alike in the Old and New Testaments. The power to raise the dead, according to the Bible, is a gift bestowed upon all true prophets, whether under the Jewish or Christian dispensation. Elijah is said to have literally restored to life the beloved son of the hospitable woman at Zarephath, who entertained him at her home, and shared her scanty supply of provisions with him in a time of direful famine. Elisha, upon whom Elijah's mantle fell, raised from the dead the son of a Shunamite woman who had shown kindness to him. Jesus raised Lazarus, the widow's son at Nain, Jairus' daughter, and others, and in giving his final commission to the disciples who were to succeed him in his ministry on earth after his disappearance from the plane of mortal perception, he declared that the works he had done they should likewise accomplish, and even do greater works than any he had performed in consequence of his ascension to the Father.

In the "Acts of the Apostles" we are told of the resurrections wrought by the divine gift bestowed upon the apostles very similar to those already referred to. Now, in these cases of resurrection from the dead, if the literal sense be strictly adhered to, not only is there no positive proof of human immortality offered, but we can scarcely behold even a faint intimation of the spiritual immortality of man. All these narratives are very popular with the Second Adventists and others who deny spiritual life, and affirm the necessity of a bodily resuscitation. Of course it would be quite possible, by means of not unfair or illogical special pleading, to argue immortality from the fact of the spirit being recalled after it had left the form; still there are so many ways of escape from this conclusion without very much verbal juggling, that in common fairness we are bound to admit that the testimony on behalf of human immortality, furnished by such narratives, is unsatisfactory because uncertain, and wherever ambiguity prevails positive conviction is out of the question among close reasoners.

These physical resurrections, in the light of modern knowledge, are intensely interesting from a therapeutic standpoint, and are therefore really more important matters to medical men than to theologians, unless theologians are willing to return to their primitive and rightful position as healers of the body as well as the soul. Though it has always been the part of true theology to minister to sin-sick souls, it is none the less its province to minister with equal efficiency to beclouded minds and ailing frames; and because it has for centuries almost confined itself to one portion of its proper sphere, instead of working throughout that sphere, it has been not only severely reprimanded, but stoutly antagonized by utilitarians of every school, who can not see even the prospective advantages of a system which does not here and now demonstrate its beneficial influence upon mankind, even to the ultimates of physical expression.

It is a singularly noticeable fact that priests and prophets in all ages have been healers of the sick. When James said in his epistle, "If any sick among you, let him call for the elders of the church," he was but complying with a usage so ancient that no student of antique customs can discover a period (say in ancient Egypt) when such practices were not constantly resorted to. Indeed, we are very much in doubt whether in olden times a priest or prophet would have been accepted by the people at all if he had not presented his credentials in this manner. To heal the sick, even to the extent of raising the seemingly dead, was one of the leading proofs of a spiritual vocation. Words and deeds had to go together, or a claim to spiritual fitness for an exalted station was not received as genuine. Of course, it may always be argued by the materialistic school that the priests of old were versed in the knowledge of drugs, and, in spite of the mystery which surrounded their practice, they were really skillful physicians. This, of course, may be and is in a sense correct but, notwithstanding all allowance which can be fairly made for this admission, the singular evidence of the prophet's gift was that he could perform works of healing far transcending the work done by the *therapeutæ*, or medical men.

In the days of Moses it appears that the manner of testing a true prophet, *versus* an ordinary magician, was at this very touchstone of his possessing or not possessing the healing gift. Pharaoh's magicians, at a period when the court was one of infamy and despotism, could do as wonderful things as Moses. When miracles were under consideration, they could claim full equality with the great founder of Mosaism, but when it came to removing plagues from the land, Moses and the magicians differed, as light and darkness, night and day. The magicians could convert rods into serpents, and then turn the serpents back into rods; they could multiply frogs, locusts, and all manner of pests; they could afflict the bodies of men and cattle in a most mysterious and fearful way; they were complete masters of the black art, but the white art of healing was altogether beyond them. We must never forget that mere wonders are no evidence of the operation of divine power. Wonders of beneficence are required to attest the action of celestial force.

That the physical body of man ought to be under the complete dominion of reason, intellect, and *will*, needs no argument, neither does it need an argument to prove that intellect in its turn needs to bow before the moral sense. The three universally recognized principles in man, the animal, the intellectual, and the moral, must be rightfully subordinated, the one to the other, or harmony, which is wholeness, symmetry, or health, is impossible.

The superiority of mind to matter needs not to be argued; it is self-evident, as evident to the practical mechanic, or the potter who molds the clay, as to the most abstract metaphysician. That the higher should govern the lower, that our higher instincts should hold our lower passions in subjection, is admitted by Colonel Ingersoll as much as by any ascetic, but with this difference, Ingersoll differs from the ascetic in his view of what constitutes the highest welfare of the race.

Now, it stands to reason that as all material achievements are wrought by the power of intelligence, or, in other words, by mental and moral action; as it is beyond cavil that in order to subdue the material world, man must at least liberate his reason from the chains of passion, it inevitably follows that the more perfect mastery one gains over one's own lower impulses, the greater will be one's influence for good upon one's neighbors.

It needs no argument to prove that if one can remove a heavy stone from before one's own door, he has sufficient strength to remove a stone of similar weight and proportions from another's door, if he have but liberty to use that strength on a neighbors' behalf, while if he is too weak to roll away a rock which bars the entrance to his own domicile, he can not possibly remove one of equal size from some one else's door.

We can not impart what we do not possess. The more we have the more we can bestow; but at the same time nothing is truer than that the best and readiest way of learning is to teach what we do know, and thus put ourselves in the true way of learning more, while the surest way to receive abundantly is to give freely to the utmost extent of our ability.

Medical science is avowedly experimental. The highest medical testimony proves that while there are multitudes of open questions, there are very few settled ones among the medical fraternity. Joseph Cook declared, in Boston some years ago, in Tremont Temple, before a very large audience, on the occasion of his memorable discourses on probation in death, in opposition to the theory of probation after death which he was combating, that an infallible test of death had not been discovered by modern scientists, and that a large reward would gladly be placed in the hands of any one who could furnish the colleges with such infallible test as they stood in need of.

Now, if a champion of orthodox Christianity makes such a statement as this, and it can scarcely be refuted, what proof is there, we ask, that any one of the persons raised to life again by Jewish prophets, Christian apostles, or the Christ himself, were really dead? Medical opinion would doubtless be that they were in a stupor; buried in a trance, or something of the kind comparatively unusual, but by no mean unprecedented. You have all read and heard, doubtless with much interested wonder, of many persons rising from their graves after interment, and to raise the seemingly dead, even those already buried, would be less a wonder in a hot country than in a cold one, and still less wonderful at a time when epidemics being prevalent, interment in the ground follows almost immediately upon the supposition that breath has left the body.

The statement that Lazarus had been buried four days would, of course, in that particular instance, add greatly to the marvel of his restoration, but even in that case it could scarcely be said that the wonder was unparalleled. The simplest exposition, by far the most reasonable, practical, and helpful one, is that these narratives have probably been culled from an immense mass of ancient testimony to the efficacy of direct spiritual healing after all external measures had proved futile.

The author of the fourth Gospel ends his record by saying that if everything which took place at the time concerning which he wrote had been recorded, the collection of manuscripts would have been so great that the world could hardly contain them, thereby leading us at once to infer that only sample illustrations were given, testifying to an exuberant outpouring of the spirit extending throughout Judea, and doubtless elsewhere, astounding the populace, arousing the bitterest ire and indignation of interested parties whose fortune was derived from monopolistic enterprises, and generally proving to the populace that even for bodily ailments there was a cure unknown to the practioners of the prevailing schools of medicine.

It is impossible to vouch for the accuracy of all the details of these narratives. They are often more or less romantic in their style. They may even be parables, but whatever they are they afford a close insight into the actual occurrences of that age. To say that they are not original, to state even that they came from Egypt, by no means disposes of them, because facts of such a nature can not depend upon time and place, but upon nature and degree only.

If such things can be, if they ever were, they can be now, provided we learn to comply with necessary requirements for their production. Their place in the Bible gives them a historic base in the minds of men, and makes them capable of stimulating hope and inquiry, if not positive faith in the minds of the millions the world over who read them. We can safely leave them in their literal sense as challenges to modern disciples of truth to put the Master's theory into practice, and learn by the three-fold agency of faith, prayer and abstinence to accomplish for suffering humanity to-day benefits as great as any that occurred, from a complete surrender of sense to spirit, ages ago in far-off countries.

But it is not with the letter of these narratives, interesting and profitable though it be, that we are most particularly concerned, for through the dimness of the letter beams the everlasting brightness of the spirit; and while the letter breaks when too hardly strained, and fails to justify itself to human reason in some particulars, the spirit to which the letter is often sacrificed, but which is never sacrificed for the sake of the letter, bursts upon us with a refulgence so glorious that we cease to care whether the letter is accurate or not, so satisfied do we become with the kernel of truth after we have broken the shell in which it has been so long enclosed.

Whatever phenomenal Spiritualists may say to the contrary, the evidences of human immortality are, in their final analysis, totally subjective; and when we say this, we do not for a moment intend to repudiate or disparage such objective proofs of spiritual action over material things as may be necessary to conduct the doubting mind, immured in sordid materiality, step by step out of the darkness of materialism into the light of true and abiding Spiritualism. We do, however, most emphatically declare that phenomenal evidences of spiritual power over mortal things are only means to an end—useful and necessary means in many instances, means to be honored and not despised, but still only means—the end not being attained till the means are no longer needful.

If all Spiritualists, metaphysicians, Swedenborgians, and others would but compare notes and be reasonable on this point, a grand, united army of spiritual workers could at once be found to storm the citadels of error, and let in the light of truth to multitudes of darkened minds. But just so long as blind and bigoted antagonisms are inflamed by hot-headed partisans of a particular view of truth, people who see from one point of view only, and persist in maintaining that what they see is all the truth there is to see; so long, we say, as such people are to the fore in any movement, whatever name and proportions it may assume, that much to be desired harmony and genuine spiritual co-operation of scattered forces so sorely needed in the present juncture of human affairs can never be consummated. One side denies phenomena, calls it all fraudulont, delusive, or debasing; the other side extols it beyond all reasonable limits, even to the extent of denying the very existence of the end to which, if useful, it must of necessity lead.

The New Testament presents to us the golden mean, and so do all rational teachers who are at the same time what all rational people should be, eminently *spiritual*. In the accounts furnished by the evangelists of the resurrection of Jesus we have, when we take only a literal view, many reasons for doubt. Thomas Paine, in his "Age of Reason," has borne unwitting testimony to the spiritual sense, which he evidently did not perceive, when he positively ridicules the account as it stands literally.

The story is that Jesus expired physically on the cross on a Friday afternoon, and that certain women remained at the foot of the cross till all was over. They saw their Master's dead body removed from the cross, or, at all events, they saw him during the very latest moments of his earthly existence. Not more than forty hours later, very early, before daybreak, the following Sunday morning, they were at the tomb, which they found empty, and when these same women, especially Mary Magdalene, saw the risen Jesus, and held a conversation with him, she had no conception that it was he; but, mistaking him for a gardener, she confided her sorrow and amaze to him, without the least suspicion, it appears, entering her mind that she was talking with the very friend of whose physical whereabouts she was so diligently inquiring.

Now, if the writers had intended to convey the idea that Jesus rose from the dead in the literal physical form which was buried, why did they not so record the event as to encourage belief, rather than provoke the most decided unbelief in this connection? If a physical form were raised, then why should the women and the disciples, in the case of the resurrection of Jesus, have any more difficulty in identifying him outwardly than the friends and relatives had in identifying those whose bodily resurrection has been already under review?

What would have been more natural than for Mary Magdalene to have been struck dumb with amazement at beholding Jesus standing beside her, and, for the time being, supposing she had seen a vision or beheld an apparition? But nothing of this nature, nor anything approaching it, enters into the narative, so far, at least, as she is concerned. He looks to her like an ordinary man attending to the duties of a gardener, and it is not until he turns to her and pronounces her name in some peculiar and doubtless characteristic way, accompanying the words with some silent, subtile appeal to her inner consciousness, that she is in the least aware that her beloved teacher, whom she mourned as dead, is talking with her,—truly alive, but not in outward appearance like unto what he was before his physical decease.

Two disciples journey between Jerusalem and Emmaus the same day. At evening they hold a long conversation with Jesus, without in the slightest degree recognizing him physically. He made himself known to them at a supper by some characteristic way he had of breaking bread, and they then remembered how their hearts had burned within them as he expounded Scripture to them while they were on the road; but physical evidences of a personal character were altogether lacking, and it does not appear that any physical proofs were given to any disciple except Thomas, whose skeptical mind required more tangible evidence in his case. To meet his necessity, to use a modern word, Jesus "materialized," *i. e.*, he produced an outward form so closely resembling the physical organism he had once worn, that even the doubts of Didymus yielded to so convincing a display of the absolute power of spirit over matter.

What became of the physical body of Jesus is a very interesting query. Most answers are totally unsatisfactory. The only really helpful one is that derived from a study of occult chemistry, and a comparison of the claims put forward by theosophists concerning the faculties of adepts, with prevalent views put forward by distinguished naturalists.

Scarcely a physiologist of any note can be encountered anywhere, who does not give seven years as the longest time for those changes to become complete which periodically remodel the organic structure of man. Camille Flammarion, a Frenchman of great eminence, declares that the entire physique is remodeled in less than one year, while many parts of the body change entirely in not more than thirty days. Now, with such testimony as this before us, how utterly futile must be every attempt to establish a theory of physical resurrection among intelligent persons.

And what is far more important even than the light thrown on the resurrection in its literal sense, is the amazing testimony thus brought forward by physical scientists to the reality of the spiritual man and the utter impossibility of the physical organism being anything more than a temporary and ever-changing instrument. The physical body, in the light of natural science, is a chemical compound, susceptible of complete disintegration; when volatilized, as all hard substances can be, according to scientific testimony,—for even the rocks as well as the osseous formations in the human frame are only solidified ether or condensed atmosphere,—the most rigorous external substances can be reduced to a state ot absolute invisibility.

When the human will shall gain such power over the physique as rightfully belongs to it, and as can be obtained by a life of complete abnegation of the lower instincts, that the higher may wield unrestricted sway, the disappearance of a physical form will not occasion much surprise, as the power of will is thoroughly adequate to separate all the particles of the structure, and compel them, one and all, to return to their respective places in the external kingdoms of which they form a part.

The body of Jesus, in our opinion, was not stolen, or in any way removed from the tomb. It was dispersed, or, as some would say, "de-materialized." When the human will becomes so sovereign over sense that it is no longer held in captivity to sensuous proclivities, death will not occur even to the outward body. When the intelligent principle which has used it for a temporary work has outgrown the need of it, then will it be thrown aside painlessly and willingly. It will not slowly decay, it will be simply cast off when it has served its use. To teach the necessity of disease, and to call decay natural before the spirit has left the body, is to teach a most damnable error, one which is afflicting the world with innumerable sorrows of man's own creation, and one which, in common justice to enlightened physiologists, it must be admitted they do not teach.

Dr. T. L. Nichols and many others have argued splendidly against the prevalent notion that sickness is natural. To attribute disease and premature passing from the mortal form to an act of nature or Divine Providence is to call darkness light, error truth, guilt righteousness, and the unnatural the natural; which is the quintessence of mischievous absurdity. The sublime spectacle of Jesus quitting the mortal form after having declared his earthly work finished, is a picture on which all need to gaze whose shallow pessimism leads them to regard the effects of their own weakness and immorality as harmonious with the divine natural order, against which their own ignorance or willfulness causes them to rebel. Illness is something to be ashamed of, and when one meets with accident, it is conclusive proof to the lynx-eyed philosopher who knows somethiug of the true nature of causation, that spiritual perception is but dim and instinct obscure in the one who stumbles and falls into danger, while if he were more foreseeing and discerning he could readily have escaped.

The Egyptian custom of embalming the dead is not one which it is well for modern nations to copy. Cremation is, in its turn, far preferable to burial, while the disposal of human remains by electrical agency will doubtless soon supersede cremation, till at length what Bulwer Lytton, in "The Coming Race," calls *vril* will at length be the agent employed in all such undertakings; while there is yet to be discerned, still farther ahead, the sovereign action of *will*, which will leave even *vril*, with all its potencies, far in the background.

But when we dismiss all questions pertaining to the outward shell, and consider as we should what resurrection means, in its higher aspect, the old Greek word *anastasis*, which has excited so much controversy, appears before us radiantly transfigured, as it carries with it no further thought of a physical envelope, but admits to our view that spiritual body which Paul speaks of as altogether separate from the natural (animal) body. There are two bodies, the animal and the psychical. The former, as an individual shape, knows no permanency whatever, at any time, but is only an ever-changing aggregation of molecules, attracted and upheld by ever-varying conditions of mortal disposition.

Beyond this outward form, and altogether independent of it, is the spiritual body, which is a perfect structural organism, beautiful and harmonious in all its parts.

In giving spiritual treatment, one is not called upon to deny the existence of the body, and to use such a ridiculous formula as for instance, "You have no head, therefore it can not ache." Quite the contrary. A perfect head, not the absence of a head altogether, should be presented to the patient's thought. It is highly important that all should learn to see beyond all external limitations, and regard the whole human family as perfect interiorly and really as regards our common essential spiritual being; and when the thought does turn thoroughly to the spiritual, and all material things are forgotten, intromission to the spiritual world is the result.

We are told that David, who mourned bitterly for his child before the breath left his body, after the child was actually dead physically, consoled himself in these words, "I shall go to him, but he shall not return to me." Going to our beloved in spirit need not be postponed to a distant day, and indeed we have no reason to expect that the dropping of the material form will introduce any of us at once into spiritual society. We must, while on earth, cultivate our spiritual perceptions, and learn to discern spiritual things spiritually, or after the demise of the physical organism we may find ourselves hovering on the earth, unconscious of all things spiritual. What more credible than that many who have dropped the garment of flesh still continue to imagine themselves encased in matter?

The principal danger attending promiscuous seances and sittings with mediums, with a view to the acquisition of material wealth, is that even though communications are absolutely genuine, they are with an order of mind not far enough removed above the stock-broking level to be really profitable to those who hold interviews with it. Editorials in the *Golden Gate*, *Banner of Light*, and other avowedly spiritualistic newspapers, have frequently pointed to the *cui bono* of spiritual intercourse as a something entirely distinct from worldly emolument, and we will go so far as to say that it is usually demoralizing to drag earthly business into what ought to be a means for promoting the noblest and most unselfish instincts of human nature.

The chief cause of sickness among well-meaning and affectionate people is sorrow. No grief can be so poignant as that occasioned by the loss of beloved friends. We are repeatedly asked, in our classes and elsewhere, how such grief can be assuaged, and by a radical removal of the cause the effects be compelled to subside. Our answer invariably is that the only salutary treatment in such cases is to direct the mind of the afflicted one to the spiritual state, to use all the moral and mental persuasiveness you possess to induce your patient to look away from sense to spirit, and if you can but get the thought finally off material things and on to spiritual reality, the outward symptoms of disorder at once give place to a placid and even joyful exterior. As light breaks in from the unseen world, immediately we cease to dwell upon external things.

For this reason, Mary's attitude is preferable to Martha's, for an inordinate concern for worldly affairs is like an insect or a cinder in one's eye. When one is traveling through some delightful country, the most exquisite scenery is imperceptible to one whose visual organs are blocked up. So may we not conclude that the only reason why we are not usually conscious of the presence of spiritual influences is because grief, repining, or some other earthly emotion keeps us absorbed in those externals, which, when they engage our attention, shut out from us all view of spiritual life. After all, all that matters is that those in sorrow should be brought out of their low estate by a realization of spiritual truth.

If the various resurrections recorded in the Scriptures are literal facts, they afford no evidence that those who were thus marvelously raised in flesh did not die again. Parents and sisters whose brothers and sons and daughters were thus physically restored to them, must ever after have been tormented with the fear of losing them again, unless some guarantee was given that their life was immortal. Our greatest source of unhappiness is our own materiality. We love the things of sense far too dearly, and thus whatever we may know of spiritual immortality, we are not content, because we sigh perpetually for companionship on the material plane.

True spiritual resurrection is not the resuscitation of a corpse. It is nothing in any way physical. It is an illumination of one's interior being, an opening of one's spiritual perceptions to discern the spiritual state. Sorrow often helps us toward this end because it loosens our hold on outward things. Thus we can comprehend Job's exclamation addressed to the Almighty at the end of his affliction, "I have heard of Thee with the hearing of the ear, but now mine eye seeth Thee." Those who are truly resurrected, in the spiritual sense, are those blessed ones who, even while they dwell on earth, are in conscious and continual communion with the spiritual realm.

LESSON VI.

TRANSFIGURATION.

HAVING received a great many questions concerning the story of the transfiguration of Jesus and its attendant circumstances, and being particularly asked to apply its teachings to modern life, we present the following summary of our views on this intensely interesting subject, and as the subject easily permitted of it, we have embodied in this address replies to several questions bearing on the proper government of refractory children and offenders against the civil law. In the seventh chapter of Matthew we find the story of the transfiguration briefly outlined as follows: Jesus takes Peter, James and John to a high mountain apart, and is transfigured before them. His face shines as the sun, and his garments appear white as the light. Moses and Elias appear to the disciples talking with Jesus. Peter asks Jesus whether three tabernacles can not be erected on that glorious height, one for Jesus, one for Moses and one for Elias, but before he finishes speaking a bright cloud overshadows them, and a voice speaks from out the cloud saying, "This is my beloved son in whom I am well pleased, hear ye him." When the disciples hear the voice they fall on their faces, and are sore afraid. Jesus bids them arise and fear not. After he has touched them and they raise their eyes the two visitors are no longer visible, they are alone with Jesus who tells them the time has not yet arrived for making public the vision, but he assures them after his resurrection the time will have arrived for publicly testifying to their marvelous experiences on the mount. This narrative is immediately followed by the narration of a marvelous case of healing of one who was oppressed with lunacy, which affords occasion for a homily on the need of faith as a grain of mustard seed (a topic of vital moment to all spiritual students), and then a practical discourse on paying tribute, which seems to open up to the earnest and intelligent meditator much important teaching on the subject of the proper relation existing between faith in God, worship of the Supreme Being, recognition of the sole sovereignty of divine truth in matters of conviction and the honorable discharge of our duties in the external state.

Let us transport ourselves in mind to the scene of the vision. Significant, indeed, is the account of its being seen on a high mountain, a figure of speech which incessantly occurs in the Scriptures in connection with states of spiritual exaltation, moral and intellectual enlightenment and conquest over enemies.

More than three thousand years ago, according to the Pentateuch, Moses received the Ten Commandments from the hand of Jehovah, on tables of stone, upon the top of an Arabian mountain, while the multitude at the base were enveloped in thick darkness. Their eyes were so weak that after Moses had come down from the mountain into their midst, they could not gaze upon his features until he had covered his face with a veil. How striking the resemblance between the glorified countenance of Moses at the time of the giving of the law to the Hebrews in the desert and the transfigured countenance of Jesus when Moses re-appeared upon a mountain top in Asia Minor.

The correspondence of a mountain is not far to seek. Mountainous districts are peculiarly salubrious. There is far less disease and far fewer early deaths on high ground than in low-lying valleys. Miasmic emanations do not reach those lofty heights. In India, during the summer season, when the climate in all the cities is so oppressive to Europeans that they can scarcely endure it, the mountainous region round about is healthy and invigorating. Scarcely ever does a Western traveler to the far Orient suffer severely from the climate if he can take refuge in the mountains during the hottest portion of the year.

In Europe, when the cities of the Italian plain lie sweltering under the summer sun Alpine tourists are encountering bracing air wafted to them from snow-clad peaks whose ermine robes are never melted, even though the torrid rays of the summer sun scorch to death every flower and blade of grass in the low-lying districts. The air is always pure on mountain heights, no matter what form of fell disorder may be raging in the valleys. So universally is this fact recognized that physicians the world over prescribe mountain air as an effectual antidote to disorders considered incurable while the patient remains on lesser elevations.

In the religious thought of the world we find the sacredness of mountain heights a peculiarly conspicuous feature. Temples were almost always built on high ground, and it was a common belief among the ancients that divinities dwelt on mountains, and specially was it felt among the Jews in olden times that God could fight for them on mountain tops, and nowhere else. One of the interpretations given of the name, Jehovah (Yahveh), by some authorities is, "the god of the mountains," a deity who was ever at home in high latitudes, but utterly out of his element on low land.

Puerile as this definition would be of the Supreme Being, if any allusion to the Infinite were contained in it, it accords so precisely with the universal beliefs of ancient peoples that it is but one out of many instances proving that the Israelites shared a common faith with the great mass of humanity, even though at certain periods of the world's history they have undoubtedly been the custodians of a particularly pure and noble monotheism, while Jewish influence the world over has liberally contributed to the advancement of morals, science, philosophy and art.

But to discard the more external meanings of Bible mountains, let us at once give way for the spiritual interpretation which lies so thinly veiled in the literal dress which drapes without concealing its majestic features that any child of ordinary intelligence need not err in learning the lessons such narratives as the account of the transfiguration enforce. As a mountain is a lofty height up which no one can climb without an effort, as when once gained it secures a commanding view of surrounding scenery invisible in the valley, as it frequently rains down into the valleys when it is clear upon the hill-tops, as clouds hang frequently about the mountain sides, obscuring its peaks and completely hiding the celestial panorama we can gaze at when on its summit, the mountain fitly represents a state of mind attained alone through earnest and oft-times laborious effort, a mental state above the doubts, fears, worries and vexations of every-day existence, a state which once reached allows the one who has attained it to gaze henceforth on spiritual glories undiscernible by all save those who have scaled the rocky peaks upon whose towers one may see the pageant of the heavens and not the dust of earth; on mountain heights we are so far above the noise, strife and bustle of ordinary affairs that we seem to dwell in a fairy region, a charmed estate where music not of earth and sights unknown to mortal observation entrance our eyes and ears with glimpses of the realms eternal.

The everlasting hills! What a sublime expression that is. How calm, strong and satisfied the mountains seem! How they appear to smile, half disdainfully and half compassionately at the little nervous enterprises of the ever changing towns and hamlets at their base.

It is not a foolish speculation which leads many to inquire if God is not nearer to us on the mountains than in the valleys. He is not nearer to us, but we are apt to be consciously nearer to Him. The vastness of the solitudes brings us into closer relations with our inner selves, and through the highest in us can we alone approach the highest in the universe. Mountain solitudes are often so terribly oppressive to the external mind that the brain reels, reason totters, and insanity ensues. We have heard of many men, some of them mere youths, who have become maniacs through tending sheep alone on mountain heights. Such experiences were frequently alluded to in ancient works on occultism, where initiatory rites were spoken of as entailing the utmost danger and distress on the weak and faltering, while the strong, persistent, and courageous neophytes grew stronger and more gifted with every trial they encountered, till, at length, they rose superior to every dread, and came off triumphant victors over sense and its seductions.

It may be in place here to allude briefly to an article published some time ago in the *Two Worlds*, an English spiritualistic newspaper, edited by Mrs. E. H. Britten. The article is entitled "Practical Occultism," and the writer is styled "One Who Knows." This article was copied by Dr. J. R. Buchanan in the January 1888 number of his *Journal of Man*, accompanied by editorial comments which are on the whole extremely reasonable, as they are to the effect that no kind of occult discipline which disqualifies one for the performance of the regular appointed duties of life, can be as much a blessing as a drawback to the progress of humanity.

This is just the point we want to emphasize, and it needs especial emphasis at this particular time when occult studies are being pursued, or, at least, looked into by the most intelligent persons everywhere, while, as may be expected, there are many bats in human form ready, if possible, to eclipse the sunshine because they are too blind to appreciate its radiance.

Esoterically considered, the New Testament agrees exactly with the Hindoo Vedas, and every other pure and ancient Scripture designed to preserve a concise record of spiritual discovery upon the earth in the exact language of precise and unchanging correspondence. The recent publication of the "Bhagavad Gita or the Lord's Lay," in a new form, by Mohini M. Chatterji, with copious annotations and references to the Christian Scriptures, has furnished a fresh proof of the striking similarity of one inspired form of teaching to another.

All inspired writers point to one only means of reaching a knowledge of truth, so far as to make it practical in every relation of existence, and that is by going up, or, in other words, going in to the mountain of the higher, which is the inner nature, there to discover the pearl of great price which lies buried in the depths of man's spiritual being, so as to be able when that pearl is found to carry it out into all the family and business transactions of life, till, at length, there is a new earth or external state of justice and purity, as well as a new heaven or higher and deeper internal realization of things divine.

To pay especial attention to the details of the story we are now specially considering, let us note the three disciples accompanying Jesus up the mountain. We find these three going with him wherever he went. John was the most beloved and intimate of all, but Peter, James and John were his constant followers and immediate attendants. They suggest to us the three representative orders of human faculties we all recognize: the moral, the intellectual and the physical, while Jesus represents the immortal soul. All our faculties must go up to the summit of the mountain, or, in other words, our entire nature, classified as it may be in three grand divisions, must be employed in the discovery, diffusion and application of spiritual knowledge to the diversified needs of our common humanity.

Every one needs a time for mountain climbing, and a place which may be to him a holy mountain so far as outward isolation from the busy world can make it so. When it is asked why the Orientals are said to attain spiritual altitudes more readily than members of the bustling communities of the Western world, the answer is invariably the same. Hindoos reply: "We live nearer to the soul of the universe than you do; we care less about money, rank and fashion; we spend less time and thought upon external things than you, and, as a consequence, we have our reward; we seek spiritual bread, and we get it; you seek the stone of wordly honors and distinctions and you get them; according to your desires, so are the answers to your prayers, for all desire and effort is prayer, and as you pray, so you are answered, no matter to whom you pray or what you pray for."

The great question for modern moralists, yes, and for physiologists also to consider is the relation of external striving to health and purity. It may sound to some a worn-out platitude that you are destroying your national health and undermining the very foundations of future greatness, but this truth needs to be sounded as with the voice of a trumpet sounding an alarm, in the ears of all heads of families and public instructors throughout the land. Morality cannot be taught successfully to youth so long as parents and teachers set the example of mammon worship. The influences surrounding a forming mind, subtle, unseen, usually unrecognized influences are what tend to develop character far more effectively than any amount of routine instruction. There is everything in a pure, healthy, invigorating, mental atmosphere. The moral air a child breathes in unconsciously is what molds his temper of thought and character, not the scholastic drill which is often a painful and unwelcome strain on the intellectual faculties.

If, as Dr. Buchanan prophesies, psychometry is to be the dawn of a new civilization, psychometry, which means, literally, soul measurement, another term for psychical perception, must be utilized in tracing the effects of unseen influences on the triune constitution of man. The question is constantly raised as to the education of sensitives. Crammed scholastically they had better never be, for the less they are burdened with pedantic technicalities, the freer and sweeter will be their inspirations. But can any one doubt that something very practical can be accomplished in the way of helping to unfold psychic powers and perceptions naturally?

In the *Two Worlds*, "Schools for the Prophets" are discussed. Mrs. Britten and many of her most intelligent correspondents are strongly in favor of doing something practical in the way of assisting sensitive persons to unfold and use their powers under the best possible conditions. Speaking for ourselves, we are not much in favor of endowed and incorporated institutions for such a purpose, as trustees and directors are too frequently dogmatic and intolerant. They may have excellent financial and executive ability in the business world, but spiritual gifts are not in the market to be auctioned off to the highest bidder. You cannot purchase the gift of the spirit for money. Thus if colleges for sensitives be established there is a danger that, falling into the hands of dogmatists, they will develop into nothing better than mesmeric establishments, in which all the subjects would be connected by means of invisible wires of thought with some centralizing and controlling power, not so much spiritual as material.

The gospel story of the transfiguration need not be considered as a literal historical fact, if one does not so desire to consider it, as its spiritual import is universal. The evangelists tell us of certain methods being adopted and certain ends obtained. We may say then, in a certain sense, a challenge is thrown out to the world; let whoever will pick up the gauntlets. Jesus, the central figure, is exoterically whoever fills the position of a great and advanced teacher; esoterically, he is the spiritual nature in all mankind. The Great Teacher gathers together those of his followers who are prepared to receive a higher lesson in divine truth on the top of a mountain, and there is transfigured before them. Far away from the strife and bustle of the noisy, mercenary, contentious world they are brought face to face with the sublimest aspects of truth the world has ever witnessed; Moses and Elias appear to them. If this is literal history, then they receive on that high altitude, in the clear, bracing air, a proof of human immortality they could never receive on the low tablelands or in the valleys. If the spirit of the story be alone regarded, then, what is Moses but an embodiment of law, or what is Elijah but prophecy personified?

Let us look at Moses in the light of law for a few moments, and then at Elijah in the light of prophecy. Flippant, would-be critics may dismiss biblical narratives with a contemptuous sneer, because the hidden treasure has to be dug out of the mine, and they have neither inclination nor ability to dig it out; but to the student of life's mysteries, to the reverent inquirer into the secrets of the universe, every page in all the Scriptures of the earth glows with the light of a hidden flame, whose guiding light ever beckons the world on to higher and ever higher attainments. The true theory of evolution is more plainly exemplified in Bible history than in all the treatises of Darwin and his followers, even the latest scientific speculations concerning natural selection, and the survival of the fittest are all magnificently illustrated in scripture stories when esoterically interproted.

There can be but little question to-day among those whose researches are something more than despicably superficial, of the existence in remote ages in Egypt of a splendid spiritual dynasty, of which the most powerful and glorious kingly dynasty was but the outward shadow. Chronologists inform us that Egypt was ruled by gods for 13,900 years prior to the reign of demi-gods, who, in their turn, were succeeded by Pharoahs, who were ordinary men, native princes.

Let us strip ancient history of all its fantastic apparel, and let ancient phraseology melt into modern forms of speech. Let us employ the gospel interpretation as a working hypothesis in deciphering the hieroglyphics of the past, contained in the words, "They were called gods, on whom the spirit of God (the Eternal) came," and we can readily perceive how the Jews (the word Jew really means any enlightened person, not necessarily a relative by blood of any special human ancestor) in the days of Moses, probably a contemporary of Sesostris the Great, borrowed and never returned, *i. e.*, carried out of Egypt, the most valuable treasures of wisdom which they locked up at length in the jewel cases of their correspondentially written scriptures. The Mosaic law was a perpetuation of a system of legislation, dating back no doubt to the sunken Atlantis, from which actual (not fabulous) country Egypt received her first impressions of science and religion. The Atlantian heroes and wise men who colonized Egypt were the gods who ruled the country for nearly 14,000 years in the long ago.

The most ancient law buried in the letter of external Mosaism, is the one divine law of truth. It is the universal, spiritual, natural law, to transgress which is sin. This law never changes; it is absolutely immutable, like its author and sustainer, God. When law is transfigured, and not till then, do we see how perfectly at one are all the religious systems and bibles of the world. The unity of law is to be found only in its spirit; its letter killeth, and that which kills also dies, while its spirit giveth life, and therefore lives forever. The great paradox of the New Testament is the presentation of diametrical opposites in the life and teaching of the ideal man. Jesus is constantly represented in the two-fold capacity of law destroyer and law fulfiller. In the sermon on the mount, he disallows the letter of Hebrew legislation in its every particular, and attributes the enforcement of antiquated customs to a spirit of servile submission to the traditions of the past.

How can the law be destroyed in letter but fulfilled in spirit? How can we in this day, in this land, completely set aside the letter of the ancient law, and at the same time enforce its spirit in every particular? Take the Sabbath law as an example. The old Jewish institutes concerning Sabbath observance are literally so repellant to the spirit of human liberty and even justice that we shrink with horror from the thought that a human being was ever put to death for working on the seventh day. We can have no sympathy with the old blue law of New England, which ordained heavy fines and imprisonment for the slightest departure from the rigorous enactments of the Puritans. Still, we all know by practical experience, that one day of rest and recreation out of every seven is intensely beneficial to all who observe such a periodical season of refreshment and repose.

The institution of the Sabbath dates back to an age and country where slave-holding was as common as hired labor is to-day. The Sabbath law was, in its intention, a humane and merciful provision against the overworking of human beings and animals alike. Read the Fourth Commandment of the Decalogue carefully through, and you must, every one of you, be thoroughly convinced that men and women, oxen and asses, as creatures who worked with scarcely an intermission, except for nightly sleep, during six consecutive days of every week, were greatly blessed by having secured to them the rest of the Sabbath. In the olden days, when men were not to be moved, it appears, by any merely human mandate, the authority of a really or assumedly divine revelation was absolutely necessary to compel tyrannical masters to allow their slaves some seasons of repose, and, as Solomon truly and wisely says, "A righteous man regardeth the life of his beast"—the Sabbath law was as stringent concerning animals, as it was concerning men, while an extension of the same law insisted that the land should rest every seventh year, and by thus resting the land, oriental agriculturists prevented the soil from wearing out, and the land from becoming sterile through over-cultivation. So wise and so beneficent is the Sabbath law in its essential spirit, that we can, none of us, afford to disregard it here to-day, and we are happy to say that avowedly materialistic papers, such as the *Boston Investigator*, are as much in favor of intelligent Sabbath observance as any Christian sheet can be.

The question which naturally arises is, What do you mean by Sabbath observance? We answer, We do not mean any sort of ecclesiastical observance, but a healthy cessation of business cares and vexations, for the whole of one day out of seven. Let people go to church if they like, into the parks, onto the water, or wheresoever they please, and if it is found necessary to employ some people on the day when others rest, an equitable arrangement might be made whereby some people should observe the Jewish and others the Christian Sabbath. Still, as far as possible, all should observe the same day, for the purpose of rendering possible a calm and quiet general mental influence due to the absolute cessation of at least nine-tenths of the work done on the six working days. Jesus, in all his teaching and example treated this question in the most practical manner conceivable. He healed the sick on the Sabbath day, thereby dedicating it to the best good of the race physically, as well as morally and mentally; and when accused of being a Sabbath-breaker, he answered, "The Sabbath was made for man, and not man for the Sabbath."

In that statement he caused Moses to appear transfigured before the mental vision of those who claimed to be devoted disciples of the great Hebrew legislator; and when we pass on to a consideration of teachings yet more vital and important, we shall find the same transfigured Moses held up by Jesus to the people in place of the old Mosaic commands, whose literal barbarity is so shockingly repulsive to the enlightened thought of the nineteenth century.

When we spoke against the hanging of the Chicago anarchists, at the time of their trial and condemnation, we took for our text, "Whosoever sheddeth man's blood, by man shall his blood be shed;" but we coupled with it many words attributed to Jesus, taken from the sermon on the mount, in which he most emphatically dissents from the retaliatory interpretation of those grandly prophetic words, the full inner meaning of which can only be comprehended by a true theosophist deeply versed in a knowledge of *Karma*, or the law of consequence. Several Boston newspapers were sent to us by friends in Massachusetts, containing lengthy reports of sermons by Christian ministers, approving of the execution of the anarchists. Almost every one of those sermons, delivered in Christian pulpits, was in downright defiance of Jesus, and justified the comment of a friend who sent us the papers. "If Jesus were on earth to-day, those very ministers would cry out, 'Crucify him.'" We ask, in the name of common sense, how can preachers or hearers be so hypocritical, or so blind to the meaning of words as not to see that their applications of old Hebrew texts to modern events are at deadly variance with the teachings they profess to regard as the words of incarnate Deity? The Christian Church will never put down iniquity, so long as it worships Jesus with the lip, and insults him in every act of legislation. Joseph Cook's oft repeated babble, "May God, have mercy on their souls, but may the Government of the United States not have mercy on their bodies," was one of the most inconsistent sentences any man professing to be a follower of Jesus could possibly utter or frame. As Moses Hull, editor of *The New Thought*, said at Mt. Pleasant Park Camp Meeting in August, 1887, Why do not these professing Christians condemn men for shaving the corners of their beards, for the same chapter in Leviticus which enforces the barbaric commands against which the sermon on the mount so forcibly inveighs, is as strict in its denunciations against shaving the whole face, as it is against adultery.

Swedenborgians interpret the old law spiritually, and thereby assist in the transfiguration of Moses; but we regret to say that even among people professedly constituting the New Jerusalem Church, there are some who advocate capital punishment. "An eye for an eye, a tooth for a tooth," is still their motto, in spite of all that Jesus said so earnestly against it, and the singular anachronism is, that the very people who advocate these awful barbarities read as a portion of the divine word publicly in their churches the most emphatic condemnation of their own acts. We do not wish to be severe, but we cannot resist repeating the words of an intelligent Oriental, who had just been studying the New Testament, "Well, it is difficult for me to see how any Christian can advocate capital punishment without being either an idiot or a hypocrite."

We have no difficulty in perceiving that the original intent of even such a monstrous act as decapitation may have been to deter others from crime, and therefore may have seemed legitimate; but that the wisest men of the East saw no deeper into human nature than to believe that doing evil that good may come, brings good to pass, is something we neither will nor can believe.

The lesson to be derived from the appearance of Moses on the Mount of Transfiguration is primarily and essentially the adjustment of our laws in harmony with the Sermon on the Mount. When the vail is removed, and law appears in its own intrinsic beauty, undimmed by false disguise, there will no longer be any need for prisons, jails and penitentiaries, but before these institutions, relics of barbarism that they are, are totally abolished, prison reform must be carried to such a pitch that going to prison will be looked upon in the same light as going to school or to a hospital.

Moral asylums are needed just as asylums for the blind, the deaf and dumb. And as visitors go frequently to these latter institutions to watch the progress made by those who, often from some unknown cause, have been deprived of some natural gift, toward the obtaining or recovery of it, so should prison inspectors take an active interest and sincere delight in the moral recovery of those who, often through infamous early training, or lack of training, have so comported themselves as to render their temporary captivity within four walls necessary for their own reform and others safety. We are not necessarians, and we do not condone offences; but what we do maintain is that love being the fulfilling of the divine law, only through loving administration is the world to be redeemed from the innumerable errors which now curse it.

What a lesson the disciples of Jesus must have learned on the top of that mysterious mount where Moses thus marvelously appeared rehabilitated in the garments of loving kindness! What a difficult lesson it was for Peter to digest, who, even at the most affecting moment of his beloved Master's surrender of himself into the hands of his accusers, thought to advance that Master's interest by lifting up his sword and cutting off the ear of the high priest's servant Malchus! How small must be the mind of any caviler who picks at the outer garb of the gospel story, and utterly fails to see how applicable are all the events therein recorded to the present day and this very land of ours. Was it, after all, enthusiasm for the Master, or was it a feeling of spiteful revenge which lifted Peter's hand? He could not have been, at that time, very brave or noble, when he so soon after denied his Master! Hot-headed impetuosity is never associated with genuine fealty and lasting friendship. The man who would fight boldly for Jesus was the man who was the most ready, through cowardice, to deny him. Physical culture dissociated from spiritual culture develops the pugilist, who is never brave. The gymnasium, and certainly the fighting ring, will develop in one and the same person a herculean body and a pigmy soul; physical giants are often mental dwarfs. To strike a blow or fire a pistol is not courageous. Courage gives the soft answer and therewith turns away wrath.

Oh! how often do we witness the saddening spectacle of men and women seeking to enforce discipline by boxing children's ears, and other cowardly and wicked practices. Children grow up sneaks and criminals, become yet viler through the machinery of a law of hate and fear, when a loving, just, and merciful regime would educate little ones, and reform criminals.

But we must revert, ere we conclude, to the appearance of Elijah, or Elias, who was the embodiment of prophecy, as Moses was of law. Prophecy is said by Paul to be the greatest of all spiritual gifts. Now, what is prophecy? A prophet is a seer, one who looks ahead, who scans the heavens, and foretells coming events; but he is, most of all, an exhorter—one possessing the power to speak directly to the hearts and consciences, as well as to the intellects of his hearers. Between priest and prophet there is always the same difference that there is between inventor and copyist, between creative and imitative genius. Priests and those under them do not usually believe in prophecy, and they often stone the prophets. A prophet can not be confined within the narrow limits of any man-made creed, he can not submit to having his wings clipped and living like an eagle in a cage. He must be free as the air, and he would rather starve than compromise. Of such pure metal was Elijah made, and of such, verily in every age and country, may it be said, "Their's is the kingdom of heaven." No earthly crown decorates their brow, no earthly honors and emoluments are theirs, nor do they seek them; their motto is ever, "For God and for humanity," and their whole life is an exemplification of the truth to which, through good repute and ill, through fire and sword if need be, they steadfastly adhere. The significance of the appearance of Elijah on the Mount of Transfiguration is far removed above that controversial speculation which disputes over the literal identy of John the Baptist with Elias of old. Whether John the Baptist was the personal Elias re-embodied is not a question of any vital moment.

Elijah is the synonym of prophecy, the representative of prophets everywhere, and for all time. When prophesy is transfigured, or, in other words, understood not in the killing letter, but in the life-giving spirit, it no longer appears as unconditional as it did before. Israel of old was so favorably situated that all things seemed conspiring together to make of the house of Israel and of the city of Jerusalem the greatest nation and the metropolis of the whole earth. Had Israel always remained true to her sacred trust, had she invariably adhered to the commandments of the decalogue, the day could never have arrived when the name of Caesar had to be acknowledged in Palestine.

It was the scheming, calculating spirit which animated the demagogues in the days of Jesus to curry favor at the court of Rome by condemning the innocent to death, that through many centuries as a deadly but most insidious poison, had been lurking in the veins of the Israelitish people. This alone it was which wrought their downfall and made it possible for the Christ to weep on Olivet. No more touching scene has ever been portrayed than that of the weeping Savior of a doomed humanity—not doomed by any cruelty of God, but self-destroyed, preferring war to peace, hate to love, falsehood to truth, vice to virtue. Is there a medical man who can not at once apply the scene to many among his own patients? Faithfully and patiently he has pointed out to them their errors, reasoning and remonstrating with them till time and language were alike exhausted, and then, when they had proved utterly incorrigible, in sadness he has turned away and lamented the idiotic folly of men and women rushing headlong to physical perdition, when the means had been placed within their grasp of working out their own salvation ere it became too late.

Prophecy is not prediction solely or chiefly, it is first of all and more than all, exhortation. The true prophet is a genuine exhorter, one who sets the truth before the world with convincing power and fervor; one who, with more than usual hindsight, insight, and foresight, knows the inevitable law of consequence more fully than his fellows, and consecrates that knowledge zealously, untiringly to blessing the world. No prophet can tell you what will of necessity befall you; but he can tell you what must inevitably acrue if a certain course of action is persisted in.

Nothing is more natural than prophecy. From a spiritual standpoint prophecy is an exact science, and the understanding of it as such is the master key to all those occult mysteries which continually beset us. When the followers of Jesus knew what prophecy really meant, all their national hopes were dashed to pieces. No longer could they regard the Infinite Jehovah as the tribal deity of the Jewish clan, almost exclusively interested in the welfare of a fragment of the human race. A broader conception took possession of their minds, and henceforward God to them appeared as no respecter of persons, but a respecter of righteousness only. This sublime view of Deity was not new; Hebrew prophets had entertained and expressed it long before, but there is little reason for supposing that the Jews as a people had ever risen to a general acceptance of the idea of a universal and utterly impartial Deity.

To apply this subject to vital issues of the living present, we have only to change the time and scene of gospel episodes to render them intensely applicable to present conditions in Europe and America. We need to press the matter still nearer home, and individualize the lesson of the story, by contemplating how poor a thing is bald prediction when applied to our own circumstances, while genuine prophecy, that gift of the spirit which Paul extolled above so many others, is the richest dower which can fall to the lot of any human being.

It requires a lecture on heredity to explain in anything like detail the working of the prophetic element in daily life. Supposing you are told your lungs are weak, and you believe it, and instead of setting to work to strengthen your system by healthy discipline you give in to the saddening thought—a thought most woefully depressing wherever entertained—that it is a part of your ill luck or adverse fortune to succumb to a terrible disorder. You fulfill a vile, and perhaps utterly baseless prediction by affiliating in thought with the very forces which tend to tear you down, while you might just as readily have affiliated with an opposite class of influences, association with which would have built you up. Now take an instance on the other side, being told that you inherit an exceptionally robust constitution, and that in consequence of being thus naturally vigorous you are bound to live a long life and enjoy excellent health to the end of your days, you fritter away your energy in disgraceful dissipation; you will most certainly fail, like the hare in the old fable, while your less fortunately started neighbor may be the winning tortoise in the race.

These illustrations are intensely commonplace, but our ambition is to be practical, not to indulge in flights of eloquence or flowers of rhetoric. Let the history of the Jewish people two thousand years ago and the history of all peoples who have once been great, but who have yielded to the corroding moth of presumptuous self-satisfaction, lead us all to yield to that glorious Elias ministry of the soul, which, in the stentorian tones of a rugged and utterly inelegant dweller in the deserts, often proclaims to us the only means of escape from all the evils which menace us, when he lifts up his voice in the wilderness, and loudly cries: "Repent, for the kingdom of heaven is at hand." A kingdom of heaven is now at our doors. We are entering upon a new social, religious, and political order. The great industrial problems of the hour, the tremendous struggle between capital and labor, between monopoly and justice, can not much longer be dallied with; the final issue can not much longer be delayed by unsatisfactory temporizing in the way of palliative concessions, when radical reform is loudly called for over all the earth. Not those who fare delicately, and are clad in costly raiment are the prophets, but those who dare to lift up their voice in humanity's cause, espousing right and liberty even though their cry shall cause thrones to totter, and shall shake the hoary foundations of a false political system until it falls about the ears of those whose material interest it is to uphold it.

Let no cringing servility to wealth or fashion seal our lips, or cause us to lay down our pens. Let one and all buckle on the armor and fight with the spiritual and intellectual weapons of persuasive argument and forcible denunciation of wrong, the demon tyranny which still holds multitudes in thrall. America, the richest, fairest, freest land beneath the sun, even you, with all your great advantages can not afford to trust idly in your luck, for if you do not speedily hold converse with Elijah on the mountain, or, to change the metaphor, lift high the banner of pure morality upon the folds of which is inscribed the sacred watchword "Justice," all your advantages will be as naught, for unerring prophecy ever declares that nation and that state which is distinguished above others for equitable government, righteous laws and a united people, shall assuredly wear the crown and wave the palm whenever the day arrives on which we shall see infinite justice in righteousness award the prize of supremacy to those who, above all others, love justice and mercy, and thereby serve the Eternal in truth, and keep His commandments.

LESSON VII.

TRUE INDIVIDUALITY,—IN WHAT SENSE AND TO WHAT EXTENT IS MAN A FREE MORAL AGENT, AND WHAT IS THE ULTIMATE OF INDIVIDUAL SPIRITUAL ATTAINMENT.

THE problem of divine sovereignty and human free agency is one of the most difficult ever presented to the human mind for solution, and we certainly do not expect to solve the problem fully so as to remove all difficulties out of the way of the honest inquirer, nevertheless we hope to throw at least a little practically helpful light upon it.

In this age when it is customary in many quarters, presumably learned and scientific, to deny the supernatural altogether, it is necessary to define clearly what truth underlies the doctrines of supernaturalism.

The word nature signifies a something born, therefore if nature is something born, the laws of nature are laws governing something born, or laws inherent in this something born, we know that nothing is born without parents and that nothing can come into existence without an adequate cause. The so-called supernatural is strictly speaking only super-phenomenal, supermaterial, super-sensuous, or super-terrestrial.

Supernaturalism arises with the conviction that there is in divine power an unlimited faculty of causation, God being an infinite and omnipresent cause, knowing no beginning or ending of his work but dwelling and working in an eternal present.

Whenever enlightened Hebrews called the Divine Being Yahveh or Jehovah, they signified by this term the Being who always was and who therefore ever will be. The Eternal One who was never made and could never be destroyed.

When a child inquires, "If God made everything, who made God?" his question is simply puerile and insignificant, because if you could tell who made God, the question would then occur, who made the being who made God? And then if you reached in your reply to the being who made God, you would have to answer still another question, viz.: who made the being who made the being who made God? You would be of necessity obliged at length to take the position that there is, because there must be, a self-existent something or some one. The entire difference between theism and atheism, and between gnosticism and agnosticism is a difference with regard to the attributes of the self-existent being.

The atheist is obliged to admit that something always was and ever will be; that something was never created and can never be destroyed. He says you can not destroy an atom, that annihilation is inconceivable as applied to substance itself, and if nothing can be put out of existence, then nothing was ever brought into existence. Theism goes further and affirms that the eternal something which never came into existence and can never go out of existence is not unconscious and therefore unwise, for it would be an axiomatic absurdity to declare that the something always in existence is less than the something not always in existence; it consequently follows that if consciousness, love, wisdom, spiritual life, in a word all the virtues, were not always in existence, you are brought face to face with the miracle of creation, of something made out of nothing. Therefore, those who deny God and substitute an unconscious nature teach the absurdity of something being created out of nothing, for if goodness, wisdom, will, intelligence, mind, spirit, soul, if everything relating to our higher being was not always in existence, how did it ever come into existence? But if that which was never made, never even made itself, but ever was and ever will be, if the Eternal Being includes all attributes pertaining to nobility of mind and soul, if all the attributes and elements we desire to be permanent, were in the eternal heart from eternity and will remain in the same eternal heart to eternity, this view induces us to regard our individual finite personal lives here as nothing other than expressions in limited form of attributes, elements and principles which are infinite and eternal in the fullness of their being.

People talk of divine existence as totally apart from human existence very often. It is not absolutely correct to speak of God's *existence*, but it is entirely correct to speak of man's existence; existence means expression. Existence is a revelation of something. God is eternal *being*, and existence which is external, is a manifestation of being. Therefore we say that we *exist* but that God *is*. In making such a statement we logically, in technical language, convey our idea concerning *eternal being* and *temporary existence*.

When we know what we *are*, we have discovered the absolute and infinite truth of being itself; when we have reached to that stage in the ladder of our journey we shall look no longer at things as they *seem* but shall behold them as they *are*; then we shall know what Longfellow meant and all that any poet could imply in that wonderful statement in the Psalm of Life, "Things are not what they seem."

As long as we dwell in the region of the *seeming* we live in a lower region than the region of *being*. When we deal with things as they appear we do not usually deal with them as they are. All the delusions and counterfeits with which we are so accustomed to deal, will pass away, and be destroyed forever; but that which is permanent, whatever is real substance, cannot ever be destroyed. Destruction of error is accomplished in the sense in which folly is destroyed by the advance of wisdom, for wisdom is greater than folly, folly being but the absence of wisdom. Ignorance is destroyed through education, for education brings knowledge; knowledge is greater than ignorance, for ignorance is but the absence of knowledge. All our frailties, imperfections, faults, and misbeliefs, all our imperfect dreams and personal vagaries, will at length be cast into a bottomless pit, and be burned with unquenchable fire, while all that is real, our true being, all that is preservable because worth preserving, will forever, in our individual consciousness, enable us in the limited circle of individual capacity to say, I am as the Eternal, embracing eternal life. Every child of God, every son and daughter of the Most High reaching the bed rock, touching the eternal foundation upon which is reared the temple of finite existence, can say forever,

"*I am.*" The realization of this divine individuality, this glorious identity of soul that forever will be man's blessed portion, is the only infallible evidence of one's entrance into the true Kingdom of Heaven, or Nirvana, to which many Orientals especially look forward with such earnest and eager quest.

Many people, in consequence of a total ignorance of genuine Theosophy, suppose that hundreds of millions of people desire annihilation, which implies that they desire that their individual souls should no longer retain identity; what they really desire is complete destruction of personal or external selfhood, or the lower nature, whose passions constantly war against the higher.

We tell you most emphatically that you have to lose your outer self in order to find your inner self. You must part with all that personality which makes you disagreeable to one another and engenders animosity and rivalry, in order to find that divine individuality which teaches you to enjoy each the other's welfare and to live in perfect peace and harmony throughout eternity as a thoroughly united family. When you attain the glorious height of spiritual perfection, when you have trod the perfect way, reached the perfect goal and won the perfect prize, you will have lost everything that could possibly make you disagreeable to any one, and every one around you will have lost whatever could possibly make them disagreeable to you, but you will retain everything that makes you agreeable and valuable to each other and you will have found in this ocean of love, infinite powers of enjoyment which you never dreamed of when you were on earth concerning yourself with external business with a view to outdoing your neighbor.

We endeavor to point our students to the higher truths of spirit, to the higher view of immortal life, so we have to tell them there are things to forget as well as to remember; there is a memory to be killed as well as a memory to be cultivated; there is a carnal selfish self that must die and never rise again, as well as an eternal identity that never can die; we assure you that the only things that can be destroyed are things that cause you discord and trouble by alienating you in interest one from another. All desire to kill must be annihilated; the desire of one nation to make war upon another must be annihilated; the disposition of one person to hate or slander another must be annihilated, with everything that makes you rivalrous and selfishly ambitious; for when you enter fully into the glorious region of the truly real, and the principle of absolute being is known and understood, you will all unite, all coalesce, so as to all form one glorious heavenly company, one divine choir: and as in a grand organ there are many stops and many parts which harmoniously blend together and as there swells forth as a result of this blending, a volume of sound wherein one cannot distinguish with an untrained ear the separate sound of each sweet note; or as in some great and glorious choir pouring forth melodious harmony you hear the music of a thousand voices, but cannot discriminate with the untutored ear, one voice from another; the reason why you fail to detect individuality is because you are not trained sufficiently in the sense of hearing to discriminate; but bring a thoroughly trained musician into the presence of ever so mighty a torrent of sound and he will tell you he hears each separate voice in the chorus no matter how many are singing at once, and if any voice is singing out of tune, he can tell which voice it is. When we have found our true identity we shall know each other as we shall know ourselves, we shall all be individual members of the celestial orchestra, each an individual member of a perfectly harmonious choir; those angels who are now able to distinguish us truly the one from the other in the sense of recognizing each of us to the extent of knowing how we are all performing our respective parts, individualize us perfectly in their thoughts and we shall all somewhere find that individuality is ours (in a far more glorious and perfect sense than now) when it is apparently to outward sense lost in the mass of perfected humanity than it ever was when we took an arrogant position of aggressive selfhood and endeavored to annihilate the individuality of every other member of the race by setting our interests in conflict with those of our brethern.

In the eternal harmonies of the universe every soul must play its own part and sing its own song; in the glorious temple of eternity every individual will be found in his proper place, and as nature has stamped individuality upon every atom, upon every globule, as individuality is the very basis of life, true individuality is consistent and compatible with perfect accord and perfect coalescence. In the divine life let us think of ourselves as all forming one great family of the Most High, in perfect harmony the one with the other, each individual enjoying the blessedness of recognition by friends and kindred, not in the earthly, but in the highest spiritual sense forever.

When we have found our souls, and not until then, have we found the purpose of our existence or the guiding principle of our life. When we have found our inmost identity, we have found that which can never desert us; but until then we are wandering on, often in complete darkness and never in a very bright light. We are all thoroughly differentiated on earth; not only are we endowed with special individuality and appointed special works, but we all differ the one from the other in our stage of development, and therefore, in our perception of the principle of being. The reason why there are so many differences of opinion in the world is simply because so many different people are obliged to look at matters from their own peculiar standpoints; no one *can* look at a matter from another standpoint than his own. All persons have not an equally wide horizon, all cannot see equally far, no matter how much they may try to; all cannot hear an equal number of sounds, no matter how intently they may listen to music; all cannot smell an equal number of perfumes or taste an equal number of flavors, no matter how much they may strive to. As we cannot all see, hear, taste, smell or touch equally much, some of us being far more limited in capacity than others, owing to some being further along the line of spiritual development than others, so all again cannot look at matters from the same side, some standing as it were with face to the north, others to the south, and others to the east and west; those who gaze northward see something that exists; so do those who look in the other directions, but they do not see the same things; but though they do not see the same things, they see different portions of the one truth; often because of not seeing the whole truth, they act like children having some blocks of a puzzle, but not all, while it is necessary to have every block to complete the puzzle or picture; therefore if you have not all in your possession, the puzzle remains a puzzle and the riddle continues a riddle. Leave out a single necessary ingredient in some compound, and you cannot form the compound until you have procured the lacking ingredient.

Different people start out in different directions and arrive necessarily at different conclusions; they ignorantly imagine all others must be wrong if they are right, while others may be partially right and they partially wrong, but all will at somo time learn they have each seen a portion of truth, and foolishly imagined the portion they saw to be the whole; this error was the whole of their mistake.

One person says, "I believe in fate"; he recognizes a portion of truth. Another says, "I believe in free will"; he recognizes another portion of truth. One says, "I believe in foreordination, in predestination, in God's sovereignty"; he recognizes a portion of truth. Another says, "I believe that every man enjoys freedom of will, and has to work out his own salvation; that he is the arbiter of his own fate, and that his destiny lies in his own hands"; such an one has also discovered a portion of the truth. Now, when we inquire how the seseemingly irreconcilable truths are all parts of one great truth, it is important for us to remember that while certain grand declarations of wisdom are irrefutable, we very often state a principle in words correctly, and then argue incorrectly because we have not understood the true application of the principle as an entirety to all its parts.

You make a statement which is perfectly true; "there is an infinite will; the infinite will cannot be thwarted; there is an infinite plan which cannot be frustrated;" but because this is true you go on to say, erroneously, that certain other things which are also true, cannot be: that man cannot have a free will because there is an infinite will for example, which is false reasoning from a true principle. The principle is sound; there is an infinite will, but you have not discovered what is the will of the Being whose will is infinite; now if it is the will of the Infinite that man should enjoy free will, though man's free will must necessarily be only so far free as the eternal will ordains it to be free, divine providence permits of the freedom of the human will, as a smaller circle enclosed within the infinite circle of divine sovereignty.

To bring this eternal and infinite question to the level of our daily actions, and thus bring it within the comprehension of the youngest child, we will illustrate by the familiar representation of parent and child, which is always the highest, sweetest and truest illustration that can be given of the dealings of the Eternal One with his children. You as a parent are physically and mentally a great deal stronger than your child; if you choose you can restrict your child's actions so that he can never take a step alone, you can so govern and command him, if you will, that he can never give utterance to a single opinion you do not approve; if you choose to hold your child so thoroughly under your control, he never can go out of doors unless you take him out, he need never be a moment out of your sight, and never deviate a single iota from your desire. You would under such a *regime* be fully carrying out your will as to your child, and in such a case it would be your will that your child should have no will of his own.

But if on the other hand you voluntarily give your child a certain amount of freedom, you remonstrate with him, reason with him, and then say, "Now, you have heard what I say and know what I wish, but you can do as you like; I advise, recommend and request you to do a certain thing, but I permit you to do as you choose;" would you not be exercising your will discretionally with your child as fully as in the other dissimilar case? In this case it would be your will that your child should exercise some will of his own.

The question for theologians and philosophers to decide, is this: Has the Eternal Will ordained that we should nave no will, or some will of our own? Has the Eternal Will decreed we should have a limited amount of freedom, or no freedom at all?

Our teaching is, that the Eternal Will wills us finite freedom as a means of developing within us nobility and grandeur of disposition. We believe that the possession of that gift is the primal cause of the soul's embodiment. Many Theosophists believe that the soul which has forever dwelt in the bosom of the Eternal Infinite, the soul being an uncreated spark of the divine fire, the child of the Infinite Spirit, awakes to the consciousnesss of its own individuality and begins to reflect upon it, when an impulse from the Eternal awakens within it the power of choice.

There is much truth in the theological doctrine of the Fall of Man, and also in the Darwinian hypothesis of the ascent of man, for man falls in order to rise. The soul does not come in contact with matter, does not take up its abode in an earthly tabernacle, and enter a terrestrial school to do nothing and learn nothing; all our earthly discipline or experience is for the purpose of developing that individuality and voluntary nobility of character which alone makes noble men and women, and at length develops celestial angels.

We may conceive of the soul prior to any earthly experience doing right from necessity; but the same soul after all its earthly pilgrimages are completed, returns to the angelic home and does right from choice. The soul before it has known earthly experience at all obeys the divine will automatically as a machine obeys the machinist, as an instrument responds to the master hand of a performer; but when the soul goes back to that wonderful home in spirit whence it came to earth, it has acquired during its term of experience a power to love and choose the right, and is therefore no longer an automatic machine, but a machine that understands its own movement, and instead of obeying the hand that works it from necessity, consciously and voluntarily obeys from love. Is there not an immense difference between unthinking and thoughtful obedience? Between reflective and unreflective adoration? Between one who obeys consciously from love, and one who obeys from necessity, without realizing any other possible course of action than the one he is pursuing?

Again to cite the analogy of child and parent, you see this truth illustrated; a very little child obeys you without knowing why; that little child is pure and innocent; you endow it in mind with every sweet and charming attribute of purity, but when you know that the many trials and tribulations of life lie before that young and tender one, though you know that ere the child grows up to be a man or woman he or she will have to fight a way through the world and may fall into many pits and pass through a veritable Slough of Despond en route to the Celestial City, you feel that out of it your beloved one will rise with added experience upon the other side, and therefore even though you knew all that your children would have to encounter in the world, you would still send them out into the world; you would not lock them up so that they could never be contaminated with a breath of impurity; you would not say they will lose their virtue while fighting the battle of life, but you still prefer to send them out to fight it; then when like valiant soldiers returning from battle, though there are scars upon their cheeks, those scars are glorious, for they are the evidences of successful encounter with the adversary; that they have been wounded by the enemy makes the boys dearer to you than they ever were before.

Do you not think that in times of war when a mother welcomes home her son who has been mutilated in battle, but who has been great and noble through all, she is more proud of him than when she rocked him in his cradle or danced him on her knee as a little babe? It may be that the young man has not always maintained a perfectly moral record; it may be that he has done many things for which he was sorry afterward in his soldier life, much that he would fain erase, many mistakes he would not repeat, but still there is more pride, more rejoicing (and more cause for it), when the boy comes home a bronzed and bearded man with all the stain of travel and scars of battle upon him, than when he was ushered into the world a sweet little infant who did not know the difference between right and wrong.

We believe so firmly that all earthly discipline is for a good purpose, that all our sufferings and trials are a part of our education, that there is a *divinity* that shapes ours ends (not a chance or a fate) that whenever we are called upon to give consolation to those in sorrow or bereavement, we feel we can honestly with our whole soul tell them that all discipline is for their good and they will rise out of it ennobled, strengthened and purified.

Whenever we meet a poor suffering creature who has sinned and suffered, who has, like the prodigal son, in the parable, reached even the swine's trough and only been brought to a right mind when famishing with hunger, we feel that when the discipline is over, when the suffering consequent upon the sin has yielded peaceable fruits of righteousness, when after having fallen into manifold temptations he has developed patience and nobility, directly he has renounced his love of evil and overcome his infirmity, borne the penalty and through it grown wiser, that we are fully justified in saying to him—for we have the evidences before us—"Thy sins are forgotten, wiped out, outgrown, overcome, go in peace." Such was the course always pursued by the meek and lowly Jesus and all the world's greatest benefactors everywhere. But remember that whilst you are doing wrong in rebelling against the higher voice, your own conscience will not allow you peace. You may strive for it, other people may pronounce it, but your conscience permits you no peace until you have overcome the love of evil; then when the dicipline of pain has awakened within you the divine love of virtue, though all the world may brand you, all the uncharitable people in creation may tell you that you are not fit for decent society, God speaks peace in your heart, the returning prodigal and repentant Magdalene feels the peace of God which passeth all mortal understanding, a peace which cannot be bestowed by the world and which the world therefore cannot take away. We have all to deal with God as a divine Judge in ourselves, the judgment seat is within us, but the mercy seat is beyond and above us where the Eternal reigns, where angels are, where bright and holy ones are who have passed out of great tribulations into realms of glory, where the pure ones are who have outgrown the love of everything but purity.

There is the mercy seat, so when we approach the higher power we approach infinite love, in which there is no reproach, but as the infinite love streams down upon us, as the light of divine mercy makes its way into our souls, telling us there is a higher and better way, ever saying, "Behold, I show unto you a more excellent way," that divine life, light and love constitute all the fire there is in "purgatory" or "hell," either in this world or any other.

Let us thank God for the "fires of hell," illustrations of which were drawn by Jesus from the pit of

Gehenna outside the gate of Jerusalem, wherein all the refuse of the city was consumed, Gehenna being a sanitary institution that the atmosphere of the city might be pure and its streets clean.

So outside of this world, or the realm of man's mortal observation there is an ever-burning fire, and when a rich man who cares nothing for his fellow creatures while on earth, who is less kind than oriental dogs, and will let the dogs pay their serviceable attentions to the best of their ability to the poor Lazarus covered with sores, without taking example from them even to the extent of giving the beggar the crumbs from his table, when such a selfish miser, who cares for nothing and no one but thinks entirely of his own personal comfort and luxury finds himself in hell and there lifts his eyes in torments, what effect does the fire have upon him? When it has burned him so severely that he would gladly fall at the feet of the Lazarus whom he had spurned, if he could but obtain from him but a single drop of water to cool his burning tongue, he outgrows his selfishness and pride, and while we are not told that the sufferings have as yet abated, before they begin to abate they have shown their reformatory nature, for that man who was the very embodiment of luxurious self-indulgence, the very personification of egotism, never thinking previously of any one but himself, or of anything beyond his own dinner, his own house and his own comfort, even though suffering intensely, exclaims, "would that an angel might be sent to my brethren lest they also come into this place of torment."

The world wants to know what Jesus really

preached, to hear the New Testament explained, instead of ridiculed, the hidden wisdom revealed, instead of listening to ignorant attacks upon ancient spiritual literature made by people who are not capable of understanding its true meaning.

Jesus taught that all suffering by fire, all torment, if you will, was God's angel of deliverance leading us to higher knowledge and nobler life. Jesus, familiar as he must have been with the opinions of the people about him, with Jerusalem and its outskirts, with the traditional beliefs of the House of Israel, with Talmudic and Rabbinical literature (having when only twelve years of age entered into consultation with the learned council of the Sanhedrim, the highest council in Israel), understood perfectly that Gehenna was a place of purification. In reading the Greek Testament, it may not be scholarly to translate the word for everlasting (as some Universalists have translated it), *long-enduring*, for in several instances the same adjective has been variously translated *eternal* and *everlasting* simply for the sake of euphony, the original being in both instances the same. Do not be surprised, when we say that we are very glad the Universalists are not right in this particular, because if the fire were not eternal, if the time ever came when the fire should go out, then those who were not thoroughly redeemed, would have to remain for eternity in their sins. The divine fire which burns eternally, burns in us, as well as without us, eternally; it torments us only until we have learned our needed lesson, and then that same fire yields us indescribable comfort and delight. The fire burns in the *moral sense*, and who is there that wishes to get rid of conscience, to blot it out so as to have no conscience throughout eternity? Not one who thinks at all on this subject, can deny that the conscience which upbraids and accuses and is the source of our greatest misery, when it applauds, is the source of our greatest joy.

If you are seemingly alone in the world, fighting for the right, with no friend in the material form to stand by you, and your conscience says you are in the right, if you feel the Eternal Being sees your heart, reads your motive, you would surely rather let everything else go than have conscience destroyed or your sense of the divine omnipresence removed.

Take away from one who has committed an act of murder in the dark (no man having seen him he cannot be led to the gallows) all sense of divine scrutiny, of God's omnipresence, he might have comparative peace, because conscience is as terrible to him as it is beautiful and blessed to the other. In the one case "Thou God seest me" saves a man from suffering; in the other case it drives him to desperation; in the one instance it supports him even though the whole world is against him; it enables him to so triumph inwardly that though his flesh were to perish at the stake he would sing praises to the Most High and know it is but a leap from flames to glory; but in the other case it compels him to throw himself upon human justice, confess his crime, or else go raving mad and die in despair, possibly by suicide. In both cases it is the same conscience, and the application of its working to two diametrically opposite states of mind is necessarily divine. Now if we follow that poor wretched victim of perverted instincts into the invisible world, even though he is condemned to execution, or though he commit suicide, even though he drink to drown his sorrow, until through temporary insanity he is run over by horses in the street—no matter what becomes of him, what sufferings he may have to endure on the other side of the grave as well as on this—you will meet him among the blessed in eternity; and when you meet him thus, no matter when or where, with all his sufferings outlived, with all his sins outgrown, with all his miseries forever vanquished, that man will possess the same conscience, the same realization of right and wrong, though in a higher degree, but it will conduce to his bliss among the angels; he will then say, "Thank God for my conscience. Thank God for that once dreaded text of scripture, 'Thou God seest me', for now I realize the truth involved in it as essential to my unending happiness."

When we realize that all that once caused us pain, suffering or sorrow is necessary to the development of our highest happiness, then we shall have made a right use of free. will; we shall then enjoy perfect freedom of will; a will to choose between our higher and lower self, a will to choose between the hosts of heaven that side with our conscience, and the hosts of those yet in darkness who side with our passions; but we shall then always choose on the right side.

We are placed here on earth between opposing powers; those who urge us up and those who try to drag us down; it all comes in the long run to this: That we must struggle between conscience and passion, for all higher influences reach us through our moral sense, while all lower influences reach us through our animal proclivities.

Let us realize ourselves as ever between the higher and the lower spheres, and remember that as our power of resistance, like the extent of our knowledge, is not a fixed quantity that can never be increased. When we are very weak we cannot move a chair out of our way, while at another time we can almost carry a piano upon our shoulders. We are continually increasing in bodily and mental strength so that we become daily the creators of circumstances instead of their creatures, and the time will come when we shall acknowledge no sovereign but the Eternal Being; when all personal wills will have lost their hold upon us, when all external circumstances will be under our government and control, and we who have been faithful over a few things will be rulers over many things.

Our freedom of will is a constantly growing quantity; but we can never be free from God's will, and when we are sensible we never wish to be. When we reach our highest condition we shall know God's will, and appreciate as well as understand it, both love and obey it, then we shall be under no earthly control. No one will then be able to enslave us, for having outgrown that condition wherein we are servants to our own lower inclinations and proclivities, and are therefore creatures and tools of lower wills, we shall be servants of God, and shall obey no other ruler. We shall obey the Eternal as he makes his will known in our souls, because we love and appreciate the perfect goodness of his will. And thus with no dread of God, but with the understanding coupled with the love of God; with no dread of punishments, with no irksome sense of being under government, we shall obey, because our own higher nature feels the beauty and blessedness of obedience; in such condition we are perfectly free in truth, and this perfect freedom of our will will be our crown and our prize in that glorious state of immortality where sin and misery are unknown forever.

LESSON VIII.

WHAT IS THE PERFECT WAY AND HOW MAY WE WALK IN IT?

"Be ye perfect even as your Father which is in heaven is perfect."

THESE words have been spoken of again and again, as implying that which is impossible. How can man be perfect even as the Eternal One is perfect? Can man be omnipresent, omniscient and omnipotent? Can man be infinitely wise and loving, pure and just and good? Can man be on a level with the great Eternal Being who is the life and the soul of all the universe and its myriad forms of existence? "Can man by searching find out God," and can he discover absolutely the very existence of the divine Being?

This is a question that scientists, philosophers and theologians have endeavored again and again to answer, but have in many instances utterly failed to comprehend.

If there is difficulty in finding God, in describing him, in making known to the world his attributes, what must be the difficulty of complying with the injunction "be ye as perfect as the Eternal?" For surely if we are to be as perfect as the Eternal we must know everything about the Eternal and shape our lives voluntarily in obedience to our knowledge.

If, however, there remaineth no longer any mystery

for us in the divine nature which our spirit has not solved, if there are no impediments in our search for God which are not thoroughly removed by the discoveries of intuition, can we not deem it possible for us in some sense to obey the commandment, "Be ye perfect even as your Father in heaven is perfect."

With all reverence we make the assertion that even God cannot be more perfect than his nature allows him to be, and, therefore, if the nature of God is an all perfect nature and God lives in perfect harmony with the requirements of that all perfect nature, if the divine thought, the divine word, the action are all in perfect union with the divine ideal, in union with the divine sentiment; then the nature of God is infinitely perfect, but it has infinite capacities, infinite powers, infinite possibilities. And however glorious our conception of the Eternal One may be, however majestic the idea in our minds, of the Eternal Majesty of the Infinite, our intuition tells us it is impossible for God to be more perfect than his nature allows him to be, and if he is infinitely perfect his nature permits of infinite perfection.

Why did an Apostle say it is impossible for God to lie, but because God is infinite truth, and a nature that is infinitely true cannot be finitely false, for infinity includes all there is, and outside the pale of infinity there can be nothing. Therefore to conceive of an infinitely true God is to conceive of a God who cannot lie and who cannot wish to lie, as the infinite will being perfectly true to truth can have no emotion in the direction of falsehood. We only say that God lives in perfect harmony with his own law, with his own nature, in all particulars perfectly good.

The beloved Disciple John said, "God is love," using the noun; he did not only say God is loving or God is infinitely lovable, but God is love itself; love is the supreme power. If that declaration is true then it is impossible for God to be unkind, it is equally impossible for God to wish to be unkind. And so with all the divine attributes, justice, mercy, tenderness, etc.; perfection, the infinitude of these attributes precludes the possibility of a desire in the infinite mind to act out of harmony with the divine conditions. Therefore the unlimited must have limitations in a certain sense and the limitations of the unlimited are infinite limitations. The limitations imposed by infinite goodness render impossible a single iota of unkindness: the limitation of infinite truth renders impossible the smallest departure from the strictest line of integrity; the limitation of infinite justice percludes the possibility of a thought deviating by a hair's breadth from perfect equity; the limitation of infinite love shuts out forever the possibility of a single dispensation of Providence—no matter how dark and mysterious—proceeding from an emotion which is not purely benevolent.

When we can hold in mind the idea of an all-perfect Being, when we can rise above all the conflicting creeds which like fogs surround us on earth, when all the perplexities and inharmonies born of our ignorance and imperfection are overcome and we see with the eye of enlightened mind—yea, with the sight of the soul itself, which is far beyond man's merely intellectual power, the vision of eternal goodness, the sight of that eternal goodness will prove an absolute panacea for all the ills to which imperfect mind is heir. Knowledge of the

Supreme Good is the eternal and infinite antidote to all sorrow, repining, discontent, misery and dissatisfaction henceforth forever. But there are many persons who maintain there are no evidences that an Eternal Being lives, and there are others who maintain that even though God exists, God is not all-powerful. John Stuart Mill fell into the miserable error of supposing that the divine power and its operations were limited, because when he looked about him in the world he thought he saw equal evidences of divine goodness and of its opposite; he thought the divine goodness had a circumference somewhere and that beyond the territory occupied by benevolence there was a dark waste occupied by evil, ignorance and hate.

We find when we look at the matter closely that almost all the religions of the world have started out with the assertion, or assumption, that there is one God and there is none beside him, and that he is all-perfect; yet they have soon divided the throne of the universe between this perfectly good God and inferior earthly deities. Without saying anything to hurt the feelings of those who differ from us and are not ready to accept the statement of pure theism, that goodness is supreme in the universe and that there is no supreme being but the eternal God, we wish to point out to you how very naturally mistakes have been made and yet how intolerable and unwarrantable they are because they are flagrant errors, direct results of human ignorance and weakness.

Our first positive affirmation is this: The mind of man cannot think beyond possibilities; there can be no fancy, no imagination which transcends the possibilities of the universe; for our imaginations are images thrown upon our minds, reflections of objects upon the retina of the mind's eye, impressions conveyed to the interior brain, from which impressions are never wholly removed and upon which impressions cannot be made unless there is something really in existence adequate to produce such impressions. So, when people say to us this that or the other is all imagination, that a person is cured by imagination or terrified and made ill by imagination, that one is saved by imagination and another ruined by imagination, we answer: it may be so, but imagination is a very important factor in our constitution, and a very important and influential element in human experience, because imaginations are always reflected images of realities; and when we are in a condition of mental harmony and health, when our inward eyes are open and we see things more as they really are, when we have learned to make the distinction which Longfellow made: "Things are not what they seem," seeing things from the standpoint of spiritual reality and no longer from the point of view of imperfect finite appearance, we shall all declare goodness supreme in the universe, and God, signifying the infinitely good, to be all in all.

No one can deny that in the world's thought as expressed in the noblest literature there is found an idea of infinite truth, infinite love, infinite wisdom, infinite benevolence, and no matter how hard and terrible the path of life may be for many, no matter how great the suffering, how bitter the misery, or how sorrowful the bereavement many have undergone, yet in the midst of the most terrible torture which men have ever experienced on earth, faith, genuine loving confidence in the eternal God, has not been shaken. Irritable and shallow people complain because of their petty worries and annoyances there can be no infinite goodness in the universe, for if God were infinitely good, if eternal goodness reigned, they would never be sick, never suffer, their business affairs would go smoothly, their friends would not be removed in the very heyday of their youth and prosperity, their children would not be snatched away while yet infants at the breast, but, oh, remember when you hear such wailing notes or are inclined thus to complain yourselves, that men, women and children have gone to the stake and been burned, have been tortured upon the rack, devoured by wild beasts, been stoned to death, and yet in the midst of the most terrible and excruciating tortures have been able to say as the ideal man said in his latest moments, "Father, into thy hands I commit my spirit." Such words have not been uttered only by one whom all Christendom has deified and acknowledged as God the Son as well as a son of God, but the first Christian martyr, Stephen, in the midst of the tortures of stoning, saw heaven open, and his beloved Master waiting to receive him. In the dark days of the persecution both of Catholics and Protestants in Europe only a few centuries ago, and indeed throughout the history of the Christian church, many noble men and women from the rack and the flame have seen angels ready to welcome them to a higher life; they have not complained, they have not felt the sufferings they underwent irreconcilable with the infinite goodness of the Eternal.

Now if men and women have actually gone through sufferings far more painful than yours, if many have absolutely experienced tortures in comparison with which your miseries are trivial indeed, and in spite of such excessive burdens have not lost their faith in God, then the trials you undergo are surely no evidences that there is no infinite Being of goodness, since those who have undergone far heavier trials have found that the divine light could shine through the densest clouds, that the infinite goodness could be made manifest even in the cruellest chambers of torture.

When we contrast our load with that of others, when instead of always looking at those who are favored and fortunate, who live in palaces, who have gorgeous apparel and beautiful carriages, if instead of always envying the great we descend into the hovels of the poor and take our station by the bedside of the sufferer who is tortured by the most excruciating pains; in such wretched places we behold oftentimes intense joy and peace, perfect confidence in God, perfect trust in the eternal wisdom, while very, very often the comfortably housed, the well fed and well clothed, the moderately prosperous, are those who, because they do not have everything they desire declare there can be no infinitly good Being superintending and controlling, for if there were they would have all their ambitions gratified, all their prayers answered, all their doubts removed.

Through the entire experience of the world, and in the history of the universe throughout all its wide domain we learn that the perfect way is not the way of sudden achievement, or instantaneous fruition. We learn in all departments of nature, that seeds must be deposited in the ground, grow in darkness and then burst forth, first into stalk and blade, then into tender ear and then at last comes the full corn in the ear. We learn that worlds are born gradually, and that they work their way slowly up from chaos and an age of fire mist, until at length they shine as radiant spheres rolling in splendor, as worlds of golden light and glory, upon which life manifests itself in perfect freedom and entrancing beauty.

The history of man teaches that man has gradually advanced from the savage bushman, who is little superior in appearance to a monkey, to a man who can control the most powerful forces of external nature so that the very elements obey him, that by mechanical devices he can command rain to fall from heaven, even employing the lightnings of Jove to convey knowledge, as he hurls the very current of life itself (electricity) through space, making it fulfill his commands and deliver his messages in all parts of the world.

The gods of antiquity were only men in perspective; the powers ascribed by cultured polytheists to the deities of Greece and Rome, were only powers which man himself possesses, and which he will at length perfectly embody and fully unfold and utilize; the gods of ancient days were from a spiritualistic point of view, merely human spirits who had ascended already to the higher realms, and doubtless, as ancient literature reveals, had once been monarchs, rulers, prophets and mighty personages on earth; the powers of gods in human form were the actual possibilities of man, and when the multitude shall have reached the high level of attainment of those who have already passed on to the true higher life, the most marvelous powers will be in every one's possession to use as he will, but only for good, as great power is not in the keeping of the basely disposed, they being unequal to its generation as well as to its employment.

The perfect way of man's development is the way of evolution, and evolution is the external manifestation of involution. Were you able to see into the spiritual realm and watch the processes of what you vaguely call creation, were you able as scientists to transfer your gaze to the spiritual realm and study involution, then you would learn first of the descent of spirit, and afterwards of the ascent of matter; then you would perceive that from the starting point of cause in spirit, thoughts and ideas flow outward until they produce cellular tissues, protoplasm or germ cells upon earth, spirit manifesting itself ever more and more until the perfect man stands before you. You would then know that spiritual power is needed to create protoplasm, and that other actions of the same spiritual power are necessary to develop protoplasm into the forms of perfect manhood and womanhood; you would know that Lamark in France, Darwin and Spencer in England, and all the grand minds that are endeavoring to trace the ascent of life, are merely beginning with the outermost effect of life and trying to trace it back to the realm of causation, as many finding the estuary of a river endeavor to trace the current back to its primal source. You can find the mouth of the Nile without any difficulty; anybody could have discovered its mouth, for where it empties itself into the sea it is conspicuous in the eyes of all beholders, but African explorers had to proceed with laborious researches year after year and perhaps century after century, to find the source of the Nile. When physical scientists speak of the source of life, of the beginning of life, they only speak of the most external manifestations of life, of the point where life discharges itself in view of all beholders, in earthly form.

But where is the source of life? The source of life, its starting point is away up in the eternal hills, where from clouds of angels the stream of existence upon earth takes its rise, and flowing gradually through a thousand forms, at length manifests the fullness and glory of its true form in perfect manhood and womanhood. You cannot go back far enough when you simply studying geology, anthropology or astronomy. You can only discover effects, and then at last you are confronted with the greatest of all problems, but where did life come from and what is life? And when you are told by spiritual scientists among whom must be numbered all truly eminent theologians and inspired spiritual teachers, manifested life is an efflux from eternal life, no one can say it is not so. Material science knows not whether spiritual definitions are correct or not. Neither Spencer, Tyndall, Darwin nor any other great physicist or sociologist dares to deny the affirmation that life is an influx from Deity; all they say is, we do not know whether it is or not. Colonel Ingersoll cannot logically go farther than that, and does not attempt to say more than that he does not know of the origin of life. All life originates in spirit, in divine thought, in divine idea, and when great and noble scientists, men who have labored year after year until they have exhausted the fire and ardor of their physical frames in the pursuit of knowledge and the solution of the most difficult problems presenting themselves to man's understanding, shall be conversed with in the realms of the great beyond, when you shall prepare such conditions of mind that you can enter into true communion with the great and glorious army who have ascended to the higher life, then there will be disclosures from the spiritual state of being explaining every difficulty, solving every problem and destroying the Sphinx of mystery, by revealing the meaning of all that was expressed in mysterious symbols, in the glorious architecture and art of the East in olden times.

When men and women come together without prejudice, ready to disarm themselves of all foregone conclusions, when they are ready to hear all theologies explained in the revolutionary light of a new revelation, when they are ready to study science intuitively as Jesus urged the Jews to read their records spirit ually; when they are ready to accept spiritual interpre tations of what science is now revealing, even though such interpretation widely differs from the accepted interpretations of universities as the command of Jesus differed from the letter of Mosaic law, "An eye for an eye and a tooth for a tooth," they will then be able to see as the best Hebrew scholars and the most eminent and liberal Christians see to-day, that there is no discord whatever between the essence of the Mosaic law and the essence of the Gospel of Jesus, that there is no conflict whatever between spiritual and physical science when both are understood. Evolution and involution, will be alike plain when men have listened to the noble teachers who speak from the spiritual spheres and give the result of their knowledge in the immortal world; these can reveal how every impulse works outward from spiritual cause to physical effect; all the difference between true theology and genuine material science is, that true theology begins with *Theos*—God, and true geology with *Geos*—earth. Working from Geos to Theos you can trace the evolution of all earth's various forms; working from Theos to Geos you trace involution as the cause of all manifestations of intelligence.

And thus, if life proceeding from God to the atom employs the involutionary pathway, and returning from the atom to the Deity employs the evolutionary pathway, then there is no conflict between thoology and geology, no conflict between the science of heaven and the science of earth. One science tells you how the life proceeding from Deity pulsates in atoms, and the other how the pulsation of atomic life can be traced to the Eternal Mind; both ways are perfect. The way of travel to the circumference is a perfect way, and the way of travel back from the circumference to the center is a perfect way; and when these two perfect ways have been resolved into the one all-perfect way, then the outward and the return journey of spirit to matter and matter to spirit will be understood as the great truth of the ages, which all religions and all science have endeavored to explain but have not as yet *fully* interpreted in any instance.

There are a few persons on earth who have found the perfect way; a few who have discovered the true relation between spirit and matter, beween cause and effect, between form and its origin in spirit. While these wonderful persons do not necessarily belong to any Brotherhood or Sisterhood, or to any secret organization, while their home is not necessarily in India, still the records of astonishingly wonderful works which you hear of as being performed by Mahatmas, Adepts and others, who have devoted their lives to spiritual development, have all been founded upon the fact that when man becomes superior to material inclinations and has put under his feet all pride, prejudice and vain ambition, he becomes as one of the gods, no longer blinded by the dust of matter in his mental eyes. We therefore recommend to you a spiritual study of theosophy as a means of theosophical development, which signifies an unfoldment in the knowledge of divine wisdom. We would not advise you to make long pilgrimages to celebrated shrines in this or any other country, or to clothe yourself in haircloth, or to walk with bare feet over jagged rocks; we do not tell you that you must leave your family and friends, and hide yourself in some retired place in the Himalayan Mountains; we do not tell you that your own country and your own daily duties are not sufficient for your highest development.

Mere asceticism has frequently developed self righteousness and vaunted superiority in ascetics, while the higher matters of the law, justice, and above all, charity, have been neglected. In all exalted teachings that have ever been given to mankind, fasting and prayer have been put forward as necessary steps toward the perfect life; perversion has occurred when the true idea of prayer and fasting has been lost sight of, and men have obeyed the letter, but neglected the spirit. A person may be no nearer the kingdom of Heaven because he eats no meat on Friday, and keeps all the vigils and ember days; but if you subsist upon short rations day by day because your means do not allow you to have all you would like, or far better, because you feed some poor hungry sufferer at your gate; if you do not eat your meat because you prefer to give it to one who needs it more than yourself, if you go about in tattered garments because you have given your clothing to keep the cold from the naked body of some one who lacked, then your charitable devotion to the necessities of others, or rather the spirit which causes you to make outward sacrifices, must elevate your soul; you walk then surely in the true way, and you have prayed to eternal goodness by cultivating divine goodness within your own breast; having risen superior to self love, and having cultivated the love of neighbor, you have demonstrated the reality of the love of God in your soul.

Whenever we act from a divine impulse, whenever we work to save and help our brethren, we render the accepted offering which is acknowledged as the only sacrifice that God requires, by the most inspired teachers of every age. It was the saying of a grand old Hebrew prophet, "What doth God require of thee but to deal justly, love mercy, and walk humbly with him?" Walking with God is walking lovingly and honestly with one's fellow beings. Now if any one has supposed that rigorous initiations, strange and weird incantations, magical circles and awful rites and ceremonies initiate persons into the perfect way, they have surely been deceived by blind leaders of the blind; many who have struggled for perfection on the road of magic have found, to their bitter cost, that the blind led by the blind both fall into the ditch. A great deal of so-called theosophy and a great many theosophists have failed because they were actuated by pride, selfishness, worldly ambition, by the desire to do something greater than anybody else, and not being actuated by pure benevolence, but rather by love of the mysterious. In their determination to exalt themselves there has been fulfilled in their experience no other promise than this: "He that exalteth himself shall be abased."

But when we go beneath the letter and touch the spirit, when we discover the deep and glorious inner meaning which lies in all the wisdom of the East; when reading wisdom alike from the Sanscrit, Hebrew and the Greek, we find that Jesus and Buddha, all the lights of the Orient and the Occident, agree in pointing out a perfect way, and we ask, what is that perfect way? Turning to the ideal life of Jesus and to the ideal life of Buddha, the Light of Asia, we read in the history of both that the great renunciation, the glorious self-abnegations, that characterized those great teachers, led them to forget all earthly honor, that they might win for humanity a crown imperishable. When they had lost sight of self and had become nothing in their own eyes, having made God and humanity everything, then they found what no penance, nor rituals, nor ceremonials could teach; they found the perfect way, they became pure in heart, and therefore they saw God.

You are told in the story of Buddha, as it is magnificently related in verse by Edwin Arnold, that the truth came to him only after he had given up all association with his royal family and the splendors of an Eastern court, when he no longer adhered to the externals of the Brahmin faith and practices, when he no longer considered it incumbent upon him to obey the ritual requirements of the East, when he overthrew caste and put down every form of tyranny and carnality, when he acknowledged all men as equals, when he was kind to every beast of the field, when he was moved by love of others and sought no self-gratification; then whilst he was meditating under the holy tree a divine revelation came to him, and he found Nirvana, not in the loss of his identity, not in the absorption of his soul into the essence of Brahm, but in the perfect union of his will with the divine will, as a drop in the ocean flows harmoniously with all other drops and yet retains its individuality intact forever; though never losing its identity, there is no conflict, no struggle between itself and any other.

If any ask, what becomes of the individual human soul? Shall I always retain my identity? We tell you that only when you cease to think of self will you find your highest self; when you are no longer concerned about your own identity you will have found your highest identity; then will you find the divine image within you, and shine forever in resplendent glory and know yourselves to be children of the Most High.

Over and over again we are told we may become children of God. We are all children of God now, but when we become children of God in a special sense, we come to know ourselves as such; when we are introduced into the knowledge of divine truth it is because our spiritual eyes open, and when our inward eyes open all the universe is seen by us as it was never seen before; when our spiritual ears are unstopped and our lips are unclosed, we hear and speak from the soul as we never heard or spoke before.

We are all possessors of divine life, but we are like men and women who are heirs to some wonderful inheritance and know not of it; we possess by right jewels and treasures beyond all price, but we have not yet found them. When you discover your spiritual possessions, when you are thoroughly revealed to yourself and know what you really are, when you have found your deepest nature that is within you, you will discover that you are each as a drop in the ocean of God's infinitude; you will then be filled with eternal joy, and will not think any more either about forgetting self or preserving identity.

But your identity is what nothing can destroy; sense of your identity is the only consciousness that can never leave you; it is the only thing that seemingly takes care of itself under all circumstances and cannot be lost; identity is inseparable from your real being which relates you forever to the infinite identity of the Eternal. To attain to perfect oneness with Deity you must all attain to perfect oneness, *i. e.* harmony with each other; you must all become co-workers, loving one another with pure hearts fervently, and not preferring yourself or your own interests to those of a neighbor; you must bow down no more to the competitive idol, but acknowledge co-operation or divine communism; enlightened minds will no longer fall into the errors of those communists who though setting out with grand and holy purpose, have spoiled their plan or seen it ruined by selfishness. Strive to enter into the spirit of those great reformers who are actuated alone by divine benevolence and you will discern the pattern of universal equity.

When Robert Owen and Robert Dale Owen, two of the noblest men America has produced, endeavored to establish communistic settlements, it was their highest ambition to do good and elevate society; they were willing to undergo privation and the loss of earthly possessions that they might help others; we cannot but admire these noble and glorious men; both of them were fully conversant before they passed into the spiritual world, of the reality of immortal life; both were spiritualists in the true sense of the word, and endeavored to enter into profitable relations with spiritual life by the cultivation of spirituality, knowing that spirituality was cultivated by benevolent disposition and action. They trod in the perfect way as far as they could find it, but then why were their endeavors comparatively unsuccessful? why was so much of their toil seemingly fruitless? why were their splendid communities castles in the air more than anything else? Surely because the men and women who undertook to walk with them were not so magnanimous as they who led the way. When magnanimity and nothing else shall guide persons to form combinations solely for the good of the race, then we shall see an ideal community; but the preaching of communism as right living, with all the eloquence and argument that can possibly be brought forward in its defense, will fall to nothingness until the spirit that imbues the workers in the enterprise as well as the founders, is a spirit of pure philanthropy.

We can see no perfect way of doing anything when we are imperfect in our thought and desire. There can be nothing perfect on the outside until there is a perfect state within; no perfect government, no perfect law, no perfect order, no perfect body until there is perfect thought within. There must be perfect thought first, as all works are embodiments of thought. External forms fall short of thought but never transcend it.

The thought must be perfect before the external can be. Consider a seed; can you put an imperfect seed into the ground and make it produce a perfect plant? No; no sunshine or rain, no process of irrigation, no enriching of soil can possibly make an imperfect seed bear a perfect plant. Perfection must inhere in the seed, and if this be the case then if all climatic influences are favorable and it receives the necessary cultivation adapted to it, it can unfold into a perfect plant. So in our own minds there must be a perfect seed, a perfect thought. "Be ye perfect;" it is within the reach of every one of you. Your thought must be a perfect seed before it is a perfect acorn, a perfect acorn before it is a perfect sapling and a perfect sapling before it is a perfect oak. So when generation is spiritually accomplished there is first a perfect babe, then a perfect child, a perfect youth, a perfect young man, a perfect man of mature years, but a babe as a babe may be just as perfect in nature and freedom from taint as the perfect man.

So all along the perfect way, in the pathway of constant progress there is growth, expansion, unfoldment, ever a further manifestation. But in the perfect way there are no worms to eat the seed, no diseases to destroy the beauty and symmetry of youth; no errors introduced to mar the plan, no wild oats sown with the vain expectation that there will never come a reaping time for anything but golden grain. In the perfect life there must be perfect attention paid to every detail of growth.

What do you call perfect? That is only perfect which is perfect in every detail, but that is perfect which during all the stages of its development is perfect as far as it extends. You may be painting a perfect picture—but what do you require for a perfect painting? First, a perfect sheet of blank canvas; then you begin to cover it, doing the first day very rudimentary work indeed, just a little marking upon the canvas, but it is perfect as far as it goes, and you go on month after month until your picture is at length a master piece in some school of art.

Now that is a sample of what our life should be; that is the idea we should put before our children; do not expect old heads on young shoulders; do not expect a child to know as much as a man; do not expect by a single leap or bound to mount up to celestial heights, but always move in the right direction; never turn back, go straight ahead; be sure you are right and then keep straight forward. That is the rule of perfection. Do the best you can each day. Let the child recite one portion of the multiplication table perfectly, and then go on and learn the next portion, and so on until he has the whole complete. Learn everything thoroughly as you go.

This is the meaning of "Be ye perfect;" perfect according to your power, according to your knowledge, according to your ability; be perfect in your resolves, perfect in intention, will, desire, motive. Never say anything unless you feel it is right to say it; never do anything unless you feel it is right to do it; never allow yourself to indulge a thought unless you feel that thought is a rightful and holy one.

"Be ye perfect even as your Father who is in heaven is perfect," because you have the possibilities of perfection, because you are in the image and likeness of the all-perfect One, because perfection is the only one thing to be tolerated in all stages of advancement.

Perfection never means transcending the order or law of growth; it does not mean ignoring the slow and steady processes of involution and evolution. Let the involuted thought and the evoluted action be alike perfect, the one the cause, the other the effect. Then the command, "Be ye perfect even as the eternal is perfect," will not be understood by you in any impossible sense, but as within the limits of the possible action of every one of you.

Our application of the subject, therefore, is this: Have only one master, and that master your highest conviction of right. Acknowledge only one God and one revelation from God, and that revelation the divine voice in your own soul. When you give your children moral or religious education, when you call them together in a Lyceum and teach them so that all may understand, never say a statement is true because it is in the Bible; never say a thing is right because you tell them so; some time they may find you are mistaken and they will grow up to distrust your authority and to doubt your position being a warrantable one. But say to every child, never do anything that will cause you to forfeit your self respect; always listen for the still small voice of the Holy Spirit within you; always listen to the divine command echoing between the cherubim of your moral and intellectual nature; always look for the Shekinah within; always remember that the highest oracle is within; that the voice of the Eternal sounds within your innermost being; do whatever you do because you feel it to be right.

But supposing you are mistaken, what will the result of honest mistake be? Mistakes will teach you wisdom. Never be discouraged and never look upon your work as evil, because that work is not immediately perfect in all the fullness of completion.

In the perfect life if one lives in harmony with highest intention, conforming himself as far as he may to his loftiest ideal, he is perfect as far as he can go, but not perfect finally because he has not traversed the whole of the way. In building a temple you may have only the foundation laid, and that may be perfect, but it is not a perfect temple; only when the temple is completed can the architect say, "There is a perfect expression of perfect thought."

Here is the true idea of perfect life. In soul we generate perfect thought, a perfect ideal; then we have to work it out, laying stone upon stone, until that perfect thought is externalized in the perfect temple of our manifested being.

And when you feel, "I have committed a sin; I am so sorry; I thought I acted for the best, but I find I made a mistake; I did wrong; I have hurt some one to whom I would have given the sweetest consolation;" we tell you, you did right, relatively, because you did the best you could; it would be unreasonable on the part of God, and, therefore, impossible for him to be angry with you. If you did not feel that your acts were imperfect, you would settle down in contentment and never rise higher. No act is properly imperfect when it is the best you can perform, under the circumstances.

Let us reverence our ideal of perfection and rest assured that the way to perfection is ever to act in harmony with the best that we know, so that we may ever do better and better and better, until the comparative changes to the superlative, and we are perfect in the purity of our every thought and perfect also in the wisdom that enables us to carry our perfect thought into perfect effect, which will ever be displayed in a symmetrical mind expressed through the instrument of a sound and healthy body. Perfect physical health is the ultimate or final consequence on earth of perfect thought in spirit, compatible with present attainments.

LESSON IX.

THE RELIGIOUS INSTINCT; ITS ORIGIN, GROWTH AND ULTIMATE PERFECTION.

THERE are many persons who now-a-days question the desirability of religion, as many consider the word religion implies restrictions antagonistic to liberty, maintaining that as religion is derived from *religio*, which signifies to bind, or to bind again, therefore to be religious implies to be held in bondage. Now while there is no necessary idea of bondage connected with religion, we must all admit in a certain sense that we must be bound in order to be free.

There are no two words in the English language which mean more directly opposite things than liberty and license, than freedom and lawlessness. No one can be lawless and yet free; no one can be unmindful of the interests of his fellow beings and live as though he were the only occupant of the world and enjoy liberty, for liberty is a pure, holy, divine and healthy sentiment, which unites man forever and forever with the eternally true, with the eternally free. "He is free whom the truth makes free, and all are slaves beside," is an utterance that has been wisely quoted thousands of times in the past, and will be quoted thousands of times in the future, as it expresses the true idea of what liberty is. Liberty is freedom to serve truth; freedom to live a life of truth in obedience to one's highest convictions of right and duty. Genuine liberty is liberty for the soul, for the spiritual nature, for the immortal mind, over which death can have no power and the grave no victory. Liberty is a divine and holy realization of our relation to divine law and order, and the willing subjection of all our material inclinations to immortal guidance. Liberty never concerns itself with the first person singular, with *my* affairs or *my* interests; liberty knows nothing of the great *I*, but always speaks of *our* interests, of *our* concerns, of *our* welfare. Liberty, therefore, is in perfect accord with self abnegation, and yet with purest self enjoyment in the spiritual sense.

Without doubt it is natural to man to love happiness, and, to search for it, it is natural to the human family to try every experiment until they find happiness; every creature seeks happiness, and it is our supreme conviction that the day is coming in this world when everybody on the planet will be happy. Our sincere conviction is, that that wonderful goal of joy looked forward to by all nations and individuals, will one day be found; that as the Eternal Parent is an infinitely happy spirit, all children of the one Great Eternal are by their very nature, by the essential and unchanging constitution of their being ordained to happiness. Our belief is that all darkness and discord, all the pain and trouble through which mankind at large is now passing and through which individual minds are passing, even beyond the grave, is never anything worse than a school discipline, and even though a school be a purgatory, it is still an educational institution.

Our idea concerning man's existence is, that every creature, without exception, is born not only with a great desire to be happy but also with an instinct that happiness is natural to him and will eventually be realized by him.

Happiness can be only attained in one way: in purity, not in impurity; in truth, not in error; in love, not in hate; in knowledge, not in ignorance; in wisdom, not in folly. And as happiness can only be obtained in wisdom, knowledge, love, liberty, truth and righteousness, no matter where we may be, either in an external form or in spirit, we must be unhappy as long as we are impure, foolish, ignorant, untruthful, unloving, unwise or unrighteous; and as all unhappiness is the result of ignorance and imperfection, it is as the grand old Grecian sage, Socrates, described, happiness, good and knowledge are all one, while evil, darkness ignorance and misery are all one and inseparable; so we must all admit that as there is within the mind of man an ineradicable desire to be happy, and happiness can only be found in the one way ordained by Eternal Providence, *i. e.* in compliance with divine order, all souls will at length be happy, all lives will eventually flow together in one divine channel and all feet march together up that great hill upon the summit of which stands the city of gold, the symbol of the transmutation of all life's perplexities into the absolute fullness of eternal harmony.

Sorrow is often-times an alchemist transmuting the baser elements into the more precious. Our perplexities and woes, and even our restless discontent, are all servants of the divine plan that works out infinite good at last; when we hear the words pronounced so often on funeral occasions, "Peace at the last," let us pause for a moment and ask, "What is the last?" The last, *Omega*, is identical with the first, *Alpha*. In the beginning God created, *i. e.*, in the beginning of the history of a planet God began to manifest himself, and at the last his manifestation is complete to all souls from that planet. In the beginning man was endowed with a pure and holy soul, immortal, ineffable, and at the last, no matter how long that soul may have been eclipsed, it shines forth in divine splendor, in sheen of glory it bursts from behind the clouds which have so long veiled it and caused shortsighted minds to deem it lost forever.

All our imperfections and errors may be compared to the mists and fogs, and smoke arising from the earth, especially from great manufacturing centers, while our souls in their union with the Eternal may be compared with the glorious lights of heaven that are never diminished or quenched, because earthly factories and chimneys fill the air with smoke.

Here on the earth we are surrounded with imperfection and error, we are living in a smoky atmosphere and the smoke arises from the chimneys of our houses and our factories wherein we do material cooking, and engage in material merchandise. We cannot see the glorious lights on high when we are in the midst of a city whose chimneys fill the air with smoke, but when we get some distance out of the city, though our traveling brings us no nearer to the heavens above, no nearer the glorious sun, no nearer the circling planets and the "fixed stars" so very far away, by it we get out of the smoky atmosphere that we ourselves have created by our own occupation and our own very imperfect way of doing business; so when we have got out of the mental smoke which befogs ideas, out of the smoky atmosphere of our doubts and misbeliefs, got rid of all unhealthy sentiments which arise from our perverted nature and which make impure the atmosphere we breathe — God will have come no nearer to us, angels will be no closer to us, divine power no more ready to bless us, but we shall see the sun where aforetime we saw the fog; the fog will clear away that hid the sun — then will the sun appear. This simile will be found very important and easy of application in almost all cases.

Astronomy teaches that the sun is much older than the earth but no matter how old it is, the earth could know nothing about it until the sun became visible to the earth. No matter how old the stars may be the earth could know nothing about them until it became ready to see them, so from man's standpoint of imperfect observation it appears as though new worlds were ever coming into existence, as though new truths were ever being born, though from God's point of view, from the point of view of the angels who have passed beyond the murky shadows of earthly imperfection there are no such new creations, new dispensations and new revelations as less enlightened minds suppose, but they understand how man in his ever increasing intelligence draws ever nearer and nearer to a knowledge of the Eternal and his works. And so when you sing, "Nearer my God to thee, nearer to thee," you must not imagine that the idea of prayer, when interpreted truthfully, spiritually, philosophically, and scientifically carries with it the slightest suggestion that God ever changes his disposition toward us; you must never suppose for one moment there is any such thing as an atonement or reconciliation offered to the offended Majesty of Heaven whereby he is importuned to have mercy upon the sinner; never suppose there can be any opposition in the divine nature between the divine attributes, so that mercy and justice are reconcilable by vicarious atonement.

But in the light of a true perception of man's spiritual nature he offers atonement who effects reconciliation, who reveals the fatherly character of the Infinite, who removes all that doubt, fear and pride which as the smoke filling the earth's atmosphere, hides the glorious luminaries of the heavens from man's observation, and as theology of old has often concerned itself with changes in God, and from the very earliest times men have engaged in propitiatory rites, in offering sacrifices to placate a hitherto implacable Deity, as men supposed that by their altars running with blood, by human as well as animal sacrifices they might prevail upon God to be merciful—they will learn in the future that God was never unreconciled to man, but man has, unfortunately, often been unreconciled to his brother man, and the reconciliation which needs to be effected in society to-day is, the unification of all races, and the identification of all human interests. We must no longer remain unreconciled to each other, and in our own individual nature we must no longer remain at discord with ourselves. Follow out this train of thought simply and logically and you will all understand the true nature of atonement.

The religious instinct in man is as natural as the instinct to walk, talk, eat, clothe ones-self or sleep. Any good phrenologist will tell you that the organs of veneration, spirituality, sublimity, benevolence, conscientiousness, and all the others which portray religious and moral faculties are just as natural as the organ of alimentiveness which disposes toward the enjoyment of food, or the organ of destructiveness which immoderately developed causes men to be dangerous to one another, but when perfectly balanced and wisely unfolded gives strength of character without which man would have no intellectual vigor or spiritual power.

The religious sentiments are born in man, and the organ of spirituality which phrenology has discovered, as well as the organ of veneration, proves the natural instinct of worship, which, because natural, may be cultivated or repressed, but never totally eradicated.

Nature worships in every flower that turns its face to the sun, offoring an act of adoration to the great fountain of energy; the animal that looks up to man, a dog or horse looking up to his master with loving gratitude, displays the instinct of veneration. And when men erect high pedestals and place upon them statues of great men and women, almost deifying heroes and heroines; while they spare no praise and stint no gratitude when asked to pour out eulogistic adoration at the feet of some benefactor of society, man though he calls himself an infidel and avows no faith in God, doubting if there be a spiritual or supreme Being, his natural instinct of veneration leads him to bow down to some superior man. In America there are men who acknowledge no supreme Ruler of the universe, who do not believe in erecting houses of worship, and who disregard all religious sentiment and worship altogether, who are ready to almost deify George Washington, Abraham Lincoln and other eminent patriots; those who read history are so profoundly touched with a sense of the majesty—we may also say divinity—of the greatest characters who appear upon the historian's page, that they consider no monument, no eulogy too extravagant when these men are brought before them as objects of respect.

There is in man an irrepressible instinct of veneration and worship, and when people talk about the time coming for worship to cease, for adoration and devotion to come to an end, we tell you if that time does come man will be born with only half a brain, but as long as he is born with a whole brain physiologists and phrenologists will still behold the outward indications of sentiments of worship within the mind.

This true instinct of worship, veneration, adoration, this continual looking up to a higher power is the lever in man which lifts him to a higher and more glorious life; that moral sense, or conscience, that spiritual faculty which is so closely allied to, and, indeed, inseparably identified with the distinction between right and wrong, or the sense of good and evil, is the magnet within man's being that attracts him to a higher life, the inpiration of the soul within him that causes him to rise to a more blessed level and without which moral and spiritual progress would be impossible.

Unfortunately, man has been so ignorant of his true nature, that what has been after all the divinest and kindest gift of the Eternal to his children, has been regarded as the voice of God's displeasure, as the anger or wrath wherewith he would smite his enemies. How very, very often in human ignorance men denounce as cruel that which in days of added wisdom they declare to be most kind of all. How very often that parental discipline which brings the most tears to the eye and the most immediate sorrow to the heart of a child in the days of its adminstration, in after years proves itself to the absolute satisfaction of the offspring to have been the noblest and kindest ministration of fatherly and motherly love and wisdom.

So when we look back through the dim vistas of by-gone years, when through the long ages we see humanity toiling up the steeps of time, and shedding blood even, for what we may now term superstition or fanaticism, we find the instinct of worship even within the savage breast, deepest down in human nature of all instincts, and destined at last to overcome all imperfections and shine forth in its native brilliancy as God's best gift to man.

Let us consider briefly some of the forms which this natural instinct of worship has already taken to manifest itself, how it is now manifesting itself, and how it is likely, indeed certain, to manifest itself in future. Our first proposition is that no one ever worshiped anything without deeming it in some respect superior to himself; no one ever bowed to any power, force or creature without endowing that power, force or creature with superior attributes; and no one ever endowed any creature, force or power with superiority until that force, power or creature had manifested something that looked like superiority to the worshiper.

Let us revert to the earliest form of savage worship, the worship of animals. Wherein does animal superiority consist? Surely in superior physical strength. No one can deny for a moment that the larger animals on earth are man's superiors physically; in bodily strength, in power to protect themselves, in power to fight, they most certainly excell. Poor, illiterate, naked savages, not armed with the weapons which intelligent and skillful nations have devised, could not protect themselves against the mauraders of the forest; they were stung to death by venomous reptiles they could not control; they were eaten up alive by monsters of the forest they could not destroy, but who mercilessly destroyed them; had they not then good reason to recognize superior strength in such creatures? Now, as they witnessed in animals and reptiles a disposition to do them harm, they discovered also that they could appease them by offering them food; that they would often eat the food given them instead of destroying them and their children; what was the outcome? Surely a system of sacrifice; even human sacrifice grew up in the world and frequently parents offered their own children to monsters; they offered one child that several might be saved; later on they frequently offered prisoners whom they had taken in war, and in still later times they offered those who were less perfect than others in order that by the sacrifice of one they might save many; sacrifices to the barbaric gods of all tribes originated with fear of animals and the elements.

When men saw creatures of savage propensities holding sway on earth, they soon thought of militant powers in heaven, of wrathful and unmerciful gods, especially as they saw nature bestowing what seemed to them her greatest gifts upon the cruel and ruthless; they soon endowed the power that brought everything into existence with attributes like those of the serpent, the bear, the lion, the tiger and the wolf, and then when they turned their eyes to the heavens above, and also contemplated the phenomena perpetually transpiring upon the earth around them, wind, thunder, lightning, volcanic eruptions, earthquakes, cyclones and all forms of devastation, which were more active in early times than now, did they not naturally endow the powers who ruled all things, with awe and majesty, with power and might, but with very little love, mercy or tenderness? And indeed to any one who is not a careful scientist, a profound philosopher, or deeply spiritual in his thought, the universe certainly suggests the idea of wrath mingled with beneficence. To any one who cannot read in the future the harmonizing and equalizing of all things, this world appears to be given over in large measure to powers of darkness, hate and cruelty. To those who look only upon the surface, there are no satisfactory evidences of a perfectly good God supreme in the universe. We do not wonder that awful ideas of devils, hells, divine wrath and fiery retribution hold sway, when we see the lightings strike the dwellings of the innocent as well as of the guilty, when the earthquake does not spare the babe at the breast, or the mother who is so necessary to the maintenance of her offspring, any more than it spares the murderer; when the volcanic eruption has no sympathy for the young and tender, any more than for those who have lived a life of sin.

There is an awful mystery in nature; a mystery which scientists, philosophers and theologians have alike endeavored to unravel and have as yet been unable to satisfactorily explain save when from the higher realms of spirit and the deepest intuitions of man's divine soul a voice has declared this is only a prelude to the oratorio, a scaffolding to the temple, which when it appears in all its beauty, crowned with light, the scaffolding removed, and the noise of the workmen hushed,—when all the forces of angry waves have subsided and there is a great calm, when the rain and wind have ceased, then you will see the earth rejuvenated and perfected. Then you will know that all is for the best, and the righteous shall shine forth in the kingdom of their Father.

There is wonder and dread all over the world, and those poor short-sighted theologians who can see out of earth into hell, but can not see through hell into heaven, who can see beyond man to devil, but cannot see beyond devil to the angel into which that devil will at length be converted, who can see the strife, discord and storm, but can not see beyond it to the day of ineffable calm and great glory yet to be revealed—such short-sighted gazers into the mysteries of human life and destiny are not merely imagining horrors or supposing calamities—they simply do not see far enough; their point of view does not reach out into the universe far enough.

Until we have more powerful telescopes and greater powers of spiritual vision, until we are longer sighted with regard to spiritual things, we shall be tormented with dread of fiends and hobgoblins and all the awful creatures which people the realms of the unknown; but when ignorance dies and we know good, all is for good, when brighter light and fuller revelation explain the mystery and solve the problem, then because darkness is no more, the hobgoblins disappear even from imagination, and in the light all will know that there is nothing to fear. When in the darkness you are afraid of everything, even of your own shadow, and often of that most of all. When Emanuel Swedenborg in the last century, and Dante centuries before saw into the hells and told of states almost too awful to be depicted, they did not describe what did not exist, but Dante, who had been educated in Roman Catholicism and had therefore been taught that there was an endless hell for those who died in mortal sin, and Swedenborg, who had been brought up in the Lutheran faith and taught that those who died out of Christ would be damned forever, could only modify their ideas of everlasting torment, they could not see far enough beyond the hells into the heavens, which all must at length reach. Anyone standing at a point were he can see but a little way before him can describe only what is not very far ahead and is apt to imagine there is a boundary line, a horizon, and nothing beyond it. A child standing upon the shore, with a field-glass, looking across the water thinks there is nothing beyond the water—it is all water and nothing but water in that direction to this vision. But those who have been over seas have found land on the other side. You can not show the distant land to the child on the shore; you can not, even if your sight is excellent, stand on the Pacific slope and look across the water, to the Sandwich islands, China,

Japan or any land whatever, but when travelers have been across the water and found land, and one comes back to tell the tale, then you accept a revelation from the land invisible; there is water indeed but there is land beyond the water. This is but a poor and faint illustration of the heavens beyond the hells, of the paradise beyond the purgatories, of the good beyond the evil, of the light beyond the darkness.

Looking at matters from your earthly standpoint, unless spiritually endowed and enlightened, or in communion with those who have crossed the seas, you know of nothing more than that which follows directly upon your present state. After a few short years in the earthly body you encounter death and the grave, and there is the end of life to physical sight or material perception. But there are those who can see beyond, and where you declare death they declare fullness of life; where you declare destruction they declare resurrection and reconstruction. Siva, among the Brahmins, is "*Destroyer*" only to the ignorant, the same divinity is both *Destroyer* and *Reproducer* to the enlightened.

The religious systems of the world must come and go, rise and set, wax and wane, and all that will remain forever is man's perception of absolute truth, and this will be perpetually increasing.

We have already alluded to the worship of the lower creation—to the worship of the dark, brutal and belligerent forces of nature, which led to sacrifices of the most fearful character—and we think we have accounted for it naturally, that man being on a material plane, and surrounded with forces he could not control, and seeing no further than his immediate environment, worshiped the physical force which was superior to his own; and there are millions of people to day, who, with all their boasted intelligence, scientific ability and literary acumen, never advance further than savages, in a spiritual direction, thus they only perceive what seems very unjust and cruel in natural phenomena.

Why do the most illumined minds refuse to bow before the blind force which is the substitute for God among atheists and materialists? Why do they not acknowledge that supreme law or infinite force, a vague abstraction in the universe, and declare that is all we can know about causation? Why do they not bow down and worship the blind "*necessity*" of modern materialism?

We have only one answer; that ideal "*force*" is not as good as we are and we will not worship our inferior, we will not bow to the materialists' substitute for God, because it is an image of clay inferior to the substance of which we ourselves are made.

We claim to have some affection, some intelligence, some mercy, some sense of justice, but a blind, unintelligent force, a mere abstraction, a something not ourselves, not endowed with any intelligence, wisdom, love or sense of justice, is infinitely our inferior, and that which is our inferior calls for our contempt not our adoration.

Instead of believing that the universe is guided by some unknowable power that brings multitudes into existence, mocks them with noble powers and wonderful endowments, cherishes in their breasts the highest hopes and loftiest sentiments, and then allows a cart wheel to run over their body, or some other accident to cause their death, and that is the end of them; instead of believing in a power which gives glorious life and then allows it to be destroyed by the blundering of a drunken cab-driver, or a careless engineer, instead of bowing before a power that gives intelligence, hope, aspiration, all that constitutes noblest manhood and womanhood, and then destroys these attributes in a moment by a falling tile or by a missile hurled at your head by a careless boy, we prefer to believe in an intelligent, controlling power that regards the material body as the most external and superficial vesture of man, and sees the man himself forever safely alive, forever in spirit.

If I am a brute, I naturally worship a bigger and stronger brute than myself; if I am merely an animal, I naturally worship a larger and stronger animal than myself, and if I am a human being, with no other instincts cultivated, no other powers developed than those I share in common with the lower creation, I naturally bow to those of the lower creation, who have attributes such as mine but more powerfully developed than mine. And thus it is only natural that as long as man is on the material plane of thought and affection, and does not recognize anything more than his material nature, he will invent a material substitute for God, which substitute is the direct result of the mammon worship of this age, a remote result of the ignorant animality of savage times. There is fully as much animality and brutality and more treachery in the respectable man of business, who does not care how many wives and children he ruins, how many heads of families he dooms to misery, and perhaps suicide by his tricks in trade, misrepresentations and gambling speculations, than in the panther or the wolf. We would rather be in the clutches of a tiger than in those of a man who lives for self and money only; we would rather trust to the tender mercies of the wild beasts of the forest than to those of a creature who has more intellect but uses that intellect solely for personal aggrandizement, recognizing nothing beyond buying and selling, eating, drinking and getting gain. As long as this worship of mammon continues, and to make a fortune is the supreme object of life, so long as education has for its watchword, competition, and your most approved mottoes: are look out for yourselves, take care of number one, there can be no spiritual revelation to satisfy the highest needs of human nature, there can be no sunshine visible in which we can bask with delight. If the air is filled with noxious exhalations and the smoke from a thousand factory chimneys. Man must get rid of the mist and smoke that is continually enveloping him. When he is no longer selfish nor brutal, then he will be able to accept a glorious revelation from the spiritual universe, which is absolutely necessary to happiness and a true understanding of the plan of the universe.

We are ready to make the assertion, extravagant though it may appear to many, that we know people who have absolutely discovered God. But if they have discovered God, have they met a person and had a personal interview with an omnipotent spirit in the guise of man who proclaimed his deity by name? We answer they have beheld the divine presence with the eye of the soul; they have become spiritual to the extent of entering into conscious relation with the divine spirit made known to them in the innermost recesses of their being. "Blessed are the pure in heart for they shall see God." A great many people quibble at that beatitude, many want to know what it means to see God. According to the statement itself no one can know what it means to "see God" until perfectly pure in heart, therefore until they are in that condition they have no means of either proving or disproving the statement. The sight of God to the pure in heart is the full perception that everything is good and for the best, that all life will turn out well and all roads lead at length to the great terminus of the celestial city, that all boats will land at length upon the shore of eternal happiness. By perceiving God we mean perceiving spiritual truth, love, wisdom, goodness and right eousness; perceiving perfect justice in the order of the universe. And when we have found divine justice ruling and governing all we do not trouble ourselves as to whether Deity has or has not an anthropomorphic form; when we have found divine wisdom, love and truth we do not care to ask how love, wisdom and truth are presented outwardly to sense or intellect, we are satisfied with the knowledge of the soul, with the perception of the interior nature.

For all discussions in theology concering God's personality or impersonality we shall care less than for the changing sands on the sea shore. It does not matter whether we can decide as to the personality or impersonality of God. There are a great many things beyond our intellectual range, even beyond our moral preception, and there are a great many mysteries in the universe that are beyond us which we do not need to settle.

But if we have found enough to content our souls in truth, if we have found enough to still the wild beating of our rebellious, sorrowing hearts, to demonstrate life immortal where we have hitherto found death, and the victory of truth where hitherto we imagined the victory of the grave; if we can stand by the side of a corpse and yet see a resurrected being promoted to a higher state of intelligent existence, if we can shed the tear of sympathy with the mourner who is bereaved of an earthly presence and yet be so convinced that the so-called dead are alive and with us, that the tears which flow through ignorance we can wipe away; if we can bring wisdom's consolation to the sad heart, if we have the certainty that though every earthly prop be destroyed, and every earthly opportunity denied, though we have lived our lives from the ordinary standpoint in vain, labored and toiled for naught, that there is in the spiritual universe a crown, a reward, a glorious result for our every undertaking that can not be observed from earth's plane of observation, then we have found the God we all need to find, for we have found infinite goodness; Infinite Good, is "God" which is an old saxon word meaning the Good One or the All Good. God then becomes a word no longer meaningless upon our lips. All human speculations concerning God and the life beyond must eventually pass away, all outward forms and ceremonies of religion will pass away, but the essence of religion will never pass away. Religion may cast aside its outward dress, its pagodas, temples, synagogues and churches may all be looked upon some day as things of the past and no longer needed; but supposing the outward church does come to an end, how will it come to an end? By growth. The church will grow so large it will cover the earth, and when the whole earth is a temple, then nobody will need a smaller temple. When the temple was small it stood on a little spot of ground, and people could easily tell you how large it was; but when the whole earth becomes holy, you can never wear your shoes anywhere if you have to remove them when you tread on holy ground.

We believe in the extension of holy ground, in the enlarging of consecrated territory so that we can find God everywhere.

Where did Jacob find holy ground? Out in the wilderness where he had but a stone for his pillow. There had been no rite of consecration, no house of worship was built there, but he was constrained to remove the shoes from his feet for the place whereon he stood was holy ground. Where did Moses find holy ground, where did he see the phenomenon of the burning bush? There was no temple built by human hands and dedicated to the Most High where he received the divine message, he was in the solitary unconsecrated desert.

Where did Jesus tell the woman of Samaria that God should be worshiped? It was not necessary to approach a holy mountain, as the Samaritans thought, with their ruined temple on its summit; it was not necessary to enter Jerusalem with its temple of unparalleled magnificence or pause within its walls, for God is everywhere. Spirit and truth are the only two essential words used in connection with his worship,

In the future the religious instinct will be entirely disconnected from fear, from all harsh conceptions of Deity and moral obligation ; the very word obligatory will be removed from the thought of religion and God will be worshiped in perfect freedom.

But some may still ask how can perfect freedom be reconciled with religion or *religio*, which means binding? Can we be religious—completely bound—and yet enjoy perfect freedom? Yes, for you can serve your father and mother from pure love, you do not fear them at all, if you love them perfectly. The youngest child can know what it is to feel: father would never punish me, nor would mother; but when they tell me what to do I do it because I love them, and because I love them I choose to please them.

The only worship God can care for is the kind of worship we have just mentioned, any other is craven, and usually selfish. When worship is offered to God for the sake of receiving something in return, is not the worshiper like a child who obeys his parents not from love, but because if he is a good child he may get a toy or some sweetmeats, such worship is not religion. There are people who are so afraid of God they worship in order to escape hell. Congregations in times of revival are thrown into hysteria at the thought of endless perdition, and then they are said to receive the spirit, having prayed for the holy spirit because they very naturally did not wish to drop into fire and be burned forever. There is no religion in such experiences. Where true religion appears is where people worship lovingly and truly the eternal God, from gratitude to the God who blesses them; where their hearts are full of gratitude to the Eternal Fount of all, and they love the Eternal with all their hearts, with all their souls, with all their minds and with all their strength, fear is gone, dread is removed from such forever.

True religion has nothing but love in it. The only reason why the men and women of the future will worship will be because they love the Eternal. Now as God wants nothing, and as you can not possibly do God a favor, add to his glory or bestow one fraction of honor upon the Eternal that He does not eternally possess, religion resolves itself into practical philanthropy; and love for the Eternal takes the form of love for all his children. Religion, rising in glorious light from its chrysalis, transformed into a butterfly, becomes philanthropy, humanitarianism. When we support religious services in days to come we shall know that others are helped by them, and that they generally benefit society; we shall do whatever we can to help our brethren to a higher and nobler life. There is a divine utilitarianism which recognizes the usefulness of whatsoever tends to promote the spiritual nature, and this will be the impetus to all religious observance in days to come. Nothing is more important than that doubting and nervous persons, in particular, should be helped to a spiritual sight of divine goodness, and assisted to realize the truth of immortality. Pains, suffering and diseases of every name proceed from doubt, fear and sorrow, and to remove these deadly enemies of health and happiness is to employ the only effective measures to overcome sickness and insanity.

LESSON X.

HOW CAN WE EXPLAIN MIRACLES SCIENTIFICALLY, AND ACCOMPLISH WONDERS APPARENTLY TRANSCENDING THE OPERATION OF NATURAL LAW?

QUESTIONS similar to the above having poured in upon us from every direction, we have felt it desirable to devote a special chapter in this work to an elucidation, as far as possible, of a problem, the very nature of which appears at first sight to challenge the ability of even the ablest intellect. But when we look carefully at the proposition, and consider thoughtfully the nature of the inquiry, we shall perceive that no so-called miracle has ever claimed to be an interference with immutable law; but only an exhibition of spiritual power overcoming the ordinary limitations assigned by human infirmity to the operation of a law, the scope of which so far transcends ordinary comprehension and discovery as to remove it as completely from the realm of general observation, as the rings belting the planet Saturn are unrevealed to unassisted mortal eyesight, but stand out in vivid distinctness before the average eye when assisted by a telescope.

Spiritual science is no more at variance with physical science than telescopes are at war with eyes. Spiritual perception enables us to see far beyond the limits of average observation, thus the only contention there can possibly be between spiritual science and physics is on the score of unwarrantable negative assumption on the part of many physicists. It was always said of Darwin that the most conspicuous feature of his greatness was his determination to publish his discoveries, and not antagonize in a controversial spirit the opinions of those who as yet were not blessed with the knowledge which had fallen to his share. Let us all emulate Darwin in this respect, be truly thankful for all the positive information we can derive from the most external source, and at the same time be ever ready and desirous to peer more deeply than the outer senses can into the realm of spiritual being which ever encompasses us, and of which we are now and ever denizens.

No one can be justified in supposing that any event no matter how remarkable is due to a suspension of law, but is not law infinitely beyond our acquaintance with it, we consider the time has already come for a clear forcible exposition of the triumphs of mind over matter, not as a contribution to the literature of dogmatic theology or speculative philosophy, but of science itself. Marie Corelli, a deservedly popular authoress, in a most fascinating work which has had a very large sale already, *A Romance of Two Worlds*, has without question, in her dissertation upon the nature and application of electricity, done a good deal to prepare the public mind, which reads science in the form of romance, gladly for yet more explicit and startling disclosures which are to follow; her method of dealing with the occult forces is far in advance of Mr. Sinnett's in his theosophical novels *Karma* and *United*, for while Sinnett deals almost exclusively when discoursing of phenomenal results, with the wonderful and almost the terrible, Marie Corelli shows how in her own case especially (if her narrative is to be considered a chapter from her own autobiography) the wonderful knowledge of the noble hero of the tale *Heliobas* is directed entirely to three most important ends: spiritual development, mental improvement and physical well being. In the same book a chapter devoted to *the Electric Creed*, explains very reasonably how Peter was able to walk on the sea while faith upheld him, but when he felt himself sinking, it was at a time when fear overcame him, and fear disturbs electrical currents and renders danger imminent. Other wonderful doings of the Apostles and the strange natural phenomena mentioned frequently in connection with telling episodes in the life of Jesus are similarly explained, *i.e.* the electrical theory is applied throughout and it works well, especially as *human electricity* is never confounded with mineral, vegetable or animal electricity and it has always appeared to us that to attribute human force to animal magnetism or to call it by that name is to insult manhood and womanhood by unduly extolling the animal emanations. Man has an animal nature which links him physically with the lower orders of existence, but this lower nature is totally unable to accomplish those super-animal results which can spring alone from the operation of altogether higher capabilities. With persons who refuse to apply the scientific method of experiment or who are so satisfied with physical limitations of the most arbitrary character that they seek no spiritual light, also with those who ignorantly and pugilistically denounce whatever is above their crude physical perception,.we refuse to enter into controversy, such people will throw down a treatise on spiritual themes with a contemptuous sneer or they will attack vigorously what they fail to understand in a manner which positively compliments the work they fondly imagine they demolish, as they only succeed in advertising publicly their own shallow irascibility and overweening self-conceit. To those alone who are in search of light, who are dissatisfied alike with theologic and materialistic husks, who can neither believe in antiquated supernaturalism nor be content with frozen materalism, should teachers and healers appeal, we only waste time in seeking to make proselytes; hungering and thirsty children of the Eternal, our needy brethern and sisters who are seeking light, health and peace, and who are willing to make material sacrifices to secure higher blessings than can possibly flow through the channels of the senses, are the only persons to whom the new illumination can come, or by whom it will be welcomed, and to these is now being vouchsafed an interpretation and exposition of spiritual truth far beyond any light previously thrown upon life, its origin, nature and destiny, and the power of man to control the outward elements and most certainly his own body. We acknowledge without qualification an Infinite Supreme Power of perfect Love and Wisdom, and to the Infinite Being alone will we submit, but while we are absolutely certain that God is the one infinite truth in being, we do not allow that we as men and women are unable to so utilize and manifest divine power as to exhibit godlike qualities even on earth. There is a passage in the Psalms, which exactly states our position: "All the whole heaven is the Lord's, the earth hath he given to the children of men," which signifies that while God is supreme in the universe as the life and soul of all, man has it in his power to subdue the earth, and therefore we do not raise any objection to the teachings of theosophists and transcendentalists who declare that man has such resources within himself that ultimately he can and will control the raging elements and show himself master of the whole earth. Swedenborg's doctrine that man lives from God but appears to live from himself is perfectly reasonable, and the necessity of man's appearing to live from himself while in reality he lives from God, is also made quite clear in the writings of this greatest of modern seers. Now as we have no intention of intrenching, in this lesson, on the views of Trinitarians *versus* Unitarians with regard to the deity or divinity of the personal Christ, we shall bring forward only such instances from the New Testament as are clearly intended to refer to the exercise of a spiritual power common to all mankind, but like every gift or talent, susceptible to cultivation and needing careful culture for its expansion.

It is a very great mistake to suppose that spiritual gifts are so miraculous that they are the possession of a privileged few who have done nothing to merit them, while all others must remain hopelessly destitute of such endowments, however much they may desire to possess and use them. The manifestation of the Spirit is given to everyone without exception, but to all the same gift is not given, and where we often fail is in seeking to obtain what we have not when it would be wisdom on our part to cultivate what we have. A formal, routine system of school discipline is fatal to normal education, as all children are not adapted to the same pursuits, but no child, with proper care and training, need become or remain a dunce, an idiot or an invalid. Abnormal, unhealthy, unlovely conditions are unnatural. All works on pathology freely admit this. Then do not fall into the error of supposing that any one exists who has not some vocation, and who can not, by judicious treatment, be brought into a state of manifested health and harmony. Jesus chose his immediate followers from all ranks and stations. Previous to their call to follow him some had been fishermen, but others had belonged to the medical profession, and sat at the receipt of custom. They continued, in some instances at least, to ply their vocations after joining the apostolic band, as Paul continued his trade as a tent-maker after the greatest orations had fallen from his lips.

Concentration of mind on a given object is the open door to success and without it genuine and stable success is impossible in any direction. Prayer and Faith must ever go together, as aspiration without confidence is well nigh useless, and belief without an endeavor to ascend to a higher interior realm is practically futile. We can pray without ceasing by unceasingly desiring to accomplish a definite result, we can continually exercise faith by refusing to allow our thoughts to be diverted even for an instant from the good toward which we unceasingly aspire, and we can truly fast or abstain by so subduing the lower to the higher nature that reason is lord over passion, while reason in its turn is rendered subject to the moral sense. These three necessities, faith, prayer and fasting can be so explained as to prove to every intelligent and fair-minded student that the words of Jesus, as recorded by the evangelists, are in exact accordance with demonstrable fact, therefore scholarly or sciolistic criticisms matter nothing, for while the scholar questions and the sciolist impudently denies the authenticity of the gospel tale the enlightened spiritual scientist assumes a position far in advance of historical controversy, a position which is in fact, utterly impregnable, for to those who understand the law governing the production of marvelous phenomena the recorded facts themselves are taken as illustrations of the consequences attendant upon a certain course of action and line of development, therefore history is ot quite secondary importance so far as it refers to time and place. It matters not whether persons believed to be dead were raised to life in Palestine 1800 or in Egypt 18,000 years ago, the question is, can the so-called dead be raised at all, is there a law which renders their resuccitation possible? History furnishes us with startling accounts of the prevalence of a power in the world confined however to exceptional individuals able to restore to physical health and vigor those pronounced dead by all other testimony than that of far-seeing intelligence consciously possessed by those alone whose lives have rendered them superior to every ordinary limitation of mortality. Leprosy is instanced as being cured by remarkable men in accordance with fixed law and unalterable conditions, and when we remember that "men of like passions with ourselves" accomplished these marvelous feats of spiritual prowess, no claim whatever being made that they were wrought only by Jesus, indeed, the exact opposite being positively stated in the Bible, we can afford to dismiss without attention the silly bombast of those rabid iconoclasts, who think they can wipe out by their absurd negations man's confidence in what he can prove for himself independent of history, if he only forms the acquaintance of a great spiritual truth and harmonizes his conduct with his understanding of it.

One of the most striking illustrations of spiritual agency overcoming what has been universally termed incurable disease, is the story of Elisha directing Naaman, the Syrian, to the mystical Jordan in whose cleansing streams every trace of leprosy was washed away. Now Elisha stood in the attitude of a guide, a teacher, a director, but he was in no sense a mesmerist, neither did he attribute Naaman's recovery to any potency inhering in his personality. Elisha was a prophet and the successor of a prophet. His fitness to take Elijah's place after the latter's translation was determined altogether by his clear-sightedness. Elijah says to Elisha, if you see me when I am taken from you, it shall be evidence to you that my mantle has fallen upon you, but if you do not see me the hard thing you have asked can not be accomplished. Here at the outset we have presented to us a correct view of what Christains might call *apostolic succession*. Elisha had been both servant, student and companion to Elijah, for a long time, during which period innumerable opportunities had been afforded him of attaining the high rank of prophet or seer which signifies one in whom the power of insight into spiritual things is coupled with the ability to proclaim truth, and lead others into paths of wisdom. Elisha had so far profited by his discipleship to Elijah, as to have developed his spiritual perception to the point of ability to see and describe what was occurring on another plane than that of sense, he proves by this that his advantages have been improved, and that he is,therefore, ready to commence his journey as a witness to truth against every form of error and idolatry, and he testifies to the divinity of his mission by blessing the city into which he first enters, changing bitter and unwholesome waters into pure and sweet. If we could pause to linger over the incidents in Elisha's ministry, we could, we think, convince you that his *baldness* was but typical of the absence of material pomp, authority and show which ever accompanies the highest type of spiritual worker. The children of the city who ridiculed him were those, (plentiful in every age and land) who deem externals all important and ridicule every truth, and all who proclaim it unless it is rendered outwardly attractive and presented with the pomp and display ever characterizing civil and ecclesiastical, imperialistic despotism. The children eaten by bears in the old figurative story to be found in the Book of Kings are like multitudes in Europe and America to-day who in consequence of slighting the only agent of redemption, the spiritual teaching which bids them forego externals and cultivate the spirit, find themselves devoured by the she-bears of the woods which Swedenborg so aptly describes as human affection for earthly and dangerous things.

Elisha represents a man of unswerving integrity,

and loyalty to principle and conviction, he therefore claims nothing for himself, and stands to the afflicted Naaman as a wise and helpful teacher and he tells this great Syrian captain to bathe seven times in the river Jordan. The name Jordan means a stream flowing from above, and therefore refers to those spiritual blessings which are obtainable only when we divest ourselves of confidence in material things, and permit the cleansing and illuminating grace of spirit to remove from us all earthly defilements. Naaman, justly proud of the beautiful situation of the city of Damascus, and attached to the broad flowing rivers Abana and Pharphar, desires to wash in them and be cleansed, but following the line of correspondence we shall see that these rivers represented external means of relief to apply to which in case of leprosy was manifestly absurd, as Oriental medicine and surgery had proved hopelessly impotent to relieve that terrible disorder. Now, as no miracle can possibly be performed except in accordance with universal law, Elisha could only point Naaman to the fount of healing, he could not heal him by any act of personal sovereignty or favor, nor in consideration of a proffered reward. All of you, who are seeking to excel in blessing others, remember always that though you can open doors and windows, and let in sunshine, you cannot create it, even though you can assist others into the light, persuading and directing them by every measure of persuasive force, you can not compel any one to avail him or herself of the means of salvation. Jesus, we are told, could do no mighty works in certain places because of the obstinate infidelity of the people, his disciples were directed to leave a sinful, sensual city, shaking its very dust from their sandals. No work of art has ever been more admired, or portrayed deeper pathos than *Christ weeping over Jerusalem*, mourning because the children of Jerusalem would not avail themselves of the only means which could possibly save them from degradation and distress. The great and leading error in modern thought is precisely the error of olden times. Call it the will of God, or maintain if you please that it is the operation of a blind law of necessity (though the latter position is insane), there is unmistakably a law in the universe which governs and regulates conditions so arbitrarily that no one's wishes are respected in any case more than were Naaman's preferences for the waters of Damascus.

If the Jordan, or what it corresponded to, possessed healing virtue, then a prophet could point out the method whereby that regenerative force could be applied to the cure of an otherwise incurable disorder, and not only the prophet but the captain's servants and friends could bring argument and moral suasion to bear to induce the suffering ruler to enter and bathe in the healing stream, but that was the extent of their united power. The folly of those who claim that spiritual scientists or metaphysical practitioners ignore the law of nature, or that those of any name who acknowledge the power of spirit as beyond that of "force" or "matter" believe absurdly that God changes or the universal order is reversed by prayer or any human effort, is commensurate only with their ignorance, and were it not for the almost invincible strength of blind prejudice it would be impossible for the merest tyro in logic, or a child who comprehends the ordinary use of language to fail to understand that so-called miracles are not in the slightest degree discordant with the immutable law and order of the universe, recognized by materialists as a blind force, but by theists as the unvarying expression of divine intelligence. Never, under any conceivable circumstances, can two and two make other than four, never can oaks be raised except from acorns, never can one type be changed into another in the whole economy of nature, but nature's resources are so little known that he is guilty of insane bombast who undertakes in this age of electrical appliances to deny that anything may not be accomplished which which does not involve a reversal of the order of nature, or state a mathematical impossibility. One can never be three or seven, but at the same time the single ray of white light can be made manifest in three primary colors and seven prismatic hues and countless tints and shades, thus the essential life of the universe is one life, but its expression may be both three fold, seven fold and multiform. When in the future direct telegraphic communication is established between this earth and the planet Mars, it will be by means of an electrical system as natural as the overland telegraph or the sub-marine cable. What marvelous intellectual prodigies those men are who conceive the idea of modern appliances: the Canadian Pacific Railroad running as it does through a territory presenting at first sight utterly insurmountable barriers to the skill of the engineer, is a solid working testimony to the fact of mind surmounting any and every material barrier as it unfolds to perceive the method of such mastery.

Now shall one accept the Brooklyn bridge and prospectively the tunnel under the English channel uniting France and England and laugh to scorn predictions of further conquests over earth and tides? Does not the wise man speak very cautiously and with infinite reserve concerning the wildest dreams of future human attainment? all who think and observe must conclude that as intelligence unfolds things formerly considered utterly beyond the reach of possibility as well as probability actually will occur. Now to apply this precise reasoning to spiritual attainments we declare that what is meant by the three-fold command, believe, pray, fast, is that through the exercise of supreme confidence in spirit, coupled with sincere and constant aspiration and a complete subjection of the lower appetites to the higher promptings to the extent that transmutation is accomplished, wonders of healing can be wrought, truth can be stated and applied with reference to the entire economy of man's finite expression in external form, equaling if not excelling the sublimest works performed in ancient Galilee. The *Esoteric Magazine*, published in Boston, constantly publishes very instructive articles giving practical directions in this line, all tending to prove the immutability of divine law and the certainty of success in spiritual directions if the affections are weaned from earth and centered in the things of the spirit. The question of *will* is one that is continually recurring and is a subject upon which more misapprehension prevails than perhaps any other. Mrs. Eddy and those calling themselves Christian scientists in general, have much to say against the exercise of personal will. *Science and Health* contains some particularly strong condemnations of mesmerism, but after all, you will note that Mrs. Eddy's particular aversion is malicious mesmerism. Now all mesmeric operation is no more necessarily malicious than all speech is malicious. If Mrs. Eddy or any one else has discovered malpractice among her students and sees a danger resulting from the views entertained by some, she is conscientiously and humanely fulfilling her duty by calling attention to erroneous beliefs and practices, but wholesale condemnation of what is usually classed as mesmerism is unwise as she herself admits it can either kill or cure. Its curative proprieties are as serviceable as the constructive action of electricity, while its destructive action may be likened to the electric flame, striking and demolishing a building or blasting a handsome tree.

Personal will must be subdued to universal divine will, or it runs riot and proves itself an outlaw, while all selfish abuses of psychology inevitably lead to the misery alike of those who operate and those who are operated upon. Hypnotism, now so fashionable, is not a desirable form of psychology, as the hypnotic state is one of subjective insensibility, but whenever experiments are successfully proven in such directions, it is because the one who entrances is more fully in the light than the one entranced. Modern Spiritualism during the past four decades has amply illustrated how much good and evil can emanate apparently from the same source. Pyschologists and Spiritualists will always be in danger till they learn that subjection to the higher is the only safeguard against control by the lower. Our paramount resolve must ever be to educate, not coerce, to unite ourselves lovingly, willingly, completely with whatever appeals to us as highest and divinest in the universe. We can not succeed as rebels forever militating against universal order; we can not turn the eternal current of infinite energy out of its course because we, like straws or tiny boats, are struggling to float or row against the stream. If, as Matthew Arnold said, there is a stream of tendency ever making for righteousness, is it not wisdom on the part of all to seek to move in and with this glorious current, not to strive against it? The prayer of Jesus, "Father, not my will, but thine be done," is the very essence of profound wisdom, for what man is there however great, who can control the Pleiades or Orion to borrow appropriate similes from the book of Job? He is a lunatic, mad with pride, staggering through the intoxication of vanity, who can gaze at the matchless order of the universe and say with the foolish ones, "There is no God." The utter puerility of atheism or blank materialism is so contemptible as to make every genuine rationalist pray that modern infidels may learn wisdom from one of their own favorite text-books, Thomas Paine's "Age of Reason," in which that celebrated deist reveals atheism in its true light and *atheism or infidelity with a ghost*, professed by some utterly illogical spiritualists, is the most hopelessly chaotic system ever presented to any public.

Now listen to the reasoning of some spiritualists who are utterly unwilling to affirm the being of Deity. They declare most reasonably that intelligence acts through force upon matter. This explanation of the phenomena of existence can scarcely be improved upon, but it at once strikes the reflective mind that every manifestation of intelligence through matter is the expression of intelligence at least commensurate with such expression. Now while there are many forms of existence below man, displaying far less intelligence than man, man is utterly unable to create. There is a law he can not set aside, immutably fixed by an intelligence far superior to his own. Now this law proves God, *i. e.*, Supreme Intelligence, as no law can exist save as it is a manifestation of mind, the being of God is axiomatically proven through this universal law, and the fact that man can discover, obey or rebel against this law but can not possibly change it, is to the thinker, proof direct of an infinite and unchangeable intelligence, for law is unknown among men save as it is the result and embodiment of intelligence. It would be just as reasonable to argue that a state was governed by law and then deny the existence of any human will back of that law producing and enforcing it, as to deny the sovereignty of Infinite Will, Eternal Spirit. Now the renunciation of our human will is not required of us. Our will is a talent to be used not renounced. The true attitude of the human will is an intelligent acquiescence with the divine will, a perfect surrender of pride and rebellion, and a loving, harmonious union with the Infinite.

In union is strength, in disunion is impotence. Houses divided against themselves cannot stand, and it is because men and women are continually warring against each other, that they are weak, sick and generally wretched and unsuccessful. To gain perfect power over the lower self, and to become strong enough to resist all defiant elements, to live above the reach of disease, is to accomplish a conscious voluntary union with the Infinite Will. Now this union with the divine is diametrically opposed to the relinquishment of freedom. Our freedom is never so great, never so dearly prized as when with an absolutely free spirit, in perfect liberty we elect to walk in paths of righteousness and peace. To love the divine law, to obey it from love, to apprehend something of its perfect wisdom, and to choose the path of wisdom and deliberately walk therein, is to follow the only course which intuition and common-sense recommend alike. Now if any of you feel sick, sad, lonely, desolate, and you turn in thought to the Infinite, your cares will be dismissed, your burdens lifted, your sorrows assuaged, while hope will immediately resume the place left vacant by despair. The *greater works* which Jesus said should be performed by his disciples, may be understood in two ways: 1st, The obvious meaning is that what had hitherto been confined to a very circumscribed area should at length cover the globe; and 2d, as the minds of men expand, they are ever becoming ready for greater marvels than would have been of any use before. No matter how much a teacher knows, instruction must ever keep pace with the comprehension of the scholars; because a learned professor can solve an intricate problem in the higher mathematics, does not prove that any among his class are prepared for its solution before them, and were it solved in their presence, it would be practically unsolved for all save the professor. If a divine voice speaks and but a few can hear what it utters, the multitude may confound the sound with ordinary thunder, the fault is not with the voice that speaks in thrilling tones of perfect distinctness, but with the deaf ears of the auditors. The voice of truth is ever speaking, but as the world only gradually advances to a point where many can interpret the voice of truth or behold its form, the voice seems to be ever drawing nearer and speaking more clearly to men, the voice speaks as it always spoke, the light shines as it always shone, the processes of nature are continued as they always were, but the hearing ear, the seeing eye, and truly understanding heart are only by continuous and apparently slow processes of growth unfolded to perceive and understand these "mysteries." Dr. James Martineau, one of the most deeply spiritual minds in the Unitarian denomination introduced a beautiful canticle into his *Ten Services for Public Worship*, commencing with the words: "Blessed be the Lord God of ages, who ever delighteth to draw more nigh. In the morning of the world he appeareth from afar, in the evening he draweth nigh to abide with us forever." This quotation conveys the aspect of divine revelation, as seen by students of evolution, but as all human perceptions of truth are relative, it is no more absolutely true that the Eternal One draws gradually nigh to his children, than that the sun draws gradually near to the earth. In the Mosaic account of creation, the doctrine of gradual and successive developments is stated in such a manner as to lead the uninitiated to suppose that whoever was the author of the Pentateuch, taught the astronomical absurdity that the earth was created before the sun. Interpret the record in the light of science and you will at once perceive that the theory is, that at the time when the moon was formed, through the separation of an encircling ring from the earth, the sun and stars began to appear, just as colors are a new creation to a man born blind when he first beholds them, and sounds are a new creation to one who was deaf from birth, but whose ears are now for the first time unstopped. Transposing the idea of revelation it is at once comprehensible and accordant with all science, but let it remain in its old groove and it suggests the idea of a fitful Deity. Once we understand that the ability to perform any wonder is ours, so soon as we discover the law which makes a result possible, once we get free of the false belief that God or nature is partial, once we behold universal law in place of chance or caprice, and nothing is any longer impossible save a mathematical absurdity.

Fear in the sense of dread is the great obstacle to human liberty, fear in the sense of doubt is the great drawback to success in all matters where confident decision is required, fear in the sense of reverence, respect, submission to divine guidance is the begining of wisdom. But in its good sense the word fear is now very rarely used, therefore we do not commend to you even the fear of God as recommended in the Proverbs of Solomon. Perfect love casteth out all fear, we can not fear what we love perfectly, fear causes men to tremble and cringe even before a partially beloved object, fear and love hold divided sway in many a heart and you are doubtless all of you able to relate some chapters in your own experience when you trembled at the approach of one you thought you loved. All that we deem superior excites to awe until through the fullness of our love, all terror is displaced. Before we can heal ourselves or others perfectly, we must have lost all fear and then with liberty to utilize our every faculty and gift we shall be equal to every emergency and ready at all times to obey the summons of the Spirit. Strive to excel in calm confident assurance that all is well, in quietness is strength, the calmer we are the more we can accomplish. Anything like haste or nervousness is at deadly variance with success. Do not seek to fight a disease, do not attack an ailment, but transfer your thought to the perfection of life immortal and let the soul act. This is the secret of power.

LESSON XI.

PRACTICAL ADVICE TO STUDENTS, HEALERS AND PATIENTS, AND DIRECTIONS FOR THE APPLICATION OF SPIRITUAL SCIENCE TO ALL THE AVOCATIONS OF DAILY LIFE.

ONE of the most misleading errors and yet a very common one into which people fall, concerning Spiritual Science, is that it is to be studied and practiced exclusively for the driving out of physical ailments and therefore that its study should be almost entirely confined to those who are seeking to identify themselves with a new therapeutic school, or are seeking to rid themselves of some physical ailment. Then again, there is a prevailing impression that the practice of healing is extraordinary, that it consists in the mental utterance of prescribed formulas, and that to heal it is necessary to withdraw from the world and relinquish all hold upon common obligations. These statements are all founded on fact and are in a limited sense correct, as they apply to special cases, but taken as a whole they are exceedingly misleading, as a very brief study of the science will prove to any intelligent inquirer. From the earliest days of which there is any written record, the healing art has been practised by persons pursuing every imaginable avocation, though in ancient times the power to heal seemed especially to inhere in those who had devoted themselves particularly to the service of religion. The elders of the church alluded to in the Epistle of James, were the wisest and most experienced persons in an early Christian association. Elders were chosen because of their spiritual endowments of a practical character, and while some pursued the work of teachers and healers exclusively, others performed even menial labor, and in many instances the most successful healers have been those utterly destitute of worldly means; who have followed a laborious occupation and in its pursuit discovered their spiritual ability through grateful recognition on the part of those whom they have been instrumental in relieving. As Felix Adler has said that teachers of ethics will be successors of the clergy, so we may state that mental healers will succeed to the practice of medical men and women. But can not a clergyman widen his views and become a teacher of ethics, enlarging his sphere of usefulness, instead of abandoning his field of effort, provided his knowledge and convictions keep pace with the progressive tendencies of the time? So may the professors and doctors of medicine outgrow their physical limitations and do far more for the relief of suffering humanity as their methods become more spiritual than they could ever accomplish when limited by external scholasticisms.

Esculapius was a divinity of the old world, a god of healing, and while it is customary to call physicians Esculapians, every one acquainted with mythology must be quite well aware that the name is derived not from a study and practice, such as the medical profession usually confines itself to to-day, but from a recognition among ancient peoples of a healing force in nature pointed out and directed by invincible intelligence. No one of any experience, be he physician, surgeon, nurse or attendant, will endeavor to deny that by far the largest percentage of diseases and accidents proceed directly from vice and folly. Subtract from the total sum of painful and distressing maladies those caused by crimes and indiscretions and you would so shorten the list that the few remaining would be resolved into the category of simple weaknesses, while accidents, proceeding as they do from drunkenness and nervous disorders, in almost all instances, are most intimately connected with vice. It is useless and absurd, indeed, it is far worse, it is positively mischievous to turn into ridicule the old doctrine of suffering as a consequence of sin, for nothing is more positively emphasized by modern experience and an ever increasing familiarity with the law of heredity. Sin is so broad a word, it covers so much both of commission and omission that many take exception to it as they confound it altogether with crime, which is an intense and more malignant form of offense. You can sin against yourselves ignorantly, you can also sin against others ignorantly, but to commit crime one must act deliberately for the injury of another. Now under the head of sin may be classed all weak errors, all mistakes, all violence done to sense of right and all opposition to the law of being. Please observe, we do not talk about *laws* but only *law*, as laws are of human device and are therefore constantly changing and in no sense binding. Law is eternal and can never be put aside. Laws of mortal enactment and variable belief are called laws of mortal mind because they are mutable expressions of mutable will. these are often more honored in the breach than in the observance and they prove themselves mortal because man can make, repeal, break, alter and destroy them.

Divine law is universal. The law of nature is no respecter of persons and can not be tampered with or evaded by human ingenuity under any circumstances whatsoever, therefore, if it were a law of God or nature that you should become ill through being in a malarial district, there could not be a single healthy inhabitant in such a place. Were it a decree of God through nature that you should catch cold by sitting in a draught or geting your feet wet, under no circumstances could you escape this penalty. Were it due to the action of universal law that you should suffer from small-pox, cholera or diphtheria, because it was in the air, no one at certain times in certain cities could possibly escape. Now, if medical precautions can be taken, if doctors and sanitary commissioners advocate antidotes, they must at once see that to succumb to such pestilences is totally unnecessary, and that those who fall victims do so because of a weakness and through a predisposition which is vanquishable. Spiritual Science steps in and traces the weakness of the physical body to a prior defect in mental and moral condition, and therefore its advocates and interpreters claim that it is utterly useless to seek to overcome physical disability without first ousting the demon of error possessing the mind. How more than useless it must be to torment an almost heart-broken widow or bereaved mother with pills and powders, lotions and bandages, when every one knows as well as she that her health was excellent before the departure of her loved one to the invisible state. How ridiculous to seek to assuage results of an accusing conscience or a perturbed mind with physical appliances, for how, in the name of reason or common-sense, can any of you suppose that an effect will cease while its cause continues in active operation? If you are treating one whose sickness originated with bereavement, argue immortality to the mind of the sufferer silently at first, then as your patient becomes composed, sleeps better, and manifests a visible attachment for you, introduce the subject cautiously in conversation, chiefly in inviting and answering questions. Never force a doctrine or religious proposition verbally upon any one, but direct the thought silently until the patient feels its influence and wishes to talk about it. The best times for giving treatment in cities are early morning and late evening; in the country, where the atmosphere is perpetually quiet, midday is as favorable as midnight, unless you have active occupation which absorbs your attention.

In seeking a healer, continue your search until you find a person in natural electric sympathy with yourself, one in whom you instinctively believe, and to whom you are irresistibly drawn. Be guided far more by instinctive and intuitive recognition of a power to bless than by any outward credentials, all of which may be misleading. The only faith in a healer necessary on the part of a patient is confidence born of appreciation. Whenever you encounter any one who can help you, you feel drawn to such an one, and such drawing is your instinctive response to good already received. Never tax the credulity of a patient, but when giving a treatment adapt your methods as far as you conscientiously can to individual requirement and demand. Persons who are fond of music can be reached musically. If you are a musician of any kind, and discover a spiritual relationship or adaptability between yourself and any sufferer, play the organ, piano, violin or cornet, as the case may be, either with or without the accompaniment of song, and cause the notes you strike to vibrate to your own consciousness, as echoes of the sentiment you wish to convey, mentally if not orally, to your patient. You can give this treatment from any distance and find it successful, provided you choose a time when both you and your patient can be undisturbed. In doing general housework, cooking and chamber work in particular, treatments can be successfully given, as you can impart your psychic influence to food you prepare, and leave your mental aura in any room you have swept or dusted. If your outward engagements are those of the clerk, you can reach those who are attracted to you, and whom you wish to benefit, by simply conveying to them, mentally, while handing them goods, the same thought you would utter in words were they to seek a conversation on the subject. In dealing with troublesome children, you must invariably hold them in mind as the very opposite of what they appear, for by so doing you appeal to and stimulate their dormant higher proclivities. Never repeat a mistake or call attention to an error; counteract and destroy it by affirming and exhibiting its direct opposite. Never seek to diagnose disease physically, so as to become acquainted with physical defects or derangements, but always insist upon seeing every part of the body perfectly whole, for by holding before the mind a perfect picture you induce an outward manifestation corresponding thereto. Do not use silly or incomprehensible phrases, such as, "You have no head, therefore it can not ache," but hold before your own and your patient's mind a perfect head, and as all form is essentially perfect in spirit, and outward symmetry is a result of inward harmony, by discarding pathology while retaining anatomy and physiology, you never allow an image to present itself to thought which you do not desire to see reflected or ultimated in externals.

When seeking for success in legitimate worldly enterprises, always remember that you can bring to pass whatever you steadfastly adhere to in thought; but your success will never be to some one else's detriment, but always in a manner conducive to the general good. If you are dissatisfied with your present position, but have no other situation to go to, stay where you are, and faithfully and unrepiningly discharge the duties of your state, but perpetually see yourself in mind where you desire to be. If you keep a hotel or lodging house, see your rooms filled with just the kind of people you desire to occupy them, and by persistently so doing you will throw out a wave of mental influence which will attract to your house the very persons who need what you have to offer as much as you need what they have to give in return. If you are a teacher in search of pupils, a professional person desiring an engagement, an artist with pictures to dispose of, a lawyer needing clients, a lecturer in want of hearers, in a word, whatever your necessities may be, do not content yourself with advertising them in public print, or talking of them to your friends, but bring into requisition that perfectly legitimate occult force with which every one is by nature supplied in some degree, and which can be cultivated by all by a simple use of judicious concentrative methods.

If any timid souls are afraid of black magic or malicious mesmerism let them silence their doubts once for all by remembering two important facts, one is that in order to be influenced by evil there must be a weakness in your own condition, which it is the special province of metaphysical treatment to overcome, and the other that ignorance is no safeguard, but on the contrary knowledge alone is power, and to be forewarned is to be in a position to get forearmed. Spiritual methods are never competitive, but invariably co-operative. No one can link himself in spirit with celestial spheres who does not banish from the circle of his immediate thought and desire all uncharitable, envious and selfish ambitions. The spiritual view of the universe and of the earth is that there is enough and to spare for all. No one needs to go hungry because another is well fed, none need be paupers because of the opulence of others. Competition and monopoly are gigantic evils, and even the entire wage system is a relic of feudalism and will soon be peacefully outgrown as spiritual principles are universally taught and applied. Whenever you seek to accomplish anything by mental methods, first assure yourself by submitting the project to conscience that it is right, then proceed at once to claim your inheritance. Why should you be deprived of light and air when there is abundance for you without depriving a living creature of any? Why remain victims of disease when you can recover without injuring a living thing by your recovery? Why not enter into the realm of truth consciously and enjoy that fuller measure of health and ampler supply of all vigor which can only conduce to the betterment of the condition of all your brethren? Discard utterly all false notions of contracting disease, render yourselves positive against disorder by boldly affirming that nothing can possibly affect you to your detriment, because you are immortal spirit and as such proof against all contamination.

Taking this firm, strong mental attidude will produce a radical change in the state of the body, affirming positively in thought with firm conviction will send an electric thrill through your entire frame. If the extremities have been cold, the lips blue, the cheeks colorless, pulse feeble and heart action weak and uncertain, you will find any one of these symptoms changed so that any medical man would instantly report a change in the pulse and bodily temperature, as all outward conditions are results of mental or affectional emotions. Though you may not diagnose a case or know or say anything about physical conditions, mental assenerations and denials change the physical state by processes identical with those which make the blood boil or turn it to ice, to use common expressions on receipt of terrifying or distressing news or under provocation of a slight or insult. The body unwittingly responds to the mental condition, thus it is not necessary to know the physical difficulty in order to remove it. Diagnosis is a subject which needs very careful handling, as from a retrospective point of view it is often valuable in convincing a patient that some knowledge derivable only by mental processes is in the possession of the healer. This evidence conduces to confidence, and provokes therefore a favorable bearing to the system presented. Prognosis is often highly objectionable, because while it is founded upon a recognition of the accuracy of prophetic prediction, it is usually utterly estranged from the true idea of prediction, which is not to the effect that certain persons must of necessity suffer certain pains in future, but only that there is a discoverable law of sequence, which can never be set aside, which necessitates certain definite effects springing from certain defined causes.

True prediction is prophetic in that it is a statement of universal law with which the majority are unacquainted. Very few people have any idea of the extent to which their lives are influenced prejudicially by courses of thought and action, they have been accustomed to pursue unthinkingly from servile devotion to custom, fashion, or habit; therefore it becomes the prime duty of an intelligent mental practitioner to give salutary advice of a strictly practical nature, in accordance with ascertained knowledge concerning the inevitable results of thought and conduct. For instance, it is very common for people to live together in the closest relationship, and yet mentally antagonize each other and that perpetually. The most prevalent source of sickness is unexpressed discord, for we must never forget that spiritual science teaches the eradication, not the repression of cantankerous feelings. No greater mistake can possibly be made than to endeavor to secure a simulation of good will not felt, for though an open enemy may be sometimes dangerous to encounter, the secret foe is always the deadliest. Open animosity can be rebutted, and the very expression of erroneous feeling is usually followed by a better state of mind, as volcanic eruptions are followed by periods when the mountain is in comparative repose. Under no circumstances permit the little foxes of secret animosities to grow to maturity and multiply to the destruction of the fruits of your domestic vineyards. Remember the sage request, "Take us the foxes, the little foxes that spoil our vines, for our vines have tender grapes." "Let not the sun go down upon your wrath" needs to be ever held in remembrance, for nothing is so pernicious as to fall asleep in a state of discordant feeling, and have one's dreams broken in upon by hideous nightmares and delirious fears. When you are bodily asleep, your minds are intensely active on the psychic plane, while less amenable to outward influences, such as words and acts of those about you, you are far more sensitive than when awake to the thought emanations which are around you, and which are sent to you from those any where who seek to influence you either for good or ill. In treating for nervous affections, general debility and chronic ailments of all kinds, you will soon learn that secret fears, inharmonious and objectionable desires are at the root of the malady. To endeavor to repress words and actions is more than useless, as the mind turned in upon itself seeks gratification in lustful and revengeful feelings, which owing to the psychic law of attraction and repulsion, bring those who indulge them into the circle of those who live in the domain of such foul influence.

Whenever you have a difficulty or grievance meet it boldly, bravely encounter your adversary in open combat. If it is in your power to argue a matter out with any one who annoys you and who is apt to be violent and unreasonable when you are alone together procure at least one wise truth-loving third party to act as audience, then demand explanation in a calm judicial spirit of inquiry. If such opportunities are denied you, write to the parties between whom and yourself misunderstandings have arisen, assuring them of your utter repudiation of all malicious feelings. Never accredit any one with evil motive, attribute sin to ignorance, and after fully and freely stating your determination to bear no grudge and never to retaliate, dismiss the whole matter from your mind. Cremate your grievances in the fire of universal charity, and from that day forward refuse to remember that you ever had a quarrel. When you rise to that state of feeling, you are like a granite rock, immovable, no matter what breakers of ill-feeling from other minds may be directed against you. "Forget and forgive" is an imperative command, for the mortal memory of error must be destroyed, that the immortal perception of truth may assert its supremacy at all times, and enable us, whenever we desire it, to have for use all the treasures of knowledge we have accumulated in our varied experiences. We complain of defective memory because we allow ourselves to remember what we ought to forget, and by retaining in our minds the recollections of what we should forcibly expel we clog our channels of communication with our higher or interior selves, wherein are deposited all the wisdom we have accumulated.

In dealing with lack of adaptability between persons who are compelled to live or do business together, the infallible recipe is to carefully look out for some one or more traits of character in those who are in many ways uncongenial to you. Fix your gaze steadily upon their good points and pleasant features to the exclusion of regard for all others and not only will you protect yourselves from annoyance, but you will be benefactors of priceless value to those whom you thus regard, for it is an inevitable certainty that whatever you acknowledge in those with whom you associate, you tend to develope in them and also in yourself. Failure to reform and heal springs from dealing with the imperfection you desire to exterminate. To obliterate drunkenness and love of improper pleasure in any one who frequents places of evil resort, never try to follow the delinquent mentally into dens of vice, but hold steadfastly in your own mind the picture of such an one where he should be, and doing his duty faithfully. Thus the wife of a gambler, or a man who is always at his club when he had better be at home, must, ere she can reform him, picture him constantly happy in her society at his own fireside. She must ever welcome him without reproaches or expressions of surprise and by constantly holding him in thought as already where he should be she will draw him to righteousness by the superior attractions of "home, sweet home." A school teacher can correct naughty children by ignoring their naughtiness and placing them in thought as already tractable and just. In a word, the universal rule is reverse the portrait of evil, and by persistently holding in mind the image of what you rightly desire to see actualized you form mental union with powerful invisible force which accomplishes its externalization.

LESSON XII.

FORMULAS, THEIR USE AND VALUE.

AS we have already given the general outline of both the theory and practise of metaphysical science as applied to healing in its widest sense, we shall only in this last lesson briefly review the ground already traversed, and try to help you to see the value of those much controverted formulas which, while nothing in and of themselves, are nevertheless as forms of sound words, calculated to confer inestimable benefit on those who use them understandingly, or who are led by hearing them or seeing them in print, to meditate carefully upon the ideas they so tersely embody. You must all have noted many times in your experience how vividly you have been struck and deeply impressed by some words you have heard, not, perhaps, meant for your ears, or by some motto you have seen upon the wall of some railway waiting room. We have known of cases where a scripture text or other motto has prevented suicide. One case in particular we will relate as a sample instance, and we are sure many of our readers can easily collect similar anecdotes. A young woman quite alone in the world, without any settled religious belief or conviction of any kind, poorly educated and inured to neglect and misery, was driven to the utmost verge of desperation by the coldness and unkindness of those who ought to have befriended her. She was traveling in search of work; everything looked blank before her, and as the train stopped at a side station where she was expecting to find some employment, but where no one met her, she sat down in a dreary waiting room alone and hungry to await the coming of a woman who had written to her to accept a hard situation for very little pay, and revolved it in her mind whether she had not better end her miserable existence in the river which was close at hand. Without trust in God or man, or in any form of spiritual protection, her eyes seemed suddenly fascinated by a hitherto unrecognized text upon the wall, "The Lord will provide," the word *will* particularly struck her; it shone out, a certain declaration, no faltering *may*, but a decisive *will*. As she gazed spell-bound at the words, which all the while seemed as though they were being burned into her consciousness by some invisible agency, the wall seemed to grow transparent, and through the apparently diaphanous substance she saw a figure pointing to a pleasant villa residence on the bank of the river farther up the stream, (which was a winding one) than the ordinary eye of a spectator could behold.

It seemed to her as though a beautiful lady was holding the text in one hand over her head, and with the other beckoning the girl to follow. So deeply impressed was the girl with this vision, which lasted for fully half an hour, that when it faded and the room resumed its previous bare appearance, she went out of the station and followed the course of the river a considerable distance without seeing any house at all resembling the villa of her vision. When almost ready to abandon what promised to be a fruitless search, and attribute her strange experience to hallucination, the effect of weariness, she saw rising before her in a most picturesque region a house identical with the one which had created so forcible an impression on her inner consciousness. Hurrying toward it, running to the door and eagerly ringing the bell, she found herself at once asking the neat young woman who answered the door whether the lady of the house was in search of some one to do plain needlework or assist in the housework. Before the girl had time to reply, a clear, commanding, yet gentle voice, said, "Show the stranger into the parlour; I wish to see her." On entering the room, she stood face to face with a beautiful lady in middle life, but looking much younger than her years, who said, "So you have answered my call, have you? Is it not better to come here and work for your living in this pleasant place, where you will always be well cared for, than go out alone among persons who do not even keep their appointments to meet strangers at the depot?" And then, looking very steadfastly at the girl, she said, with intense but most kindly emphasis, "The Lord *did* provide not a grave in the river, but a home in the valley, for His tired and sorrowing child." At these words the girl, who had been standing silent and motionless while the stately lady was addressing her, impulsively burst forth into eager questioning: "But, madam, how *could* you know what my thoughts were, or anything about me; you have never been to Binghampton, where I was born and reared—have you?"

The lady replied, with a sweet and knowing smile, "No, my child, I have never been to Binghampton, and I never saw you until to-day, but there are many ways of getting acquainted with people, of which you, as yet, know nothing. But you must rest to-night after you have had some refreshment. Louisa, the young woman who answered the door, will provide you with all you require, and at nine o'clock to-morrow morning I wish to see you and tell you many things it is important for you to understand, with reference to the position I offer you in my household. I know you are willing to perform its duties and will serve your employers faithfully." With many protestations of fervent gratitude, the weary, but now hopeful and almost happy girl, left the presence of her mysterious benefactor, and after a good wholesome supper retired to bed and went to sleep in the prettiest room she had ever occupied. The apartment was simply and inexpensively, but beautifully because artistically furnished. Everything spoke of order and method, but not an unnecessary article could be detected anywhere.

The following morning she awoke precisely at seven o'clock hearing her name called, "Marie Florence Hepworth, it is time for you to rise." Here was another surprise. How could anyone in that locality know her name? She had always been called Mary, occasionally her ears had been offended by that grating mispronunciation of the soft and lovely Italian *Maria* which seems to be spelt *Mayryre*, but Marie Florence carried her back on the swift wings of childish recollection to a delightful little *chateau* in Normandy where a tender mother, who passed to the unseen state when she was less than five years of age, said with departing breath, "God bless my little Marie Florence and keep her forever true to truth" As she was dressing these words repeated themselves again and again to her inward ears, *true to truth.* What a sublime and comprehensive expression! She resolved to relate her experience of this morning to the kind lady in whose house she was for the first time in fifteen years beginning to feel what truth expressed through love might mean. At breakfast, which she took with the servants almost in silence, for her heart was too full for many words, she seemed to feel a presence looking at her and almost touching her, and as she felt that presence beside her or bending above her, her food seemed filled with a subtle essence of life-giving power food had never possessed for her before. She felt palpably stronger with each mouthful, and her mind seemed to grow clearer with every particle she partook of. After finishing her meal she went into the large and beautiful garden which skirted the river, and enjoyed the songs of birds, the perfume of flowers and the general loveliness of the almost enchanted scene until the clock on the village church rang out nine, when she immediately returned to the house and presented herself to the noble lady to whom she was already so deeply indebted, and toward whom the deepest and tenderest emotions of gratitude were already stirred in her bosom. The lady received her with a gracious smile and inviting her to be seated said, "Now we are ready for serious conversation, and as I have much to say to you, I have given orders that we shall be quite undisturbed for at least two hours. Come with me to my private apartment where I do all my specially important work, we can there talk without fear of interruption. Entering the charming boudoir, fitted up with that peculiar grace and elegance which seems the natural habitat of truly refined people, the girl was at once struck with a magnificent illumination between the windows, "The Lord Will Provide." These words stood out in flashing brilliancy, as though traced in letters of moving fire. From the earthly standpoint only a cunning contrivance of the decorator's art, but when viewed spiritually, capable of opening up a field of mystical research which ages can not fully unravel. Taking the girl very gently by the hand and kissing her softly on the brow, the lady seated her in a chair exactly in front of these wonderful words, and requesting her to remain quite passive for a few moments, said, "relate whatever impression or vision comes to you." After about five minute's silent gazing upon the words which riveted the attention of eyes and mind at once, she started visibly, and exclaimed, "Why, Madam! I see a thin, white, shining cord running through the air all along the road between here and the railway station, and it ends just with these same words traced upon the wall of the waiting-room where I sat yesterday and felt you calling me, for it must have been you, or I should never have been led as I have been, to this beautiful house." Finding that the girl was truly receptive to mental influence of a high and practical order, the lady gave her valuable directions and much advice of inestimable worth, warning her of the danger of dabbling with occult forces for vain and sordid purposes, but dwelling chiefly upon the tremendous power for good inherent in thought, which is the greatest of all forces, and of which electricity is the first born child; she then proceeded to explain how concentration of gaze helps concentration of thought, and how it is possible to establish phsychical connection between distant persons and places by means of what is sometimes called occult telegraphy. The telephone, microphone, audiphone and other marvels of nineteenth century skill are all products of a spiritual wave of enlightenment now sweeping over the earth and inciting inventive genius to outwardly portray in some degree the mighty silent power of intelligence which, in its higher modes of manifestation, accomplishes by invisible methods what physical inventions feebly externalize to the perception of mortal sense.

As we have no space to continue this narrative which will be published in full in a story* setting forth the practical workings of the mental telegraph we must ask our readers to content themselves with pondering over this mystery of the connection between the texts in the lady's boudoir and the depot waiting room. While cabalistic incantation, crystal seership and other marvels and mysteries of ancient occultism may be disregarded by multitudes to-day as degrading superstitions or devices of the evil disposed to lure the unsuspecting to their doom, we ought never to forget that the vilest form of black magic is nothing but a reversal of the purpose of beneficent mental operation. As you do not advise the destruction of the tongue or any other member of the human body because of its fre-

*The Electric Age, a romance of to-day, by W. J. Colville, now in press.

quent perversion, so we are foolish indeed if we raise a cry of alarm either at the approach of spiritualism or theosophy, for both those systems contain so much of truth, and are expressions of so much hidden power in nature, that because the unscrupulous abuse their gifts and the ignorant sometimes get into trouble, is no reason whatever why intelligent people of every phase of opinion should not unite to clarify the air of mental pestilence by vigorously setting to work to comprehend and utilize the divine power of thought ever at their command. If the unscrupulous do occasionally deceive the unwary, if mercenariness does sometimes eclipse sense of duty in those who make gold their idol, the great majority of those who are practically engaged in the work of teaching and healing by mental methods are striving to obtain a clearer insight than ever before into the mystic law of spirit which is fathomable by us only as we knock on the door of the temple of knowledge by earnest longing to bless rather than to be blessed.

A formula or set form of words should always accord fully with the convictions of those who employ it or it cannot be faithfully made use of. In treating general cases, and in striving to keep yourselves fortified, terse, simple, comprehensive formulas are often useful.

NEGATIONS.

God is Omnipresent Good, therefore there is no evil.

Matter has neither intelligence, sensation nor substance.

There is neither sin, sickness nor death in Real Being.

God is working through me both to will and to do His good pleasure, therefore I need fear no evil.

AFFIRMATIONS.

God is Omnipresent Good.

God is infinite love, wisdom and truth.

God is Omniscient, Omnipresent, Omnipotent.

God is infinite life and substance.

God is our Father and Mother.

God fills all time, space and place.

I am in God.

At the center of my being I am one with God.

As man or woman I cannot get out of God.

In the Real Being I am Well, because God is my health—and He is working through me to will and to do His good pleasure.

These sentences, most of them compiled or selected by Mrs. Sara Harris, of Berkeley, Cal., are a good sample of formulas of value.

Our special word of exhortation shall be: Do not permit yourselves to be blindly led by any human authority, however admirable. Remember that every great man and woman the world has ever seen was in one sense an original theorist. Imitators and copyists have never been the great ones in the ranks of science, literature or art. And as we admire originality wherever we find it, as original genius, rather than imitative, places the crown of unfading glory upon the brow of those who have possessed it, while we do well to pay deferential heed to all who would bring us words of truth or encouragement, let us acknowledge *divine principle* and not *outward appearance*, as our guide and director at all times and in all things.

With love and good will toward all, and malice toward none, realizing that the weapons of our warfare are spiritual and not carnal, let us go forward in our work, hand to hand, shoulder to shoulder and heart to heart, and let us ever remember that in union, but not in uniformity, there is strength. We do not desire all voices to sing anthems in unison, but we all desire to weave glorious harmonies in the anthem of our work. We desire to create symphonies rather than for all to carry the air. When we learn to symphonize; when we learn to harmonize, and thus fill in the different parts in the song, and play the different instruments of the orchestra; when we can be like great organs with many stops and pedals, producing many variations in sound—now soft as the gentlest zephyr, and now wild as the roar of the ocean on the occasion of some great storm; when we learn to appreciate the bright red of the poppy and the geranium, the purity of the white lily, the modest purple of the violet, and the lovely family characteristics of the lily of the valley and the little blue forget-me-not; when we can learn to appreciate and imitate the grain of mustard seed, which is the tiniest of all seeds, and know that from the smallest beginning the greatest result may be evolved, then, never faltering, but always pressing on, we forget the things behind, we forget all discouraging circumstances, and bravely press ahead to the radiant goal of perfection, which enamors our delighted vision, and spurs us on to the overcoming of the gravest difficulties, if we do but keep our mental gaze riveted upon it. We implore you not to look back, but to ever look forward.

When the hosts of Israel had crossed the Red Sea, and had placed their feet upon the borders of another country, the words came from Jehovah to Moses, "Speak unto the children of Israel that they go forward." Not that they look backward, nor that they stand still, nor even that they *look* forward, but that they *go* forward. Let us take this motto for all our work: "Go forward," and let us remember that while in the letter it may be an allegory, in the spirit it is always a fact that Lot's wife, who looks back, is converted into a pillar of salt, a warning to those who come after her. Do not let us put our hands to the plow and then look back, and thus become unfit for the heavenly kingdom, but let our career be a continual forward march, and if it is such our success is inevitable.

If any one character in poetry represents true metaphysicians more than another, it is Longfellow's Alpine climber, who, in that charming lay, "Excelsior," represents the true and glorious child of God and nature, who presses on to ultimate conquest, even over seeming total defeat. Longfellow's "Excelsior," is the representative of all true, noble workers. It stands for every true worker and his enterprise. The youth sees a high mountain before him; he determines to climb it. The worldly wise come to him and say: "Try not the pass." They speak with the wisdom of age and experience, and they say: "Other people have been dashed to pieces; try it not! It is mad folly to attempt it." The girl who loves him represents the affections of the lower nature. She comes with all the allurements of earthly affection, and urges him to desist from his enterprise, and rest with her, enjoying the sweets of life on an earthly plane. He is deaf to the entreaties alike of the sage and of the maiden, and pressing on and on, he still holds in his hand "The banner with the strange device, Excelsior." He still sings that song, "Higher ever higher."

It seems at last as if he were utterly defeated, but when the monks, engaged in their devotions, and the dogs which are employed to ferret out travelers who fall asleep in the snow among the Alps, find the body of the beautiful boy, stiff and cold, ere they bury it there comes a voice from the heavens above, with all the light and brilliance of a descending star, and the word "Excelsior" is echoed from the heavens. Thus, from the uttermost confines of seeming defeat, the shout of eternal victory rends the air with the old glad note of triumph.

That same old word which the boy sang in sadness and joy and in every hour of loneliness, we too, may sing as we press to the same dizzy, but glorious, height he so nobly won. In the final verse of Longfellow's "Excelsior" are expressed the reward and certain victory of all true workers, embodied in the sweetest song. All works and all workers, who will place before them the highest and the noblest and the best, whatever their earthly end may be, whatever the seeming victory or defeat, must eventually triumph. Of one thing we may be sure, that all true, valiant heroes, all noble, conscientious, never-to-be-dismayed workers, become at length like Longfellow's melodious star, whose shining gives light unto others, and encourages with the glorious notes of accomplished victory, bidding them ever to come higher, because, even though it be through earthly defeat, genuine victory is sure, and though earthly things may fail us, we enter through true devotion the light which ne'er grows dim.

Let us take for our motto, then, "Excelsior." And when that word enters into the very fiber of our thought, and becomes one with the very blood and sinew of our enterprise; when we are no longer content with lower things, and never gaze backward, but always forward; then for each and all, helping on the good work everywhere, victory of the only kind that can be loved and appreciated by true lovers of humanity is a foregone conclusion, an inevitable certainty. And thus let us endeavor to consecrate ourselves and make our homes places where the silent influence of uplifted thought may bless all who cross the threshold; let us all follow our highest inward light. Be true to the noblest within you; look to things eternal, and not to things temporal; delight in service to humanity, and not in present and private gratifications; and love not too well the things which perish in the using.

Hearing one day a company of fashionable people discussing a musical entertainment given the previous evening before a large and brilliant throng composed chiefly of the *élite* of a fashionable society in a great and wealthy city, we were particularly struck with a criticism passed upon the performance of a young artist, whose rendering of an old, well-worn ballad was such as to give the old, familiar air a new and deeper meaning than it had ever seemed capable of conveying before. As he proceeded with his solo, he introduced some charming variations, which, to the quick ear of the very few present who had known what it was to be introduced in some slight measure to the inner sphere of music, (of which mechanical performers and professional critics know nothing,) he interpreted divinely beautiful thoughts never before associated with the song. "I should never have known it," was the remark made by several who were commenting upon the performer's skill, but how different a meaning did the same words convey uttered by two persons who both ventured to pass an opinion on a rarely beautiful musical effort — an effort in which inspired genius blended with the results of careful study and diligent application to *technique.*

In one case the hard, cold, metallic, musical mechanician demurred at anything she could style an interpolation or change of original score; on the other hand, a perception, in some degree, of the *spirit*, rather than the *letter*, of harmony, enabled the other critic, who might more justly and reasonably be called a grateful and sympathetic disciple of genius, to respond to the electric thrill which always vibrates through an atmosphere pervaded with a subtle force, generated only when combinations of sound are effected by a performer who transcends the stereotyped limits of technical exactitude.

When the mind is enveloped in a thick shadow of externalism, higher voices than one is accustomed to hear produce the rather disagreeable effect of thunder on a nervous ear, and this rumbling noise causes aversion rather than promotes delight.

To all who are seeking to work in harmony with superior thought, our counsel is, do not estimate your success in any measure by the amount of appreciation you win from a mixed multitude. If you succeed in reaching an unusually high goal or summit of attainment, you will not be appreciated by the masses as well as though you stood on a lower level, and were nearer their plane of thought; but it is only by reaching this sublimer elevation you can scientifically demonstrate that all disorders of the mind and body can be successfully vanquished through the operation of a power entirely beyond the physical. When you reach nearer than the multitude to this high station, your presence will heal all who are ready to receive a blessing through the introduction of purer thought into their mental sphere.

Perfect tranquility of mind, complete absorption in one's work through the love of it, and total indifference to the world's censure or applause, are absolutely essential to every student who would succeed in giving that evidence of ability to demonstrate spiritual science, which is indispensable to the truly successful practitioner.

MISCELLANEOUS QUESTIONS.

UNDER this heading we have replied to a number of important queries from all parts of the world in the order in which we have received them. Owing to their great number and the amount of ground they covered we found it totally impossible to attempt any more definite classification.

QUESTION. No. 1. *What is really meant by Metaphysical Healing?*

ANSWER. Metaphysical Healing does not properly speaking mean anything more or other than the power of thought to overcome all physical derangement. Without entering into any lengthened dissertation concerning the reality or unreality of matter, before we can comprehend the theory of Metaphysical Healing we must understand the meaning of the term Metaphysical, which signifies "*beyond physics, above physics,*" and "*mind over matter.*" The above definitions are sanctioned by the best lexicographers. If then at the outset we simply concede the sovereignty of mind and the subserviency of sense we shall be prepared to logically admit that no physical condition can offer an insuperable obstacle to mind. An intelligent Metaphysical Healer who knows something of occult science may readily understand how every human thought is a magnet attracting kindred, and repelling antagonistic thought. If we think bright, happy, useful thoughts, we gather or accrete to us a force like unto that we send forth into the ambient psychic atmosphere, we thereby are related to whatsoever is true, pure and harmonious, but just as surely, if we entertain sad, erroneous thoughts, do we draw to us mental influences of a darker hue.

This fact is pretty generally conceded at present among students of psychic matters, still it is very necessary to persist in affirming this continuously, when called upon to treat those in whose minds, knowledge of spiritual law is at best but an uncertain light.

The germ theory of disease now so much in vogue in medical circles, and said to be in many instances proven by the microscope, offers no impediment in the way of accepting Metaphysical ideas, for the very fact of multitudes escaping when contagion is in the air proves beyond question that we must be in a receptive state, or we cannot take in *bacteria*.

Now, while all physicians allow that susceptibility in one instance and non-susceptibility in another answers the query, "Why do some people suffer from infection while others escape?" it is only the Metaphysician who leaves the bodily condition behind and goes in search of a mental cause for such varied physical states. We do not deny that persons take cold and suffer in various ways because of their bodily condition, but what we do most persistently maintain is that physical states are invariably the result of mental.

Seek the cause of physical susceptibility or weakness, in indecision, fear or some still worse emotion that has lowered the tone of your vitality. Succeed in changing the thought radically, and the physical state alters of necessity.

QUES. No. 2. *Will you define the nature of thought and how it acts on the body?*

ANS. To fully define the nature of thought and state just how it acts on the body would indeed require much ability, time and space, in all three of which necessary commodities we feel ourselves in the present instance, at least, sadly deficient.

If "a word to the wise is sufficient," we trust to all our readers being wise enough to let the following brief and humble word drop as a seed into the fertile soil of their receptive minds, in which it may quickly germinate like a grain of mustard seed into a prodigious tree. Thought we conceive to be generated by idea, through a process of mental friction; as two hard substances being rubbed together emit sparks and kindle flame, so two ideas, either two ideas of the same individual, or one of the individual's and one of another's coming together, produce a result, and that result we call thought, which is less than idea, though it must be a partial expression and outcome of some idea. We sometimes generate thoughts, and oftener still do we receive them; when we receive them we frequently call them *impressions*, but nothing can make an impression on us unless we are in an impressible condition.

Matter is not necessarily a myth, but whatever it is, it is less than mind and is included in it. If matter in its last analysis is force, then what is force? Thoughts are things, and therefore can be felt, and under favoring circumstances can be seen and heard also.

A thought can strike your mind and wound it just as a stone can strike your body. By dexterous mental movement you can often dodge an unpleasant thought when you feel it coming, as you can avoid being hit by a stone flung toward you by physical dexterity. Those truly appareled in Spiritual sheen are like knights coated in armor of mail through which a bullet cannot pass. Again we must refer to occult science to prove our reasoning. We are constantly generating an aura which perpetually surrounds us. If this aura is of the higher type, the result of exalted modes of thinking and aspiring, it renders us absolutely impervious to the attacks of disagreeable thought, thus we become lifted to a region where we are no longer wounded or made angry by anything or any body.

All outward things commonly called material are correspondences and results of things invisible, thus as our mental state governs our mental susceptibility it reactionally and ultimately determines our physical state.

QUES. No. 3. *Can we treat ourselves metaphysically for our own regeneration in the same way that we can treat others?*

ANS. Most decidedly we can, though it must be admitted that it is a more difficult task to treat ourselves than others for the obvious reason that when we most sorely need treatment we are in the worst condition for giving treatment. Regeneration is a very large word and means vastly more than we can now explain in detail, but as it certainly includes the idea of development and reconstruction we can simply affirm and will content ourselves with affirming that regeneration is most readily accomplished by deliberately retiring from the outer world in thought as well as action, and then in some calm retreat at some convenient hour, either quite by ourselves or in company with some exceedingly congenial friend, fix our mind on whatever we most earnestly desire, and this object of our desire we must look upon with our mental vision as the artist gazes upon his picture, the architect upon his plan, the inventor upon his machine, as already perfectly externalized while yet not a single step has been taken in the visible execution of the design. Are you afflicted with grinding poverty, then see yourself in comfortable circumstances (we will not advise immoderately rich); are you physically crippled, then see yourself straight as a dart, hold the image of perfection in the direction in which you particularly seek it persistently before you, and if you will persevere in this mental exercise, most especially if you will insist upon seeing this image and none other before you at night before you fall asleep, you will soon relate yourself to a sphere of thought which will so invigorate your mind as to render actual in your body the condition you desire.

QUES. No. 4. *Metaphysicians tell us to deny all limitations and affirm their opposite. Will you please tell us how we are in truth in doing this?*

ANS. Regardless of what any persons may say, let every one speak and affirm what he individually feels to be the truth. No metaphysician should be regarded as infallible, nor his word placed in the stead of the voice of one's own conscience; therefore, never affirm anything which you may deem untrue. Nevertheless as we grow in the knowledge of spiritual things we attain to a realizing sense of what we are in truth, in absolute reality, and then we find out that we are perfect and immortal Spirit. The whole secret of success in treating is to get oneself and patients out of material thought, *i. e.*, thought about material things. When we realize our higher selves we do not think about our lower, and it is only in that exalted frame of mind that we can become oblivious to pains, vexations and limits and feel ourselves free as birds in the open air. We affirm literally nothing and we deny literally nothing concerning our physical organisms when we are "in the spirit." You have probably all known what it is to experience at least occasional and transient absorption of thought in other things than those about you. The mind needs to rest and recuperate its forces by consciously bathing, as it were, in a spiritual ocean, from which celestial bath it returns re-invigorated to perform the varied and often irksome duties of the outward state; for this reason profound slumber, undisturbed sleep, is so necessary that insomnia leads to mental aberration. When you enjoy unbroken rest all night, you awake in the morning mysteriously strengthened and refreshed and often quite buoyantly happy. This mental elasticity is due to your having enjoyed a temporary sojourn in the spiritual realm unvexed by mortal cares. When giving or taking a treatment you need just this perfect release from material sensation. We can only explain it by saying that you must endeavor to travel in thought to the infinitely happy, free and rich; you must journey in mind to the absolutely perfect, and there bask in the light of the highest ideal which the mind can contemplate. Strive to feel that the immortal *ego*, the deathless *I* is perfect and possesses all things, and rest assured that only in this manner can you so relate yourself with the infinite as to overcome the limitations of the finite. Your ailments have departed, your sorrows have fled, your pains have vanished and yet you did not see or feel them go, but they went by reason of your mental posture; you took a spiritual sunbath, and the heat melted the ice and the light drove away the vapors. Place before yourself your highest possible conception of ideal humanity and you become negative to celestial and proof against infernal influence; you invite constructive and repel destructive force. You are well, you are pefect in your immortal being, which is the center of your life. Direct your thoughts to this true vital center and you will behold truth.

QUES. No. 5. *You say every expression is a manifestation of God; disease is surely then a manifestation of God. Are not such manifestations necessary? If not, how can they be avoided?*

ANS. We do *not* say that every expression is a manifestation of God in a direct sense, but if we do believe every natural expression to be divine, we cannot thereby include diseased or distorted expressions of mortal error. Every work on pathology we have ever come across declares disease to be abnormal, it is never a natural and therefore healthy condition of affairs that is designated disease. Perversion produces the appearance of disease, and God is surely not the author of the act of perversion if He be the creator of the force which man either willfully or ignorantly perverts. Students of this subject can glean much under this head from the writings of Swedenborg whose arguments are very logical and whose deductions are very clear as to the cause and nature of so-called evil.

The writings of Henry James, an ardent admirer of Swedenborg, can be consulted with great profit by those seeking light on this subject, but as the theme is intensely profound and at first sight intricate, considerable time and attention must be given to it before the problem will appear solved. To give a patent illustration, you may conceive of all things as essentially, intrinsically good. All is good, there is no evil, but though all things are in their essence good, every separate thing is good for something and not good (therefore relatively bad) for something else. Abuse is inharmony which does not necessarily imply imperfection or error anywhere except in the use to which an instrument is put. The ability to err is doubtless a necessary part of discipline. We do not belong to that school which looks upon all physical expression as a mistake, we contend only for the possibility of so learning to employ everything aright that evil shall be utterly abolished and discord shall utterly cease. When you are suffering the best attitue to assume toward your suffering is that it is a stepping-stone to a height beyond, you thereby rob it of its sting. The uselessness of pain adds to its bitterness. Make it serve an end, transmute it, regard it as a consequence of some past experience remembered or forgotten, and, therefore, a factor in education. But whenever obstacles and sorrows present themselves remember we encounter them only to gain strength by rising superior to them. What we cannot agree to is the theory that we should tamely submit to be crushed by them and call our weakness the will of God. We can only avoid falling into misery in the future by learning wisdom from past experience and so conducting ourselves mentally as to draw to us only purely healthful and beneficent influences.

QUES. No. 6. *Is the laying on of hands ever advisable?*

ANS. The laying on of hands is advisable when you feel it to be so, *i. e.*, when you feel an influence unmistakably good impelling you to so act. The word hand is frequently used in Scripture in a figurative sense, and thus it is often straining a point to infer that whenever the phrase "laying on of hands" is met with, it signifies any form of bodily contact. We do not wish to appear illiberal, therefore, we are particularly careful to state frequently in public places, that we know many healers do great good who lay on hands in treating, at the same time we are most careful to state that in our opinion it is not the act of manipulation, but a spiritual force going with it that accomplishes the cure.

If one is confined to any external mode of action, one's usefulness becomes painfully confined, for this reason we do not advocate manipulation. Then, again, bodily contact is often productive of two serious evils—in the first place, it renders the patient's mind too active on the outward plane, and second, it frequently exposes the healer to the danger of contagion. We would, however, allow the utmost reasonable latitude in all such matters. No one should strive to be a law unto another. If you treat in the way you conscientiously feel to be best, the divine blessing will accompany your effort, whatever it may be. Pure motive is the essential need, and wherever the intent is pure, good must follow.

QUES. No. 7. *Of what use to an animal is the suffering that it endures? We can understand that our suffering raises us spiritually, and that it is through us that animals suffer, but as one creature ought never in justice to be sacrificed to another, the suffering that we cause them to undergo ought in some way to benefit the .*

ANS. There is indeed much room for speculative inquiry with regard to this interesting and complex subject, and it would be no difficult task for us to occupy many pages in a labored attempt at its satisfactory elucidation. Desiring, however, to be as brief and practical as possible, we will content ourselves with remarking that the whole gist of theosophical teaching is to the effect that everything is slowly wending its way upward to a higher expression than has yet been evolved. If the theory of involution be studied in connection with evolution, it will be comparatively easy to trace the benefit accruing to all sentient creatures from the sufferings to which they are involuntarily subjected. Woe is ever pronounced against him by whom an offense cometh, not against those who are the victims of such offense. Inexorable divine justice through the perpetual out-working of the undeviating law of Karma or consequence ordains that those who perform an act of cruelty alone suffer for such act in the long run. Appearances are often so deceitful, and it is so hard for us to clearly distinguish between real and apparent loss, that we often fail in seeming evil to trace the good, but all unmerited suffering, *i. e.*, all suffering not brought upon ourselves by folly of our own, redounds inevitably to our highest interest by accelerating the processes of our development, and let us remember that the law of Karma works in the animal as well as in the human kingdom. Animals as well as men, are all traveling on to a higher bourne than they have yet attained, and as this is a fact known to those familiar with the ancient wisdom now being presented to the world at large, the problem is solved, immediately we see the law of compensation operating on behalf of animals as well as men. Dr. Anna Kingsford, that noble woman and true Theosophist who did so much to enlighten the world on the true basis of moral conduct, argued with overwhelming force against the eating of flesh and particularly against vivisection on the score of these practices being subversive of the highest interests of human welfare, as they are in flagrant opposition to our deepest moral instincts, but though we who err must incur a penalty in our own deterioration until we have expunged our fault with bitter suffering, the innocent victims of our inordinate selfishness only lose their mortal envelopes and doubtless in every case receive an impulsion forward through the sad experience which has removed their outward forms. No philosophy which does not carry the thought of infinite retributive justice in every department of the universe can be ultimately satisfactory to mankind, and for this reason, if for no other, we should defend the doctrine of a future existence for animals and allot their sufferings a place in the order of their progression.

QUES. No. 8. *Are not consequences of human experience often totally disproportionate to the error which induces them? as for instance, a man mistakes a toadstool for a mushroom and dies in consequence.*

ANS. No act can possibly be solitary and unrelated to other and previous acts, therefore the gathering or eating of a toadstool in mistake for a mushroom and being poisoned in consequence is an experience which can only be correctly understood by one who has traced out the relations of cause and effect to an extent far beyond the attainments of the majority. Say that the act standing alone is a very trival mistake, a simple error of judgment in no sense criminal, a philosophical inquiry of momentous import at once presents itself, viz., what has induced a state of mind rendering such an error possible? Is not the ostensible act only the first visible expression of perhaps a very long and important chain of unknown antecedent causes? If the spiritual perceptive faculty was in any way keen such a mistake could not occur, and why is not the intuition keen enough to avert such a catastrophe, is a very pertinent query in this connection. We continually attribute the gravest consequences to the most trivial acts solely because we do not see behind them into the mysterious past whence they sprang. We see a flash of lightning and hear a clap of thunder, these are the first intimations we often have of a terrific storm which has been, all unknown to us, for a long time slowly brewing. We are out in the storm without even a wrap or an umbrella, totally unprotected, surprised and at the mercy of the raging elements, or we are in a railway carriage or on a steamboat and an accident overtakes us so suddenly that we are instantly maimed beyond probable recovery. These things we say are casualties which cannot be prevented, and yet in every instance had we only developed our psychic perception to an extent we have not as yet done, we should have been forewarned, forearmed, protected, or in some manner saved entirely from the affliction which has befallen us. Belief in special providence and absolute miracles has arisen entirely from a failure to account for exceptional occurences in the light of relative psychic culture.

QUES. No. 9. *Do we understand you to maintain that accidents as well as diseases are all preventible and therefore quite unnecessary?*

ANS. Accidents are invariably the result of folly or ignorance when they are not the fruits of lawlessness or crime. An accident must have a cause, it must be the effect of someting, it does not originate through the arbitrary caprice of God, neither is it a freak of fortune. What occasions for the most part those events commonly termed accidents? Drunkenness, frenzy, fear and a host of other vices and follies coupled with recklessness and a lack of skill on the part of somebody, will account probably for 90 per cent., while the remaining 10 per cent., even though seemingly beyond human control, are simply beyond that limit of control which ordinary men and women have yet gained over their surroundings. Now we wish particularly to call our readers' most careful attention to the following important proposition, which is that all mishaps are avertible, provided we are sufficiently developed spiritually to heed those numerous and instructive warnings which invariably precede disaster. Just as the weather prophet can, by scanning the face of the sky, which others can not read, foretell the impending tempest, just as the shrill whistle or clanging bell signals the arrival or departure of a train though a deaf person hears no sound at all, so unseen, and to the ear of flesh inaudible influences are perpetually warning us to get out of danger's way, but alas, the *prenez garde* of our unseen friends is heard by comparatively few of earth's children. The great practical advantages attending and resulting from psychic culture are that with our interior vision more fully opened we shall be able to see things in their true proportions, and thus avoid making mistakes and falling into pits of needless sorrow. The following clipping from the *Golden Gate* serves to illustrate in some measure what we are seeking to convey. The editor of that valuable weekly says: "One of the first fruits of the 'gift of the spirit' is that of being able to sense the spiritual status of those with whom one comes in contact. He reads his fellow-beings, whenever he chooses to do so, as from an open book. He can not tell you how or why, but he *knows*, and that knowledge is almost infallible. In the higher unfoldment of this wonderful faculty one may ever know in whom to put his trust. Armed with this power how many of 'the rocks and shoals of time' may be avoided." If this be true, as it unquestionably is in the main, in all particulars, can not we easily extend our view of this entrancing subject until it embraces a realization that we can so foresee coming events as to avoid painful experiences? The literature of clairvoyance abounds in striking illustrations of this power, but until recently the prevalent opinion has been that clairvoyance in its widest sense is a special gift, a dower bestowed by heaven on a few, but utterly unobtainable by the many. The present trend of advanced spiritual thought is toward the demonstrable conclusion that every one can in some measure develop his own inner nature so far as to be able to anticipate danger and thus avoid it. There is nothing arbitrary in the scheme of the universe. Immutable law shows no favoritism. He who has ears to hear and eyes to see can walk securely, and those who, mentally and spiritually speaking, are as yet well nigh destitute of these fundamental organs of perception can by diligent prosecution of befitting methods develop these much-to-be desired avenues of information.

QUES. No. 10. *Is it possible for a healer to remove a patient's desire for liquor or love of tobacco without the person knowing it?*

ANS. It is not possible for the patient to get rid of any habit unless he makes an effort. But how is the patient to be induced to make the effort? As effort is necessary on the patient's part, you must treat him with a view to his making the effort. You must break down all indisposition. When persons will not work, idleness is their disease; you therefore have to treat for idleness. Many treaters fail because they hold their patients in error. They seem to settle down under the conviction that their patient is not willing to be convinced. If you hold any thought of idleness over any idler it makes him still more idle; your belief that he will remain in error strengthens the bond of sin around him. What we have to do in such cases is to treat ourselves for our beliefs concerning our patients. That seems to be the hardest work of all, for many practitioners. They can only with great difficulty obey the wise injunction, "Physician, heal thyself." Ladies have often come to us and said their mothers or other relatives never would accept spiritual truth; there was a statement most unspiritual and groundless. Married women have often said: "My husband never will accept the truth." What influence do you suppose people exert over their companions by entertaining such views of them? If they are giving them treatments they are certainly malpracticing. A daughter takes to her mother the idea that she never will look favorably at certain things, and while the daughter is crying over this, her own belief, the mother is kept in a state of antagonism by the unconscious mental influence of the daughter. A woman going around telling of her husband's untruthfulness, keeps him untruthful, though of course she is not aware that her conduct keeps him from improvement. If a person is given to drinking or smoking and you tell everybody so, though you are not aware of so doing, you are keeping the one you wish to see reformed under bondage and preventing his reformation. Healers must pluck the beams out of their own eyes ere they can see clearly to cast the motes out of their brother's eyes. It is limitation in ourselves that we have to fight against. You can not successfully treat any person whom you hold in false belief. You must hold no less favorable thought than that your treatment is inducing the patient to make all necessary effort, and treatment does not take genuine and permanent effect unless patients make efforts themselves to hold their lower appetites in rightful subjection, only if you always hold good thoughts do you treat in the right way. It is certainly easier to lay blame upon others than upon ourselves, but Jesus had no patience with such self-flattery. Some of his disciples complained to him that a certain person could not be cured, and he said to them in reply: "O ye of little faith!

if you have faith as a grain of mustard seed, you can say to mountains, be removed and cast into the sea, and it shall be done, and nothing shall be impossible with you." If we only break ourselves of this detestable habit of holding our brethren in error, if we persistently hold mental pictures of harmony before our eyes we shall soon be universal public benefactors. But so long as we acknowledge and dwell upon error in others, we impose limitations upon them and prevent them from making the effort they otherwise might in the right direction; we disqualify ourselves from helping them to make the necessary effort. If our mind reaches them it holds them in error, and as we encourage erroneous thought concerning others, it holds us in error. We must not think toward any one. I wish you would make an effort, but I feel sure you will not. Encourage only the thought that sees them perfect. We must see mentally whatever we desire as accomplished already. Just as the artist sees his picture in mind before it is put on canvas. It is complete, mentally, before he takes up pencil or brush. So in the mind of an architect, the perfect building is seen. It is all completed before the draughtsman touches pencil, or the first stone of the material fabric is laid. So before the first really practical and effective step has been taken toward the improvement of your patient, you must see him in thought perfectly well. By holding this mental image you do the thing necessary to make him appear well. First, see him perfectly well in mind, then set to work to build the external in harmony with the mental design.

QUES. No. 11. *What effect has treatment upon the law of Karma?*

Ans. Whenever treatment takes effect, it causes the patient to make good Karma. If the patient had never made any bad Karma in the past, he would not be feeling ill now. Karma manufactured in the past has borne fruit in the present. We are what we are in consequence of what we have been. Successful treatment is to so act upon a patient as to cause him to make good Karma, and that destroys bad Karma. The past being irrevocable, you find different patients in very different conditions of receptivity when you first treat them. As you succeed in bringing them out of bad conditions you succeed in helping them to make good Karma, which is only the Buddhistic name for what the Christian calls a good life. You can produce the result of good Karma by inducing the patient to follow truth instead of error.

[Note.—Karma, only means consequence, and is a Sanscrit term employed chiefly by those designating themselves Theosophists, who study Oriental works of mystical import.]

Ques. No. 12. *Is it always possible in the present stage of development to overthrow crime?*

Ans. If you feel after earnest effort to overcome it that it is not possible in the case of a certain patient you may conclude that it is no part of your particular work to treat that particular patient. We have often to make a selection, for we cannot treat everybody. If you feel you cannot hold a certain individual in the highest and purest thought, then leave the case alone. Acknowledge that it may be no part of your special work. We have had many experiences where we have felt: Well, whether a desired result can be attained or not, we shall not attempt to decide, but it is clearly no part of our special work to bring it about. Therefore we don't take in hand such a case at all, but are perfectly willing any one should, who feels it is part of his mission to doso. Wedo not know to what extent every one can be influenced, but one thing we do know, and that is that we can never influence patients for good until we can hold them in the thought of good. When we have reached a plane of perfect good we can perhaps hold all others on that high level. There seems to be no definite Karmic limitation mentioned in the New Testament. Jesus was astonished at lack of faith, he wept over Jerusalem and cried," O Jerusalem, Jerusalem, how often would I have gathered thy children together, even as a hen gathereth her chickens under her wings, and ye would not!" We do not believe any one is obliged to make bad Karma. We do not believe any one is obliged to reject truth, but all have liberty to do so. If we deliberately reject truth when presented to us we voluntarily create evil Karma. If it appears that Karma sometimes operates so as to prevent certain persons from seeing truth, you as healer may be perhaps allowed to feel: "Well, I have done my duty, I must leave results to God." Sometimes you may have to shake dust off your feet. Jesus said, 'Go ye into all the world, preach the gospel to every creature." The preacher must be swayed by no doubt as to whether some people can receive his message whilst others can not. If we entertain a belief that some people cannot be healed, we impose limitations upon ourselves we should be much better without. If we do our duty faithfully we shall always be blessed. If you undertake some cases and fail, (as you say,) you do not fail utterly because you have certainly been of some use to the person you treated and to humanity at large. You have sown good seed. Whenever a person speaks a good word, though it may not make any appreciable impression upon the person for whom it was intended it effects somebody for good, we know several cases in point, one of which we will quote: Two ladies were walking on the street, one of them pleading earnestly with the other. A woman whom neither of them saw or knew anything about was walking behind them, and her whole future was changed by what she overheard. We never know the extent of our audience. We cannot tell when treating how many minds we are reaching. Do not narrow down your treatment to a single patient, but remember always that our work is bound to be of service to humanity at large in ways too subtle for objective analysis many times. Only by doing good to others can we make good Karma for ourselves.

QUES. No. 13. *What would be your explanation of poison coming from minerals or vegetables?*

ANS. Because of their being improperly used A taxidermist finds arsenic very useful in stuffing birds. He has no disagreeable thought with regard to arsenic. He knows it is not intended for food. He knows if he puts it where it does not belong it will become relatively evil. Every so-called evil thing must be put in its own place and allowed to do its appointed work, then will it prove itself good in its manner. The thought of poison in plants and minerals proceeds from a derangement in ideas. Everything has its place. Certain things fit into certain grooves. When error results discord must have been created. Looking at poisons from another point of view Mrs. Grimke says: "If there were no calumny in mortal mind there would be no arsenic in visible effect." Many say there would be no poisonous plants if erroneous states of mortal mind had never caused them. Some people kill valuable plants by destructive thoughts, others again sustain noxious weeds. We know a lady who can make nothing but weeds grow in her garden. Another lady's garden has no weeds. It simply comes to this: The emanations from the one lady nourish weeds, while the emanations from the other nourish flowers. Of course there is truth in the theory of magnetism, but magnetism is primarily spiritual or mental power. If any one benefits another by magnetism, it is really by mental action or thought transference. Magnetism far too often associated with material beliefs which convey ideas not in harmony with spiritual science. It seems to us that, taking the world as it is, we can justly entertain three ideas concerning poisons. In the first place, everything is good provided it is rightfully related, and not otherwise. Therefore you do not think of eating everything. And if you do not eat everything you use, why should you eat certain vegetables, or take certain minerals into your system? Then another view is, that everything is produced in obedience to a state of mind we sometimes recognize, but often fail to recognize, and so long as certain states of mind continue so long will their expressions continue. If we cultivate higher thoughts we shall starve out poisonous plants and animals. If such gigantic creatures as the mammoth and mastodon no longer exist, why should not poisonous insects, reptiles and plants die out? They certainly will ultimately disappear under the law of the survival of the fittest. The third view is that all these things need not affect or move us. We are so far superior to all minerals, vegetables and animals that if we only realize our true relation to God, and also understand our right relation to the inferior or external world, we shall be always safe. In treating one who has been poisoned you must make your patient fully realize his relation to God, he must also realize his relation to the external universe. Your relation to your friends in truth is that of co-operative harmony. Your relation to angelic influences is that of true spiritual communion. But your right relation to every form of error is the relation of controlling power to the thing controlled. Many people talk about mind and matter so as only to confound language. They say matter is negative and spirit positive, but after they have declared this they make spirit negative, and matter positive. They say matter can influence mind and make persons ill. They affirm that influences below man can overcome man. But there can be no real health apart from spiritual understanding, the understanding and realization that we are children of God. When we truly realize our sonship to the Eternal we can completely subdue all below us; we are then in a condition not to dread reptiles and other creatures equally below us. In that state, if a viper lighted upon your arm it could not harm you any more than it hurt Paul. Our most effective work consists in exorcising demons from our own breasts. If we practised stricter self-discipline or self-control we should soon render ourselves invulnerable and no longer care for lower things. We should then no longer dread the viper or the upas tree. We might remove them for the sake of others, but we should ourselves be in no danger from them. When we get on the high ground of spiritual victory we have outgrown the infantile condition of the mind which, being negative even though innocent, renders its possessor susceptible to danger.

QUES. No. 14. *Do you think one mind can rise superior to the universal mind in relation to poison?*

ANS. There is no universal mind except the mind of deity and God's mind is alone infinite; when we trust God fully we become one with God. One finite mind alone can not resist all danger. When you realize your relation to God you feel the force of the words, "I and my Father are one." The infinite can surely overcome the finite, but the finite can not vanquish the infinite. You say when in the bondage of sense and therefore fear the strength of evil, "I am but one mind contending against a host of minds." But is it not easier for you to contend against all there is of finite mind than against the infinite mind of God? God is on the side of health and good, disease is opposed to Him, fear of poison is rebellion against the mind of God, or at least it is utter distrust of God's sovereignty. Trust in God is necessary to our deliverance from fear. If we don't trust we remain in fear, because we think of the multitude of evil influences about us. But how many good angels are there? Are there not more angels than devils in the universe? Then why should anyone be overcome by evil? Which is the stronger—evil or good? Health or disease? Poison or spiritual influx? If we only turn our thoughts to angels instead of devils; if we only think of the power of God instead of the power of evil, we gain the victory. A young man in ancient story was affrighted when he saw the enemy, but when he saw the host of God he feared the enemy no longer. David never was so strong physically as Goliath, but when Goliath attempted to fight David he was conquered. If David had trusted in any other power than the divine he could not have conquered Goliath. If you have intelligently read Bulwer Lytton's story, "The Coming Race," you will know that the *vril* he speaks of as being carried in little frail sticks by those mysterious people who live under the earth, and who he says are to become the future inhabitants of the upper world according to that romance is nothing other than will power. A boy of twelve encounters a tremendous monster, but on directing his little vril stick towards him, the creature is consumed to a cinder. Vril possesses a power like lightning. The one who carries it feels that he has indeed a magic staff in his hand. We all have a similar feeling when we realize that in spirit we possess that which can destroy every form of error. Instead of fearing poison we know that we can give error a dose of truth that will destroy it instantly. We are never safe till we trust entirely in the divine light we derive from the infinite, the electric fire of the Holy Spirit.

Ques. No. 15. *To what occult force does vril correspond?*

Ans. It signifies the human will as superior to the animal will. It is generated by the enlightened mind of man when man's sixth principle is developed. If man exercises his sixth principle nothing can injuriously affect him. The human soul (fifth principle) versus the animal soul (fourth principle) always conquers, but vril is discovered only though the sixth principle (spiritual soul), for until reason and intellect are illumined from above (within) we cannot truly discipline and employ our fifth or intellectual principle in subduing the fourth and its correspondents, which take in the entire range of the animal and yet lower kingdoms; we must unfold the higher to guide the next below.

QUES. No 16. *What is prophecy? Wherein consists the chief difference between priest and prophet? Why did Paul place prophecy above all other spiritual gifts? Can we all attain to a development of it? Has Astrology any connection with genuine prophetic insight?*

ANS. The chief difference between prophets and priests consists in the fact that the former are seers, while the latter are but echoes, so far as their teaching is concerned. This statement is not intended as in any manner disrespectful to the priests of any religion, many of whom are noble philanthropists; it simply embodies the self-evident conclusion that those who look to ancient canons of authority for all their wisdom, must necessarily refuse to allow that the still small voice speaking within the soul of each individual is that individual's rightful and only absolute guide.

A prophet is a revelator and an exhorter. Prediction, in the ordinary sense, is not always true prophetic insight; a prophet is not a fortune-teller, but one who sees so deeply into the realm of causation and the soul of things as to be able to state the inevitable outcome of a certain course of procedure. Prophets know more of cause and effect than other people, and may be compared to men standing on lofty heights, commanding an extended view of the surrounding country. Dwellers in the valleys can only see a little way before them, and thus, through ignorance of where different roads lead, make many false steps, and go in the opposite direction to that in which they need to tread. A man on a mountain can call down to them from his exalted station, and his voice may be that of a true guide and savior, because he is in a position to see whither roads tend, the destination of which can be viewed only from a lofty elevation.

True seership is the most practically useful of all possible endowments, and therefore Paul eulogized it beyond all other gifts. How can we cultivate it, is the important question to answer. It is necessary to retire into silence, to give no heed for awhile to external voices, to cease interrogating our neighbors, to desist from consulting the world's oracles, then if we remain mentally still for a short time, fixing our thoughts and desires intently upon the object of our search, we shall learn that we have inward eyes and ears, and that spiritual voices and divine intuitions can lead us safely over innumerable difficulties, under which we should, in our ordinary condition, sink.

Prophecy is insight, hindsight and foresight, and is in truth nothing other than a penetrative perception of the law of necessity. A prophet is not a fatalist, he does not affirm that there is a private destiny marked out for each human individual. He deals with the race destiny of man, and with the inevitable sequence of events, which does not at all imply that men and women have no power to shape their own ends.

Ignorance means bondage, while knowledge is indispensable to freedom. By increasing knowledge the prophet increases the responsibility of man, as it is his sacred mission to so instruct the world that ignorance, which aforetime was only weakness, at length becomes criminal.

All true teachers are prophets. It should never be our ambition to pry into the future so as to forestall either joy or sorrow, and live as though we were the creatures of luck and not of effort, but to so learn the relations of cause and effect, as they concern our daily life, that we may be able to prevent accidents and avert catastrophes. To foretell impending doom in a blank sense is not edifying, it is depressing and enervating. The old adage is true, "forewarned is forearmed." If we know that certain events are likely to transpire, true seership will enable us to prepare to meet them. By means of it we can conquer obstacles to which, in our blindness, we should yield.

With reference to astrology the words of an enlightened astrologer may be quoted with profit: "The wise man rules his stars, the fool obeys them." By this it is meant that just as meteorology enables coastmen and farmers to protect their belongings and secure general public safety against the coming of storms, whose approach can not be warded off, so those who are warned by intuition or clairvoyance may be in a condition to guard against wrecks or disasters, which need not follow if proper precautions are taken, but which must inevitably supervene unless some skillful mind is ready against an emergency. True prophecy calls attention to the leak in the vessel or the hole in the roof. It detects it and proclaims the direful results which must inevitably ensue if it be not attended to in time.

A true prophet would deliver his message to captain, engineer, or other officer in charge of boat or train, and, by foreseeing danger, stave it off, and thus win the lasting thanks and honors of a saved multitude; or if his message were unheeded, the doom which befell those who refused to hear, would be a calamity for which they had only their own obstinate obduracy to blame.

QUES. No. 17. *An eminent occult student in a private letter, says: Everything in nature is real to those things involved therein, hence pain is as real as we are. Will you please explain the discrepancy between this and your teaching (if there is any)?*

ANS. Innumerable controversies have arisen in consequence of persons using one word in several opposite senses. The word *real* is certainly susceptible of more than one definition. When in the highest metaphysical sense, Spirit is spoken of as the only reality, while matter is declared to be unreal, the thought intended to be conveyed is that Spirit alone is eternal. Now pain may appear as real as pleasure on the external or sense plane of existence, but we must never forget that our sensations are transitory, and so far as they appear to arise from external things, they can not be everlasting. Pain as a sensation may be regarded as an educator, we do not necessarily disagree with those who call it the voice of an alarmist bidding us see to what is wrong, that having our attention called thereto, we may rectify an error. As to saying pain is as real as we are, we consider it a most unscientific statement, unless by "we" is meant simply the lower or earthly nature which the higher and abiding "we" hope some day to outgrow. If we are replying to a student of theosophical literature we should ask him to consider pain as an emotion of the inferior principles in the constitution of man. The higher principle does not and can not suffer, as it never errs or sins, and pain is a penalty, educational, redemptive, necessary we admit, when we have fallen into error, but the higher principle does not fall into error, and consequently neither needs nor endures such reformatory chastening. A brief consideration of the three distinct principles which enter into the constitution of man, and of which we are all more or less deeply conscious, may throw some light on this seemingly perplexing problem. We, as intellectual beings, are living between the spiritual and the animal in us, and suffering is occasioned by the struggle or conflict continually going forward in us as well as around us. Paul graphically describes this in the seventh chapter of his epistle to the Romans, which may be very profitably studied in this connection. We shall undoubtedly all suffer pain until we no longer require such discipline; pain therefore, in its place is good, it serves an end, and when its use is made plain it is no longer the hopeless enigma it was previously. We must outgrow a condition which necessitates suffering, and true spiritual treatment assists us to do so. A right treatment helps a patient to grow, mentally and morally.

QUES. 18. *Do you agree with the following from the same writer? God is not only love and intelligence but He is everything that exists on earth and anywhere else. Cause and effect are one and the same thing—they can not be separated. Man and God are the same, hence this physical nature is as holy and sacred as the angelic.*

The points raised in the foregoing statement, which is not a question but an assertion, are far too profound and numerous to be entered into here at any length. We regard the statement as decidedly pantheistic, and as we are not pantheists we fail to endorse it *in toto*, at the same time the ultimate of such assertion is agreeable to the genius of an enlightened philosophy, and can not be said to differ from the New Testament doctrine that the human body is God's temple. In essence everything must be divine, there can be no other life than the one infinite life which is the life of God. Such a view is calculated to elevate rather than depress our view of existence, and is therefore largely beneficial. We must get to the root of all things to find their real divinity. We must touch the bed rock in the nature of our patients before we can treat them successfully, and were we called upon to treat a person holding the opinions under review, we should scarcely seek to supplant them. All is good; there is no evil, is ultimately true in every instance.

QUES. No. 19. *Why is it that men often grow more mercenary as they advance in life? Generous boys often make stingy men.*

Why are we so sordid, and why do we grow more so? If we are all spirit, why such earthly natures?

ANS. We must never forget that so long as we are subject to mortal influence at all, we shall remain to some degree the creatures of our surroundings. While the supreme truth concerning man as an immortal spiritual entity is that he is pure spirit, we should not allow our eyes to close against the fact that we have a mortal mind to educate and develop, until it becomes the fitting channel for the expression of the inmost or highest principle of our nature. The lower principle or animal soul in us is not essentially or intrinsically evil. It is, indeed, very good when rightfully subjected to the higher principle, and our earthly discipline can only be said to be complete when this lower nature is completely subservient to the higher. Now, this lower principle is the nature we share in common with the animals, all of whom, without exception, manifest a lower type of affection than that which bespeaks the spiritual man. Self interest, self-preservation, love of approbation and particular regard for those who bestow favors on them are marked characteristics of many, if not all the lower creatures who serve us and with whom we associate. Now, in man these animal traits are always conspicuous until the loftier spiritual manhood pertaining to the higher principle, which animals do not share with man, is made manifest. What then is the sordidness of which so many complain? Surely it is nothing more or other than an intense, indeed, an overweening regard for one's personal comfort and social standing and that of one's family, without thought or regard for the equal advantages due to others. "Thou shalt love thy neighbor as thyself," introducing as it does, the singular number in both cases, suggests to every attentive mind that the command, when fully interpreted, tells us that it is our duty to recognize all men and women as our brothers and sisters, even to the extent of acting out the sublime principle of fraternity, so far as to think no more of our individual prosperity, than that of any other human unit in the great mass we call society. This is where spiritual science, or true theosophy, antagonizes human selfishness and calls forth the bitterest and most scornful denunciation from selfish and self-sufficient egotists, who will not tolerate the assertion that the rights of our common humanity must never be set aside to favor the caprice of an ambitious individual. If we can but grasp, in some measure, the glorious idea of God's universal parenthood, we have a base on which to build securely a sound philosophy of human brotherhood and sisterhood. But until this conviction becomes deep enough in every heart to make it the moving principle, the mainspring of all conduct—until man becomes angelic enough to live in the love of heaven, caring more for his brethren than for himself—not, indeed, neglecting his own culture or disregarding his own needs, but placing himself in such relation to all his neighbors as to consider any two human entities of twice the value of one, even though himself be the unit under consideration—until then, the love of hell, which is nothing other than inordinate self-love, greater regard for self than for neighbor will continue to plunge men and nations into all the awful depths of crime and convulsive throes of anarchy, which at the present moment so sadly terrify and depress many gentle and most amiable persons. Now, the only possible remedy for these gigantic evils, all springing from human selfishness, is a purely spiritual, but at the same time intensely practical system of moral education. Moral education need not lead to asceticism, and it certainly does not tend to fanaticism in any direction. It is purely and simply the culture of the higher dispositions of our nature, and by a constant direction of all our energy toward spiritual growth, instead of toward the accumulation of earthly property, it diverts the mind from selfish dreams of personal aggrandizement and fixes the eye of ambition on the shining mark of spiritual advancement. False standards of wealth and honor easily corrupt the morals of youth. Fine houses, extensive lands, elegant equipages, handsome clothes, expensive jewels, these and many like vanities are regarded as the highest good by multitudes, and why? Surely because, as a rule, we all show respect to those in affluent circumstances, while we show disrespect to those of far greater moral and mental worth who have not these baubles to display. Riches exert a powerful psychological hold on the minds of men and women, because of their immense purchasing power—and what can they not purchase in society as at present organized? If they could only buy collateral advantages of an external kind, many who now dote on them would at once despise them. But alas, they purchase in so many instances the respect, esteem and homage which by rights belong only to superior character. When our standard of value is reversed and we esteem people for what they *are*, not for what they *have*, this sordidness must disappear like murky vapors before the day dawn. Many men who seem intensely sordid in business circles are most kind and lovable at home, and try to live up to the Golden Rule; the world's temptations in the commercial sphere are however so strong that they succumb. Let it be our work to reform public sentiment so as to deliver such from evil.

QUES. No 20. *What influence is it that prompts noble men and women to so far interest themselves, even to martyrdom and violent deaths, in the momentous questions of the day — to the advocacy of Anarchism in America and Nihilism in Russia. Is not their devotion to these causes of disruption a misinterpreted inspiration?*

ANS. We regard the persons referred to as blundering reformers, many of them without doubt are endeavoring, as best they know how, to correct prevalent abuses, but so under the dominion of the lower principle are they, that they fail altogether to detect the only true means, whereby reform can be brought about. Co-operation, not competition, is the natural order. Children are falsely instructed when led to gratify an emulous ambition to rise above others. Poverty is quite unnecessary in America, but it will never be fully abolished as long as the wage system continues. This old system, a relic of feudal institutions, can not, however, be swept away by violent aggressions on the part of laborers upon the persons and possessions of capitalists. Reform can only be attained through processes of social and industrial evolution. Anarchism and Nihilism are the children of despotism. They are the offspring of systems of injustice and inhumanity which give birth to desperadoes, who destroy their own parents. Evil invariably destroys itself. In these times of excessively rapid motion the work of destruction is accomplished by violent measures and at a high rate of speed. The chemicalization of error must needs continue until every vestige of selfishness and animality is purged from human thought and affection, and while we may bemoan the measures taken to rectify wrong, and leave no stone unturned to show our erring brethren the better way, the only proper attitude to be taken in these days of angry revolt is that error in destroying itself is manifesting its true inwardness. We may learn from present disasters how absolutely necessary for the maintenance of social order and domestic peace are the spiritual truths, which are now engaging the attention of profound thinkers throughout the world. One evil may destroy another, as one poison may be an antidote to another, but it takes an enunciation and demonstration of the principle of true science to upbuild a republic of the nations, in which every citizen will enjoy a comfortable competency as the reward of his own industry, which is possible immediately the demon of selfishness is cast out of mind.

QUES. No. 21. *To a person whose happiness of the higher sort on earth has been entirely centered in the exercise of the affections, does it follow that nothing of this is preservable in our future states except those feelings which have a direct reference to religious or spiritual philosophy? Is not love imperishable?*

ANS. All true affection is spiritual, and therefore immortal, but surely none will deny that much that is called love is nothing but self-love. If we love others in a purely earthly manner by reason of the happiness they give us, our affection can not pertain to the immortal state, but if we love one another purely and unselfishly we may take the words of Jesus, recorded in the fourteenth chapter of the Fourth Gospel, and apply them to every human case. Individuality is the basis of life. We do not teach or believe that a time will ever come when the soul's identity will be lost. Neither do we anticipate a day when those who are truly related in spirit will be forced asunder. Darby and Joan, who after fifty years of wedded bliss are dearer to each other than on their wedding day, can surely with confidence look forward to a continuation of their mutual love beyond the grave, while those whose affections are sensual and selfish will assuredly drift apart and eventually discover that what they called love on earth was only a delusive chimera. Unhappiness in married life comes from inordinate exaction on one side or the other. The true spiritual scientist must not demand affection or live to be blessed, but bestow affection and work to bless others. Angelic love is all unselfish, the love of heaven that seeks no return is the love that reaps so glorious and plenteous a harvest, that indescribable bliss fills those souls to overflowing who, thinking not of any reward, find the truth of the statement, most perfectly exemplified in their experience, that to give is more blessed than to receive. If our affections are of the earth we must be wounded through them, as, being mortal they must die, and we suffer in their death if we cling to them. All *true* affection is eternal.

QUES. No. 22. *What is faith? Is it necessary that the patient have faith in the healer?*

ANS. Faith, from the Latin *fides*, which gives us the English word fidelity, does not by any means signify that blind credulity or unreasoning belief, which many people so erroneously dignify with the name of faith. In the old Hebrew sense of the word, faith invariably meant integrity, and thus the upright man was always styled the man of faith. In business circles, rather than in religious ones, we find this word still employed in its uncorrupted meaning; no etymologist would so far misemploy it as to identify it with gullibility. Faith is a grace, a moral excellence, a virtue of the highest ethical importance. Belief is secondary to faith and has a value quite distinct from faith, faith relating to the purpose of life from a moral standpoint, while belief can be only a matter of intellectual conviction at most. To require genuine faith of a patient is to demand nothing unreasonable, as it is only to require honesty of purpose, sincerity of desire, etc. Now as to belief, no reasonable person can expect another to believe without sufficient evidence, as he himself can not yield assent to any unproven proposition. It is not virtuous to believe, neither is it vicious to disbelieve. When a stranger makes his appearance and puts out his sign in a new city, the inhabitants rightly inquire into his credentials before they take him into their families. So, when a novel theory comes before the world, wise people neither endorse nor condemn it off hand, they earnestly and dispassionately investigate it. Patients are often tired of experimenting with medicine. They have suffered much at the hands of various schools of practice, and hearing of what seems to them a new and wonderful method of healing, especially when importuned by friends to do so, they are quite willing and often anxious to give it a trial. Such people can not approach a mental or spiritual healer in perfect confidence that his system is the only true one, nor can they feel absolutely sure of receiving benefit, unless some very strong influence or evidence is brought to bear upon them to produce such a result. Now a healer should not crave impossibilities or endeavor to exact what is unreasonable from an inquirer. Let the works speak for themselves. Let faith follow rather than precede demonstration. If anyone expects another to believe in him, he must generate and dispense an influence which compels grateful recognition at the hands of the sick and sorrowful, and the true healer invariably does this. You have doubtless all felt a subtile, pervasive atmosphere surrounding particular people, a "virtue" going forth from them in some indescribable manner, reaching and blessing you, which has compelled you to acknowledge that they are dispensers of a power which ordinary people seem not to convey. Now if you are in some such manner attracted to a healer it is because he has already treated you and you have felt the beneficial result, which always accompanies and follows the establishment of harmony in your mental sphere. Some people possess this gift in marvelous degree, and only those who can help others unconsciously by reason of this helpful force going from them to others, are really well adapted to become professional healers. As in many lines of business good address goes a great way, and persons of considerable intelligence are frequently unfit for prominent positions where they have to constantly meet and converse with many people, because of their lack of all that goes to make up what is commonly called "good address," so a public healer who would make healing his life work, as physicians devote themselves to the pratice of medicine, should invariably be one who can inspire confidence and regard in the great majority of the sufferers he encounters or who come to him for advice and treatment. What is often regarded as necessary on the patient's part is at first inseparable from certain qualifications in the healer essential to induce it, so while oftentimes stumbling blocks may be placed by the patient in the way of his own recovery by his own obdurate bigotry or folly, it frequently happens that the "too little faith" is in the healer as well as in the patient. The Gospel narratives amply illustrate this fact, as they record a variety of cases where the disciples failed to heal because of their own imperfections, while many other cases present the fact of the fault being on the side of the invalids. Faith of the right sort is required on both sides. The healer needs to be so well grounded in spiritual conviction, as to be above the doubts and fears which so readily assail the ordinary individual, while the paitent often needs that stimulation of faith which contact with a more thoroughly convinced mind frequently supplies. Prejudices must be laid aside, the patient must endeavor to let go of bigotry and give the healer a fair field, though a true healer asks no favors. Faith in the sense of belief is a response to a blessing already received, while faith in its deeper sense means perfect straightforwardness, honesty in thought, word and action. If you find yourselves inspiring confidence in yourself and the system you advocate, even among people who have hitherto been totally indifferent and skeptical if not positively antagonistic to spiritual methods of healing, you have evidence that from you has gone forth to them a force as palpable to their interior sense as a flower's fragrance is to your exterior sense of smell. When you can arouse faith in all its meanings in those to whom you fain would minister, you are showing indisputable credentials vouching for your genuine ability to heal.

QUES. No. 23. *What is chemicalization? Is it a necessary stage in unfoldment?*

ANS. Chemicalization is equivalent to crisis and ferment, it occurs when new thoughts are actively engaged in conquering old opinions. All physicians speak much of crises and declare them to be the turning points in the conditions of their patients. Chemicalization is often inevitable though no one is justified in assuming that it is invariably necessary, for many cases have been known to yield instantly to spiritual power, without the patient suffering anything of the nature of a crisis. To explain the workings of the various forces, all operating upon a patient, from most discordant sources, would require a lengthy discourse, and, as in reply to a question, we can do little more than hint at the solution of a complex problem, we must request our readers to ponder our remark long and carefully, that by setting their minds upon the subject under consideration they may induce a mental state favorable to the reception of ideas through their own interior avenues of perception. We all speak and hear much of the force of habit, and those of us who are at all familiar with psychological influence, must be more or less aware that when a practice, be it desirable or undesirable, gains powerful hold over a person's mind, it is in consequence of a (usually unconscious) establishment of psychical relations between his mind and the minds of others. Let us look for a moment at habits and their formation. Almost without exception habits are forced on sensitive people, very young people, and children in particular, from without, they seem rarely to be evolved from within. Many of the most pernicious practices to which men are addicted, do not seem indigenous to the natural mind, they are artificially induced through contact with people who influence those younger and in some respects weaker than themselves. Drinking and smoking as well as the filthy and detestable habit of chewing tobacco, with many other forms of impropriety, are usually pressed upon a boy by older companions, into the net of whose vile mesmeric fascination he is ignorantly drawn. Whenever one does anything one feels to be degrading or even unpleasant, because of an outside influence urging him to do it, he is yielding to a psychological influence of the baser sort and forming mental associations of the most dangerous character, from whose grasp he may find it difficult in the extreme to struggle free in future years. As men follow each other in paths of vice so do even virtuous women follow each other in the paths of folly, and in many things allow themselves to be led wholly by some stupid fashion or prevailing custom, which in their hearts they thoroughly despise. These weak yieldings to extraneous influence so far impoverish the will and render people unnaturally susceptible to every foul thing about them, that when they least expect it they find themselves overtaken with some pestilential, though fashionable because prevalent, disorder. Now when spiritual force operates to break the chains and loosen the bonds which hold the prisoner captive in the clutches of degrading error, a conflict ensues, the devil struggles to keep his prize in his embrace, while the Christ works to take his victim from him. Many instances in the New Testament forcibly illustrate this experience. Take the unclean spirits tearing the demoniacs when they came out of them. You probably all know the ancient Oriental theory of disease, it was invariably attributed to the action of powers of darkness, and thus, loosing the bonds of wickedness and delivering people from demoniacal possession (a process often called exorcism) played a very conspicuous part in all Eastern methods of healing. Modern Spiritualism has thrown much light on some of these ancient records by starting a theory of obsession, which is practically identical with the old belief in demoniacal possession. Such theories, while they are not wholly true and are terribly subject to exaggeration, being frequently pressed so far as to make them ridiculous as well as dangerous, nevertheless contain sufficient truth to explain much which would be utterly incomprehensible without their aid. Chemicalization is simply a modern expression recognizing exorcism in a more intelligent form, as belief in evil is now being greatly modified in all enlightened circles where psychology is receiving the attention it deserves. We can readily see how all the influences which tend to degrade man may have been massed together by ancient philosophers, who styled them collectively man's "evil genius," and how all of an elevating character have been similarly massed and designated "good genius." Now the true spiritual healer stands to the patient as a representative of the good genius, while all that opposes his enlightenment and recovery stands in the attitude of evil genius. The struggle for ascendency between the true and the false, the wise and the foolish, confidence and fear, love and hate, etc., is chemicalization.

QUES. No. 24. *Can you present to us any other certain method of developing the moral fruitfulness in man's nature than that which is laid down in the Scriptures, where the physical and intellectual developments have failed to bring spiritual life to light? Is there any theological creed, ancient philosophy, or modern "liberalism" which has or can change one soul from slavery to sin (i. e. passion, revenge, etc., etc.), to that freedom of spirit and soul which was promised and is still given by the Holy Spirit through faith in the Son of God, who alone ever claimed to do the will of God or to forgive sins?*

ANS. We do not pretend to give any teachings in opposition to those contained in the New Testament. It is simply our desire to arrive at the spiritual truth enshrined in its letter instead of clinging to its outward husk that causes us to take issue with prevailing orthodox opinions. Our view of Scripture is that all ancient Scriptures which have been and still are highly venerated by multitudes, in their letter reflect the general sentiment of the times in which they were written, but in their spirit they deal with essential truths of vital moment to mankind at all times and everywhere. Now as to a certain method of developing our moral nature, we should most decidedly take ground that it can only be developed at all by a sincere and determined effort of *will* in the direction of its development, and by *will* we mean affection putting forth an effort to reach its object. In the Athanasian Creed the opening words *Quicumque vult* signify whoever *wills* or earnestly desires salvation must hold to the universal faith, and it has always been a tenet of Christianity that the *will* must be perfectly surrendered, and that lovingly (not through fear) to the Divine Will, or salvation, for which regeneration is but another word, is impossible. Now it is a self-evident conclusion reached by all students of human nature that nothing can be successfully accomplished in any direction apart from persistent effort in that direction. The *will* must be directed toward the cultivation of muscle, intellect or art, or culture in those lines is impossible. The only unpardonable sin is blasphemy against the Holy Spirit, which means a deliberate steeling of one's affections against truth. It is certainly a correct view to take of education that mere secular training is by no means adequate to secure the highest welfare of humanity, but spiritual culture is not brought about by dogmatic theology or by the enforcement of creeds, but solely by the influence of moral suasion in its highest sense. As to changing a soul from slavery to sin, to a state of freedom and righteousness, we should pronounce all creeds and institutions inadequate to the accomplishment of this divine work, which can only be brought about by the liberation of the spiritual man from bondage to the mortal belief which makes of evil an abiding reality, a potent force in the universe, either personal or otherwise, and thereby creates a dread of its power. To destroy all fear of evil and all belief in its potency is to deliver men from its clutches. We yield universally to what we fear as well as to what we love, and where the love of sin appears not to exist, the fear of it, and particularly the dread of its consequences, leads to its commission, not through deliberate intent, but through weakness, which is always at one with abject susceptibility. As to faith in the Son of God, we can understand the Swedenborgian expression that we must be *adjoined to the Lord* by affection for good, but the ordinary evangelical interpretation of faith is to our mind extremely unsatisfactory. Faith means fidelity to conviction, and springs from love of truth, not from a mere intellectual assent to propositions of truth. As to the forgiveness of sin, sin never is forgiven in the old ecclesiastical sense. It has to be outgrown in every sense, and to forgive it as Jesus forgave is to destroy the love of it and prevent its re-commission, not at all to deliver the one who has already committed it from the reformatory penalty.

QUES. No. 25. *Please explain in condensed form the practical teaching of Christian, Mental and Spiritual Science when freed from the points of difference over which special parties wrangle?*

ANS. Probably most, if not all our readers are quite well acquainted with the names "Christian Science," "Mental Science" and "Spiritual Science." Metaphysical healing is now practiced under these different names all over the world. The essential truth presented by this system is that mind is entirely sovereign, matter being totally subservient to it. All take the ground which has been taken by philosophers from time immemorial, that all is mind, and therefore there is no matter. This statement is certainly astounding to the ear of an ordinary listener. The statement in one sense appears groundless, because it seems to destroy all our confidence in our senses. But when we realize that all that is necessarily implied in such a statement is, that there can be no effect without a cause adequate to produce it, and that all material things are simply phenomenal effects, while there is a great spiritual power behind everything, we are only called to look upon the external universe as the shadow of the spiritual, which is the substantial universe. The substantial is immortal; it can never die or fade away. The shadow comes and goes, while eternal stability pertains only to that which is as deathless as the Eternal Being who has spoken all things into existence.

Now, when man realizes himself as one with eternal life, he knows that the only life of which he can be conscious is the one life which fills immensity, there being no void nor emptiness anywhere. Our views of life are hereby lifted entirely above the material plane. We are carried in thought beyond all perishable forms of clay and made to realize that we are spirit, that we all belong to one great family, and that we have—in the last analysis of our subject—no parent except the eternal God, and no destiny except to enjoy conscious relation with the eternal soul of all life forever.

The word metaphysical means *beyond physics*, and *mind over matter*. It really means, in its fullest sense, everything included in the vast domain of what lies beyond the reach of the physical senses.

While metaphysicians do not call themselves Theosophists or Spiritualists, and do not take any sectarian name, or join with any particular creed or party, we may safely say that their universal object is to investigate the realm of soul, and learn all they can concerning spiritual being, to distinguish between outward existence, which is at the very best transitory and evanescent, and that *being* which is eternal and immortal, which never changes, and can never pass away

As the word theology literally means the science of God, and of all things divine, as truly as geology means the science of the earth, or of terrestrial things in general, equally may we affirm that spiritual science means the science of the spiritual man, the science of the spiritual universe, yes, and the science of God also, for there is no sublimer and clearer definition of the Supreme Being to be found in any literature, ancient or modern, than in John's gospel, where Jesus, in conversation with the Samaritan woman at Jacob's well, declares "God is Spirit, and they that worship Him must worship him in spirit and in truth."

Now when the Jews and Samaritans were disputing among themselves whether God should be worshiped in the temple at Jerusalem, or from the top of the mountain where the ruined temple of the Samaritans was still standing, Jesus said practically: It matters not whether in the temple at Jerusalem, or on this mountain-top; whether in the open desert, or in the solitude of your own inner chamber; whether in the crowded streets and busy thoroughfares dedicated to places of business, or in halls devoted to amusement. You can worship God everywhere by doing all things to the glory of God.

Now, the real object of metaphysical instruction is to help people to put into practice Paul's affirmation that we should pray without ceasing. We can do *all* things to the glory of God, whether we eat or drink, or whatever we do. It does not need to be explained that God does not need anything at our hands, God is never hungry nor thirsty, nor in want of any kind; we can not minister directly unto Him, but His children all around us are in need, and when we give to them we are presenting an acceptable offering to the Eternal Being, who can only be pleased as we bless the children of His love, who are our brethren as well as His children.

We agree with all true Theosophists who explain that the basis of Theosophy is universal brotherhood, and that all true philosophy must be built upon this one foundation. We must recognize the unity and brotherhood of the entire human race, so that every man is our brother and every woman our sister. We must not only *believe*, we must *feel* this, and there can be no true metaphysical work done so long as we unduly respect wealth or even intellect; so long as we divide ourselves into aggressive knots and groups and parties, looking down upon some as inferior, while we regard others as superior; so long as we look to the outward form and fashion of men; so long as we care for a long line of hereditary descent, for what is commonly called blue blood flowing in our veins; so long as we reverence the god of gold, to which so many bow in servile adoration; so long as we care for vain fashions and frivolities, and consequently raise our voices in concert with the multitude, "Great is Diana of the

Ephesians," if she be the popular deity of the hour, we may be spiritual scientists in abstract belief, but we shall ignominiously fail in practice. But when we learn to truly respect ourselves so as to live in accordance with the light which shines in the innermost recesses of the soul, when we direct our path by the voice which speaks within us, then we shall be free indeed, free in truth, and our freedom will not consist only in freedom from the fear of death, but also from sickness and the recognition of death altogether.

It may sound strange to many persons, even if they have read Mrs. Eddy's work, "Science and Health," to be told that there is in reality neither death, sickness nor sin in all the universe; but we must learn to look away from all things perishable to divine realities; we must learn to find within man that which is alone enduring, which is never sick and never suffers, even the divine soul which never dies. It certainly sounds very strange to be told there is no sin, no sickness, no death, while we see so many prisons and reformatories, which cause us to say with much show of reason, "It is, indeed, a reality that sin abounds." While hospitals are filled with sick people, is not sickness a reality? Is not death a reality when we are requested again and again to officiate at funeral services, and cemeteries are filled with dead bodies? But we ask, what is it that sins? What is it that suffers? What is it that dies? It can only be an external adjunct to man. Man surely is a deathless entity who can neither sin, nor be sick, nor die.

This great truth concerning man is surely apprehended, or, at least, vaguely recognized, when we talk of our better moments. We all realize that we have a higher self, and we all talk of our better moments. What are we talking of, if not of our real, cardinal nature, which is the foundation of all our existence? Is not this our true and imperishable being? And is it not desirable that we should become practically oblivious to external things, for the sake of more fully appreciating the real and ever living spirit that we are here and now?

We shall not become spiritual entities after we have dropped the mortal form. We shall not go to a spiritual world when these mortal forms have passed into dust. We shall not then become the sons of God, but we are such, here and now, and when our mortal forms have passed away nothing will have passed from us save an outward garment of flesh.

Now, when we undertake to treat patients in harmony with spiritual science, we find ourselves obliged to direct the patient's thoughts away from external things altogether; therefore, instead of dwelling continually on outward signs and symptoms, instead of highly regarding the body, and always quizzing it to find out, if possible, in what condition it may be; instead of administering medicine at certain hours, and endeavoring to keep a room at a regulation temperature, and performing a variety of outward ceremonies, we know that liberation from disease is to get out of the thought of these material works, and forget, at least for the time being, that there is anything external.

Now, in order to get out of the external we must get into the spiritual. You can not think of nothing.

you can not long do nothing. Every person will occupy himself in some way, if not profitably, then mischievously. Our minds will never remain still, and therefore to say we must not think of matter, we must not regard the flesh, and leave the statement in so unfinished a form is to preach a doctrine which practically means nothing, because no man can long comply with its requirements. But when we say, "Fix your thought upon spiritual form; maintain that all is life, all is good; look within, take a glance at your own immortal soul, and find yourself face to face with the stupendous reality of spiritual being," we know that your mental gaze can be so riveted upon the immortal that you will completely forget the mortal. Your whole thought will be concentrated on the eternal, and so you will become unmindful of the material, and of all outside the interior realm, where your higher consciousness forever dwells secure.

Speaking of outward aids to interior development, many people inquire, "Of what possible use can a talisman be?" We do not ourselves believe that sacred words have any efficacy of their own resting in them. But as for thousands of years people have worn or otherwise employed them, as many Jews have placed texts of Scripture in little houses, upon their foreheads, and upon their arms, that they might be perpetually reminded of divine truth; and while among enlightened Jews there never was a time when the *tephilin* were considered of talismanic value, they being only used as reminders of great spiritual truths, so all outward assistants are, from a metaphysical standpoint, regarded as valuable only in so far as they direct the thought to a desired object. The words, "Hear, O Israel, the Lord our God, the Lord is One," whenever their eyes lighted upon the Hebrew characters they wore, would remind them of the great central truth of all religion, the Divine Unity. So when we are giving treatment, either verbally or silently, by presenting a thought we direct attention to a certain plane of idea. Now if you look upon illuminated texts such as "Honesty is the best policy," or "Charity never faileth," or "Do unto others as you would that they should do unto you," you are at once reminded of truth which perhaps you had temporarily forgotten. If in a church a prayer is spoken or a hymn sung in your hearing, you are reminded of what perhaps you had forgotten in the multiplicity of your household cares.

While it is impossible for us to do any work for our brethren in their stead, we can assist them to arise and work for themselves. The great work of the truly efficient metaphysical healer is the work of one who is continually presenting to a patient or student the line in which thoughts should march. When a line of march is indicated to us, when the right way is pointed out, and a voice says to us, "This is the way; walk ye in it," there comes along with the pointing a subtle, restraining and inducing power; it is not mesmeric; it is not psychologic in any ordinary sense; it is not one mind controlling or exercising authority over another; for the true metaphysical healer is an educator, an enlightener of his brethren; for when we undertake to place truth before our patient, we desire to make that patient realize it and follow in that way which is pointed out to him by his newly awakened sense of spiritual discernment.

Spiritual science proclaims liberty for the individual enlightened by truth, to walk in the light of the truth as he himself perceives it. Multitudes of people love truth, but have not yet perceived it very clearly. Multitudes are longing to see some brighter ray before them, to hear a voice directing them where to go, and to discern a hand pointing in the true direction, and it is to help all such, to help all who are struggling into light, that we should work.

QUES. No. 26. *What is really meant by Metaphysical Healing, and how is cure effected if not by magnetism? How can prayer heal the sick?*

In reply to the ever recurring question, what is meant by metaphysical healing, and what are the means by which cures are accomplished, we answer there are three means of healing plainly revealed in the New Testament; at all events the three necessary requisites are Faith, Prayer and Fasting. Jesus says, "This kind," meaning the power to heal all manner of infirmities, "cometh not forth except by prayer and fasting." And He also says: "According to your faith be it unto you."

Now, when asked to define prayer, we say prayer is our recognition of divine good, and our earnest endeavor to enter into intimate relation with it. Montgomery beautifully defined it when he sang, "Prayer is the soul's sincere desire, uttered or unexpressed." Prayer is mental asking, mental seeking, mental knocking.

Whenever we induce people to seek, to knock, to ask in a definite direction, whenever we help them to aspire toward the light, we teach them to pray rightly.

Prayer, therefore, can be continued without ceasing, and if we are cured of any ailment through the agency of prayer, we do not consider that any such cure is brought about vicariously or in any unnatural manner. Individuals are simply directed into channels of thought in which they continually aspire toward spiritual light. Desire is prayer; moral effort to attain to virtue is prayer; but the prayer of faith is the only effectual prayer, as it is aspiration or desire after virtue and does not allow the word "cannot" in its vocabulary. It maintains that whatever is right for us to have can be received by us just because it is right for us to receive it. Faith in its grand old sense means fidelity, honor, straightforwardness of character, nobility, integrity; it means everything that stands for grand and noble character, not mere belief, concerning which contentious persons are ever wrangling and disputing, but noble virtue, moral excellence, ethical worth. Then fasting, what is it? Not going without food at stated intervals necessarily, but the complete subjugation of lower to higher impulses. We must deny our lower selves—sacrifice our lower appetites, that we may gain true freedom to fulfill the desires of our nobler instincts.

Now, if all students realize that they must pray, exercise faith and fast—in the sense in which we have defined these terms—we know that to-day there may be a spiritual outpouring as great as there ever was in ancient Galilee. It rests with ourselves as to whether, when we teach or attempt to heal, the result is or is not a truly pentecostal one. We must all remember we have still very much to learn. While the writings of Mrs. Eddy, Dr. Evans and others, may assist many to the light, the source of light is within us. In every human being dwells the divine word; therefore every essential word of truth must come from within, not from without. The living oracle, the ever-speaking word of God, must be recognized, or success can not crown our endeavors. We need more reliance upon our own spiritual nature, and far more direct, communion with the source of all light.

Spiritual science will tend to make us calm, quiet, strong with quiet strength, less dependent upon legal measures, outward modes of attack, controversial argument and money, and infinitely more dependent upon that silent, spiritual power which is strictly invisible and absolutely potential. Many live like people who have long subsisted upon fruitful soil and land which contained valuable ore, but have known nothing of their possessions, contented with scanning the surface. Now, though our land has become no richer, we are told of our hidden possessions, of the wealth of our mines, and we discover that our land is highly arable and can yield beautiful flowers, delicious fruits and golden harvests of grain.

Now, let us set to work and plant our vineyards and olive groves. Let us get our mines to work and our wells in operation, and though formerly our resources were as great, and our possessions as large as now, we knew nothing of them, so we now commence for the first time to enter consciously into our inheritance.

Thus do we find the golden key which unlocks the inmost secrets of our nature, unfolding to us our priceless latent treasures, which, though adding nothing to our capabilities, brings to light hidden things divine.

The science of spirit is the golden key which opens up the spiritual heaven to all, just as civilization, with all its discoveries and implements, reveals to us the treasures hidden within the earth, and beneath the ocean wave — treasures which have been there for centuries, but of which we knew nothing until our atten tion was called to them and they were placed at our command.

Feel that there are spiritual gems of every hue lying buried in your inmost nature, as old Greek philosophers would express it, your latent knowledge only needs to be brought out by education; and ever as you seek to bring forth the treasures which are embedded in your soul, remember there are just two effective modes of digging, delving and diving, and these methods are love of truth and practice of charity.

If you are lovers of truth and also lovers of your fellow-beings; if you can bear to stand alone, face to face with your own interior life, and not quail before its revealments, then you can rise superior to every mortal passion and the consequent ailments proceeding from sensuous indulgence.

TEACHINGS

OF SPIRITUAL SCIENCE CONCERNING OUR TREATMENT OF THE LOWER ANIMALS.

THAT noble and glorious reformer, Anna Kingsford M. D., (Paris) having passed from the mortal form, leaving behind her many works of great value which have never been published or in any way re-produced in America, though the Esoteric Publishing Company, 478, Shawmut Avenue, Boston, issues a very good edition of her marvelous treatise entitled, "The Perfect Way," at the moderate price of $2. We have ventured to incorporate into our present work some of this saintly and heroic woman's carefully digested and eminently scientific views on "Unscientific Science," which, when contrasted with the human teachings of a gracious and merciful spiritual science, will serve to show the utter irreconcilability of cruelty in any form with the work of even physically benefiting humanity. The most serious attention of our readers is particularly called to Dr. Kingsford's unanswerable plea for "philosophic unity" which is expressed in the following words at the opening of her lecture entitled *Scientific Aspects of Vivisection*, a lecture replete with the most valuable and authentic testimony gathered from every available source in Europe. It is with deep regret we find ourselves unable to insert it in this volume:

"The century in which we live is one of investigation, criticism and thought. Dogmas and traditions are no longer accepted upon hearsay, or even upon authority. Everything is canvassed, discussed, verified, tested by reason.

"The reign of autocratic power seems to be in decadence, and that of philosophic force begins to assert itself. Men are awakening to the fact that the true glory of humanity consists in the faculty of reason, and that that which constitutes the human being is not a special physical conformation, but a mind enlightened, enfranchised, and capable of lofty aims.

"I posit then, this fundamental principle, that the truly human and reasonable life is based upon an exact philosophy. The basic idea of philosophy is to reduce everything to Unity; to make of the various facts and diverse interests of our existence a synthesis, a consistent whole, harmonious and equilibrated in all its parts as a sphere of which the radii all converge to one and the same central point. Now it is this condition of equilibrium in the mind which constitutes *justness*, and it is the faculty of recognizing and comprehending the necessity of philosophic unity which is the distinctive appanage of the reasonable and enlightened being.

"It follows from the premiss thus announced that no method of judgment ought to be considered correct which opposes the interests and indications of science to those of morality, which causes discord between the aims and objects of physical welfare and those of the spiritual being, which creates confusion between certain supposed material utilities and the necessities of the moral nature of mankind. From this point of view, and guided by this principle of philosophic unity, let us examine the theory and art of vivisection as it is practised by modern biologists."

Dr. Kingsford's lecture on "scientific aspects of vivisection" concludes with the following reference to the testimony of one of the most noted physicians Great Britain has produced:

"Sir Charles Bell, warned by the unfortunate results of his own and others' experiments, devotes eighty pages of his 'Exposition of the Natural System of the Nerves of the Human Body' (1824) to the study and explanation of clinical and pathological cases. He regards artificial experiments as superfluous and without value in presence of the precious facts which every hospital ward and *post-mortem* room yield to investigation. And he cites examples calculated to call attention to the fact that frequently the true interpretation of experimental results altogether escapes the operator, because the animal on which he experiments is incapable of recounting its sensations, and its mere dumb gestures may, as often as not, give rise to false impressions in regard to their cause. In confirmation of this view, he relates many clinical cases of nerve-injury which served as a basis for his researches and discoveries, solely on account of the explanation given by the patients themselves of their personal experiences and sensations."

UNSCIENTIFIC SCIENCE.

MORAL ASPECTS OF VIVISECTION.

BY DR. ANNA KINGSFORD.

Apologists of the practice appear to think that the desire of knowledge is in itself sufficient to vindicate all the cruelties and injustices imaginable. They do not seem to recognize the fact that every branch of intellectual research has its *moral limits*, and that the quest of pleasure, of wealth, of power, or of knowledge must never, in a civilized state, be permitted to outrage justice or the law of humanity.

In the ancient religious mysteries of all the nations of the globe, it is said that the fall of man ensues when he sacrifices moral obedience to the intellectual desire to *know*. Ah, it is primal and profound truth, and for this reason it finds its place in the initial chapters of the occult Book. *There are certain means of acquiring knowledge of which man can not make use without forfeiting his place in the Divine Order.*

We know well that there exist many practices which are extremely profitable in their results, but which are not legitimate, and which civilization does not tolerate,

In former times human lives were sacrificed to the interests of the fine arts. It is related that a certain painter of celebrity, wishing to sieze the effects of violent death, caused a negro slave to be decapitated in his studio; and that another artist, famous for the talent he displayed in the interests of the Church, crucified an unfortunate youth in order to secure a faithful model for an altar-piece portraying the expiring Christ.

Such acts as these are not in the category of legitimate practices, whatever may be the artistic or other value of their results; and the same may be said of many other pursuits constituting so many sciences invented by man to enrich, to amuse, or to aggrandize himself, but which are, by the *consensus* of modern opinion, discountenanced and outlawed.

It is necessary that men should understand the mere plea of "science" to be insufficient as a justification of human action. There are sciences of a legitimate and civilized nature, tending toward light, wisdom and righteousness, and there are others which are neither legitimate nor civilized, and whose results can only end in the obliteration of sentiment, the negation of humanity, and the destruction of true science and true civilization. The progress made by vivisection is an advance upon the downward path.

And here we are brought face to face with the fact that the vivisecting school is pre-eminently the materialistic and atheistic school; while the school of spiritualistic thought is, by the very nature of its philosophy, opposed to vivisection.*

The materialist has no fundamental notion of Justice. For him everything is vague, relative, inexplicable. He is acquainted only with physical atoms, chemical elements, protoplasm and the theory of the evolution of forms without aim and without order. In his view there is only a blind force acting in the midst of darkness. Consequently, morality is not for him a determined and positive quality, having its source in the divine and inviolable Mind which directs and dominates all material manifestation ; it is but a matter of human habit and convention, differing according to the particular time, place and race concerned. The man who adopts this view of morality of course accepts the civil law as the soul arbiter of action, and regards conduct as repre-

*Of course I use the word "spiritualist" in its real and original sense, as opposed to "materialist."—*e. g*, regarding the universe as having a spiritual and intelligent basis. I do not employ the word as a synonym for any special doctrines other than this.

hensible, or the reverse, according to the light in which it is popularly viewed by his own nation and era. The sentiments, such as honor, justice, courage, pity, love, loyalty, are for him but idiosyncrasies, varying according to such and such a temperament and depending for their manifestation and development on physical and accidental causes. Naturally, then, he laughs at appeals to sentiment, and boasts of being inaccessible to the "hysterical attacks" of "sensitive and weak-minded fanatics." When he says this, and other similar things, he simply means that the words "pity" and "justice" have no sense for him. There is but one only thing in the world which appears to him worthy of desire and attainment, and that is knowledge—knowledge always, and before all things, without any restriction or limitation of the means employed in its attainment.

The materialist does not understand that the Source and Substance of every series of phenomena, material and physical, the origin of which he seeks so eagerly to interpret, is equally the necessary Cause of the evolution which has produced humanity, whose distinctive appanage is the *moral nature.* To think otherwise would be to create illogical and absurd confusion between science and morality, by opposing intellect and intellectual interests to justice and the interests of the psychic being.

Thus is brought about the inevitable negation of philosophic unity.

But it is no uncommon thing to hear partisans of vivisection meet the charge of injustice and immorality made against the practice by the reply that it is a work of the highest intrinsic merit, because it has for its object the welfare of humanity.

Let us stop and consider what is meant by "the welfare of humanity." What is the signification of the word "humanity," so often used, so little understood? For the materialistic and vivisecting school we know very well that humanity imports nothing else than the special physical form of an animal belonging to the family of apes, a creature having such and such conformation of cerebral convolutions, skeleton, and organs. It is the body, the physical form, which constitutes humanity, and that is all. But for the spiritualistic school of thought, humanity means the manifestation of certain qualities and principles which find no expression among irresponsible beings—a condition raised above animality in virtue of a special moral capacity. Consequently, even were it true (which it is not) that *physical* human life could be saved, and bodily advantages obtained by means of cruel and tyrannical practices, such practices would still be, from the human point of view, completely unjustifiable. ✓The human race can not be saved or enriched by acts which destroy and rob humanity.✓ The physical life and health of individuals would be too dearly preserved or bought by the sacrifice of the high qualities which alone constitute man's superiority over all other creatures. The champions of vivisection demand the abasement of the moral standard of our race to the level of the primitive instinct of purely animal existence—the preservation of the body at any cost. Such a surrender would involve the destruction of that which is infinitely more precious than our physical life, of that which gives to this life all its worth and all its glory,—the dignity of human sentiment, and the privilege of responsibility.

What would be said of any person who, being sick or in pain, should cause a number of highly sensitive animals to be tortured for hours or days in his presence, on the remote chance of thereby discovering some means of alleviation for his own malady? Who among us, hearing of such an act as this, but would say that such a man was not worth the saving? And why should the motives of a whole people which act thus in accepting the practices of vivisection as the means of healing its physical ailments be held worthier our respect than those of the individual?

There can be but one reply. The human race, once beggared of all the attributes which alone enrich and elevate it, has no claim to royalty over the animals, and its salvation can in no wise profit the world.

For tho unjust king is no longer a king, but a tyrant.

Vivisection has upon its hands the blood of violence and of abuse of force. No man ought to seek the relief of his suffering or the advance of his power at the price of the agonies of his lower brethren, even if such relief or advance should be really proved possible by these means. But it would seem that some physiologists of the modern school are only anxious to prove our common origin with the animals, and consequently the ties of brotherhood which link them to us, in order the more tranquilly to claim the right to torture and misuse them.

To vindicate the practices of vivisection by appeal to the "law of Nature," and to the habits of certain beasts who live by carnage, is to seek to regulate the conduct of the being highest in the series of evolution by the manners of those beings which are lowest in the scale, and to degrade the code of human morality to the plane of that of the wolf, the tiger, or any other irresponsible and noxious creature.

What is the good of being a man—of being a "king"—if this high rank, this glorious title, imply no superiority to gross natures and to the common lot? What is the meaning of all the mystery of development and of the transmutation of forms which, according to the teaching of science, have occupied so many thousand ages of painful evolution, and by which alone we men have gained our majesty of moral force and responsibility, if at the bidding of the vivisector we are to abandon our royal privilege, and sink again into the slime beside the last and most obscure of our vassals?

Ay, and lower even than they. For the "struggle for existence" among irresponsible beings, about which the vivisectors talk so much, rarely implies torture, but only death. The claim of the vivisector is for the right to inflict torture, in which but very few animals, and these the most ferocious and loathsome, appear to take pleasure. If, then, it be true that man has the right to kill certain animals, as he has that to kill certain men, this right does not involve the infliction of prolonged and horrible suffering. At the present day, in civilized countries, condemned criminals are given over to death, but never to the flames, never to the rack or the *oubliette*. We have no right to inflict upon innocent animals torments to which pity forbids us to subject guilty men.

The force which ought to dominate the world is not physical force, nor even purely intellectual force; but it is, above and beyond all other, moral and philosophical force, which alone differentiates man from the beast and distinguishes the civilized being from the barbarbian.

In fact, the distinctive glory of humanity is based on the sentiments — those divine qualities which have ever inspired all the noble and worthy actions of our race, and which are everywhere recognized as the most precious heritage of mankind.

It is probably because the beliefs of materialism stifle the sentiments in its devotees that they fail to perceive how inapposite are many of the comparisons drawn by them between the practices they defend and others recognized as useful and necessary to the State. A favorite argument is that which likens the craft of the vivisector to the profession of the soldier. Yet what is easier than to see that sentiment here enacts an enormously important part, and that there is all the difference in the world between the courage which gives itself of its own accord to danger and to death, and the cowardice which, at its ease at home, maltreats and martyrizes dumb and inoffensive creatures.

Where is the analogy between the vivisector's laboratory, with its gagged, bound, and trembling victims, carved to death in cold blood, and the field of battle, where every man in each contending army fights for home and country under the inspiration of enthusiasm, ambition or the desire for renown?

Neither is there any resemblance between the practices of vivisection and the great enterprises of civilization, such as engineering, exploration in unknown seas, and similar undertakings of a perilous nature, by appeal to which it has been sought to justify the scientific torture of animals; for these last do not voluntarily devote themselves to the knife. Men who take part in difficult works of construction, adventurers who traverse the arctic wastes or engage in other hazardous enterprises, are volunteers who follow the interest of their own satisfaction or personal profit at their own risk.

There is a complete contrast between the free sacrifice of oneself for the good of others and the enforced sacrifice of others for the good of oneself. The first is divine; the second is infernal. And vivisection represents a sacrifice of the latter kind.

Moreover, as already has been said, death is not torture. Let us remember that the right of vivisection differs from every other right assumed by men over animals by its peculiar nature, and that its defenders, if not wholly illogical or ignorant, vindicate the propriety of inflicting, not violent deaths, nor average pains merely, but horrible and prolonged agonies, such as that of the curarized dog cut to pieces by inches, and lingering, hour after hour, in the silence and darkness of the night—dying in torment in the laboratory of Paul Bert, the *moralist!*

It is vain to appeal to the vivisectors themselves against the cruelties daily perpetrated in their chambers of horror. Formerly, when the priests of the mediaeval church burnt and tortured men for the salvation of souls, under the auspices of the Holy Office, it was not to the eminent deans and prelates of the sacred hierarchy that the world addressed itself in order to obtain the abolition of the Inquisition and of its infamous practices. The priests of the religion of the middle ages, like the priests of science to-day, found fine phrases with which to defend themselves as a body of conscientious and disinterested men. Nevertheless, the question between the Church and the world was decided by the laity against the members of the ecclesiastical corporation, and there has never yet been reason to regret the loss of stake and rack and dungeon.

A science based upon torture can no more be true science than a religion based upon torture can be true religion. It is a new Reformation that we want—but this time in the domain of science!

For the rest, the instruments used in our laboratories of vivisection are much the same as in mediæval times. The modern arsenal is fully as complete as was that of the days of Torquemada, or Isabella of Spain—only now the dumb and innocent dog replaces the Jew or the heretic, and creatures which man judges his inferiors are bound to the wheel and tortured, with the hope of extorting from them the secret of life, in blind ignorance of the fact that Nature, outraged and agonized, replies like the human victim on the rack, more often by a lie than by the truth.

Attempts have again and again been made to dissuade anti-vivisectionists from the crusade they have undertaken, by inviting their attention and that of the public generally, to other abuses more or less grave, with the inquiry, "Why do not you kind-hearted people occupy yourselves with reforming the cruel practices of drovers, cab-drivers, sportsmen, slaughtermen, and their like? Why do you not try to solace the misery that everywhere reigns outside the vivisector's laboratory, before you think of attacking the methods of men of science?"

To all this we reply that we do most strenuously occupy ourselves with these matters, but that every such effort is paralyzed by the fact that not only is vivisection by its very nature the most cruel of all cruelties, and therefore the head and front of offending, but that it is, alone of all cruelties, protected by State legislation, although other and minor barbarisms are officially condemned. So long as the *principle* of cruelty is thus encouraged and kept alive by law, in the highest walks of science, all attempts to extirpate lesser cruelties elsewhere must prove unavailing.

✓ How, for instance, can we teach our children the duties of humanity toward dumb animals, when, in the course of their studies at school and college, they learn what horrors are perpetrated in the work-rooms of science by the masters and professors they are expected to revere and to imitate? ✓ Or how can we profitably interfere to check the barbarities of the streets, when it is in the power of the brutal carman or drover to retort that, no matter how he may maltreat his beast, he can not approach the cruelties of the physiological laboratory which have the full sanction of the law? How can we urge him to cease working some old and worn-out horse, broken down by fatigue in the service of man, when the result of our charitable interference may possibly be, not the well-earned rest of a life-long toil, nor even quick death under the blow of the knacker's axe, but a long and horrible agony in some infernal school of vivisection for the benefit of "science"? Alas, we can but stand by silent, praying only in our hearts that the poor, ill-used creature may rather be worked till he drops dead in his harness, than be delivered over to the tormentors to end his innocent life of faithful service in the pains of hell. Everything, rather than the scalpel, the saw and the hot iron of the vivisector!

We demand justice! Justice not only for innocent and defenseless animals, but for men themselves.

The present law of this country is a law manifestly unjust and cowardly. It attacks the dwarfs and respects the giants of cruelty. The poor man who, in the interests of his livelihood, accidentally over-drives his horse or his donkey, is punished by the very Legislature which protects the learned professor who flays and burns alive scores of living creatures systematically.

The law ought to be administered equally to all men, whether rich or poor, professors or laics, ignorant or learned. Either it ought to be admitted that there is no harm in illtreating animals—and in such case a law which protects them is ridiculous—or the man who cuts up a dog alive in a laboratory merits punishment as much as the man who flogs a horse in the street, and in such case the law ought not to favor the social rank or pretext of the first malfactor at the expense of the last. If vivisection is to be permitted, encouraged and endowed by the State, then societies for the protection of animals from cruelty have no *locus standi*, and ought to be abolished as anomalies at once absurd and illogical.

A good Christian once said to me, "I should never be happy in the joys of Heaven if I knew that other souls were condemned to eternal torment. Such a thought as that would render all my own felicity bitter to me." Well, this is something like the feeling of anti-vivisectionists with regard to the suffering of the victims of the physiological laboratory. The frightful thought that every day the rising sun will witness the commencement of hundreds of long drawn martyrdoms of inoffensive creatures throughout Christendom; the thought that every evening when we go to our rest the silence of night will but bring to these unhappy beings prolonged suffering, terror and agonizing death; the thought that such things take place, not by accident, or by nature, in far-off uncivilized countries, but here, in our midst, in the heart of our towns, next door, maybe, to our own home, by deliberate, organized, systematic law-abiding act—this is what tears the heart, embitters life and forces us to the reflection that, after all, human civilization and human progress are but fever dreams, futile, meaningless and grotesque.

And this is why, when the vivisectors ask us angrily, "What right have you to meddle with the researches of scientific men?" that we turn upon them with greater anger and retort in our turn, "What right have you to render earth uninhabitable and life insupportable for men with hearts in their bosoms?"

It is not the fact, as the partisans of vivisection are never weary of declaring, that the public has shown itself incapable of judging scientific necessities, but rather that the scientists have shown themselves incapable of recognizing the obligations of public morality. If in matters of technical physiology it be fair to regard the public as "profane," it is equally correct to regard the experts of vivisection as "profane" in relation to the principles of moral conduct. Does the diploma of physiologists entitle them to pose as the exclusive arbiters of morality? Or is it not rather the truth that, being themselves indifferent to the interests of morality and incompetent to deal with psychic considerations, they assume the defenders of these to be ignorant of scientific exigencies and incapable of understanding them, solely because of their own moral blindness?"

Now, the fact is that the question is quite as much of moral as of physical interest.

If society be right in refusing to recognize the infallibility of a purely ecclesiastical caste in matters affecting the public conscience—as, for instance, in respect of religious persecution—it is equally right in refusing to admit the assumption of infallibility on the part of a caste exclusively scientific and materialistic in matters similarly affecting the public conscience. It was in the teeth of powerful vested interests that the world rejected compromise with the Inquisition and with the slave traffic, and the same considerations which influenced civilized men in dealing with these institutions must equally influence them to-day, face to face with the claims and interests of vivisection.

It is vain to urge that the majority of modern torturers for science's sake are educated, intelligent and eminent men, illustrious savants, venerable professors, who are themselves the best judges of what is necessary for science—who may safely be trusted to act for the best, and who are pre-eminently humane and sympathetic in their conduct and methods. Precisely the same was said with equal truth of the majority of torturers for religion's sake. They, too, were the learned, reverend and eminent men of their time, and like the vivisectors, were often genial and polished members of society, chiefs of distinction, dignitaries of high importance in the State. And there is no reason to doubt that the atrocities of which they were the eager authors and contrivers were instigated, not by a love of cruelty, but by zeal for the honor of religion and for the advance of the church, and by ardor for the good of humanity.

Every custom that the world has seen, whatever its barbarity, has found apologists, simply because of its being a custom.

History shows us that the abolition of human and other sacrifices in religious cults was in its time denounced as a menace for the faith, as an evidence of morbid sensibility and a symptom of degeneracy. Gladiatorial combats, cruel and barbarous amusements of all kinds, formerly popular, have in their turn been suppressed, and always in spite of the clamorous protestations of persons interested in their maintenance. No pretext based on the pretended utility of vivisection ought to exempt it from the category of practices unworthy of a civilized era.

The abuse of force is an inexcusable crime and shame in those who claim despotic authority, and to seek to justify such abuse by representing it as a means of attaining a praiseworthy end is to argue, as did a certain celebrated brigand, who attempted to excuse his acts of violence by saying, "If I have committed robbery, I have robbed only heretics with the intention of enriching the coffers of the true Church."

Cruelty is always cruel, and only Jesuits and Paul Berts will dare to rehabilitate the sophistry expressed in the ecclesiastical axiom, "The end justifies the means," even when the "end" is "scientific progress," the means "suffering the most atrocious that the imagination can conceive," and the victims, beings incapable of defending themselves or of avenging their wrongs.

Happily for humanity, the arbiters of the national conscience are neither the ecclesiastics nor the biologists, but the people.

I reflect on the history of the inquisition, of slavery and of despotism, and I have confidence in the future!

There is a better gospel than that of intellectual science, there is a higher law than that of physical utility. Do not let us fear, any of us, that by living up to the best and noblest in us we shall miss any good thing that might have been ours by baser means. The greater includes the lesser, and the science of Heaven encompasses all lower knowledges. Only let us seek first the kingdom of God and God's justice, and all these things shall be added unto us. There is nothing the righteous man may not know, for the spirit in him is divine, and able to unfold all secrets in their order.

For love is the universal solvent, and love's method is in all its unfoldings consistent with its object and intent.

In conclusion, I recommend specially to my brethren of the medical faculty those brave and worthy words which Dr. Samuel Johnson addressed to the physiologists of his day:

✓ "May all men of heart who follow the noble science of medicine, the aim of which is the relief of suffering, publicly condemn the practices of vivisection, for they are of a nature to discredit their profession, and will end by extinguishing in their votaries those sentiments which alone deserve the confidence of the public, and the absence of which is more to be dreaded than the worst of physical evils."

A FORM OF TREATMENT.

[CONTRIBUTED BY MRS. SARA HARRIS, BERKELEY, CAL.]

I am Spirit divine in essence and included in the Universal. In the inmost and True Being I am not and can not be diseased, for *I am* perfect in the image and likeness of God. Over me matter has no control, for matter has neither sensation, intelligence or substance; the real is spirit; only truth is eternal. The beliefs of the race, the current thought of the day, the influence of those around me, both seen and unseen, my own error, ignorance, grief, fear, malice, envy, revenge, murder, jealousy, shall no longer reflect disease in my body.

God is my life, and I can not know death; God is my health, and I can not know disease; God is my strength, and I can not know weakness; God is my peace, have no fear, be not afraid, for God is working through me both to will and to do His good pleasure. God's good pleasure is that I should have peace of mind, health of body and purity of life. This is already true of me in the Real Being.

And now, in the name of the Universal Spirit of Truth, and through faith in omnipresent good, I declare all that is good, true and beautiful of me in spirit to be true of me in body. Error and ignorance have held me in bondage; the truth of the Real Being shall set me free.

LEAVES FROM STUDENTS' NOTE BOOK.

SPIRITUAL SCIENCE CATECHISM.

What is God?

Infinite Spirit. All Good.

What is man?

The offspring of Infinite Spirit.

What is matter?

The most external or lowest expression of universal substance.

Is it necessary to study pathology?

Spiritual healers require no such study.

Please define Mortal Mind.

Changing states or conditions of human belief.

Is God the Author of Sin, Sickness and Death?

Decidedly He is not.

What is error?

Misapprehension of Truth.

Is diagnosis necessary?

Not in all cases; it is, however, often desirable.

Should treatment be silent, and how long continue?

Silence is the greatest power. No stated time.

Some assert that our Systems of Religion are governed by our Systems of Medicine. What is your opinion?

They are in turn influenced by each other.

What did Jesus mean when he said, "The works that I do, ye shall do also"?

Exactly what he said.

Is a sick person the image and likeness of God?

The real man is never sick, only the mortal appendage of man, which is not God's image, can be sick.

Is it possible to always avoid physical suffering?

It is, provided you understand and obey the divine law of harmony.

How can we best overcome fear?

By boldly facing whatever we regard as calculated to inspire fear, then bravely defying its power to harm, which can only be successfully accomplished through unfaltering trust in Infinite Good.

Does the suicide find a friend in death?

Suicide is arrant folly, and folly can not promote our welfare.

Is soul in the body?

It is not, but spirit uses the body as an instrument or machine.

Should we forsake all for Truth?

Decidedly, but we must ever remember that truth only calls upon us to sacrifice error, and error is to truth what commonest glass is to purest gems.

Does chemicalization always follow treatment?

Not invariably when it does it marks a conflict between truth and error, and truth must triumph.

Are nerves the source of pain or pleasure?

Nerves transmit the sensations they can not produce, as electric wires convey intelligence they can not furnish.

Does spiritual science ignore all medicine and hygene?

It does not rely on medicine, which it far surpasses,

and it includes the soul and practice of genuine hygiene.

Must a healer be well educated?

In the sense that educated means morally and mentally unfolded, yes; in a scholastic sense it is not necessary.

Do you believe in heredity?

So far as mental and physical leanings are concerned we do, but all hereditary taints can be eliminated.

Can obstetrics be practiced in this science?

Not only can be but must be.

Do you object to mesmerism and mediumship?

Mesmerism is vastly inferior to Spiritual Science. Mediumship is a blessing when rightly understood.

What are the prime causes of sickness?

Ignorance of the Law of Health; lack of individuality, and too great love of the senses.

Is not metaphysical science important from a secular point of view?

Unquestionably, as metaphysical methods are the only ones which permanently efface crime.

Can we treat animals successfully?

Without difficulty, if they love and respect you, they respond very quickly to your every thought.

Do our departed friends assist us?

Your "departed friends" are only "departed" in mortal belief, they are as truly your assistants in every good work as though you could see them physically.

What is the cause of a relapse?

Relapses are consequent upon imperfect acquaintance with truth and nervous susceptibility to one's surroundings.

Can we always resist disease, and ward it off, if we know how to do it?

Just as truly as you can make a roof water-tight or a ship seaworthy.

Is Repression one of the causes of nervous prostration?

Repression fosters crime, sickness and insanity. Eradicate evil desires, gratify lawful ones.

Please explain the words of Jesus, "He, that believeth in me, shall never see death"?

In the simplest interpretation of these words the fear of death and the pain accompanying physical dissolution is intended.

Do our spirits dwell within or without our bodies?

The spirit itself can not be wholly limited by the body, which it simply vitalizes, and through which it expresses itself.

What is the relation between the spiritual and the material body?

A relation similar to that existing betwen a performer and an instrument, or a man and his clothing.

What is the Odylic flame seen by clairvoyants?

Odylic, from *Od* (all pervading), means the astral, or emanating flame of vitality.

How do magnetic healers differ from metaphysicians?

In that they rely too much on bodily emanations and too little on mind.

What are mesmerism and magnetism? How do they differ?

Mesmerism is Anton Mesmer's limited system of psychology, which is founded upon a recognition of animal magnetism.

What is mind?

Intelligence manifesting in reason.

What is spirit?

Life itself; being; self-existent intelligent principle.

What is soul?

The innermost or affectional element in spirit, mind being the rational.

What is disease?

Inharmony; discord; lack of equilibrium.

How can we avoid contagious disease?

By cultivating a mental state which generates a counteracting vital force.

Why is disease more easily overcome in one person than another?

Because some persons are more tenacious of error, and at the same time more weakly susceptible than others.

Is there any definite rule as regards the length of a treatment?

Certainly not; for in order to treat or be treated successfully, you must forget time and place.

Why are some patients considered incurable?

Because spiritual perception of the means of their cure is lacking.

How does chemicalization differ from the crises of the hydropathist?

It differs only in this: that metaphysicians consider the mental cause, hydropathists the physical effect.

How can we avoid being drafted by those who are mentally, physically and spiritually starved?

By feeding on truth ourselves.

Is God in us, or are we in God?

The finite is in the Infinite.

How can we best attain and maintain perfect health?

By persistently acknowledging good to the exclusion of its opposite.

What are the qualifications necessary for a successful healer?

Supreme love of truth, coupled with intelligent liberality of sentiment.

How far has a physician the right to control the patient's will?

No right at all. Truth is submitted to conscience and reason, and must be embraced willingly.

What law governs the will, and how can we best direct it?

By concentrating our thought and affection upon that object we most desire to reach, and that persistently.

Is not pleasant, harmonious conversation often one of the best methods?

Converse with patients whenever you can without arousing opposition.

Is it necessary for the physician to be morally and spiritually superior to the patient?

It is difficult to gauge superiority, but no moral and mental standard can be too high.

Is it absolutely necessary that the patient should be receptive or negative?

Receptive to truth, yes. Negative to mortal belief, no.

Why is silent treatmennt best?

Because it does not arouse excited controversy, and gives the most phenomenal proof.

Are hereditary diseases (so-called) the most difficult to heal?

Not unless belief in their ineradicability is firmly rooted in the patient's mind. Much depends on the healer.

Should we always call the disease by name in healing?

Not unless the patient often thinks of and mentions it by name. When such is the case, deny it by name often and vigorously.

Is the subjugation of the bodily senses necessary?

The senses must be governed by reason. Where appetites dominate the will disease is inevitable.

Should we ignore our indvividuality in our treatments for any set rule?

No, never use any formula nor adopt any rule which does not appeal to your sense of right.

How can we best discover truth?

By cultivating a willingness to forego all else for its possession.

Is not the personality of the patient often the object ve error that must be overcome?

The idiosyncracies and prejudices of the patient must be vanquished, and particularly all unkindness and animosity in thought, word or deed.

Is there any law of adaptability more potent than love and sympathy?

Love manifests itself in inevitable, spontaneous sympathy which reveals true union.

What is to be understood by perfection? and is it attainable in this life?

Perfection in its relative sense only implies perfect obedience to the highest truth perceived; this is practical.

Which are the most desirable teachers, books, experience, or conversation with superior minds?

Books and conversation are valuable only as they help persons to gain experience. Experience is the highest teacher.

Can the dead be raised?

In a figurative sense they can; those "dead in sin" can be raised to "newness of life." In a physical sense those seemingly dead can often be restored.

How can we best overcome selfishness?

By steadily fixing our thought and affection on universal human welfare.

Why are mental healers often called mercenary?

Probably because, like all other persons, they are often obliged to receive compensation for their services, and mercenary people, who are not true scientists, have invaded the ranks.

What is matter, and is it recognized in metaphysics?

Matter is the lowest expression or manifestation of mind.

Is matter a cause or effect?

Decidedly an effect, of which the cause is intelligent mind in every instance.

Do you teach metaphysical healing to be a recent revelation or discovery?

No, for it was well known to the ancients. It is only a recent discovery on the part of the masses.

Is this new phase of healing similar to what Jesus practiced and taught?

It is identical with the healing work accomplished by inspired teachers and prophets everywhere, in every age.

What is meant by the true Christ?

The essential life; divine inmost principle of human nature; God manifest.

Jesus said: "Greater works than these shall ye do." What did he mean by greater?

That whereas his work was literally confined to Palestine, similar work should at length be accomplished everywhere.

How many senses has man, and how many discovered or recognized by the masses?

Seven; for in addition to the five recognized universally, clairvoyance and intuition are clearly distinct.

Are metaphysical teachings mental, sentimental, scientific or inclusive?

Inclusive in the broadest sense of the word; but not so sentimental as scientific when thoroughly sound.

Is it wise to disregard natural laws?

True metaphysicians love, honor and obey divine natural law. Laws are human inventions.

Are anatomy and physiology taught by metaphysicians, or is an understanding of those subjects necessary to the successful healer?

Anatomy and physiology are valuable studies, but not always necessary.

Is there any difference (except in name) between metaphysicians, Christian scientists, mental scientists, mental healers and spiritual healers?

Very little real difference, save that some Christian scientists make of Mrs. Eddy a final authority. Mental science is not so broad and inclusive a term as spiritual science, while the phrase spiritual healing is correct, but scientifically inadequate.

Can wasted lungs be restored?

Under many circumstances they can be; but it is difficult to decide how far medical diagnosis is accurate.

Can we learn to overcome fatigue?

If we live in harmonious thought we shall sleep naturally when we need rest without feeling exhaustion.

If a belief exist that climate and atmosphere are unhealthy what is the result?

Nervous and susceptible people are made ill through imbibing prevailing fear.

Do you believe in contagious diseases?

Everything is contagious if we are susceptible. We believe in contagious health, which is the antidote to all disorder.

What, in brief, is the cardinal truth of metaphysics?

Good is infinite and eternal. Evil is only a mortal inversion.

Is it possible to overcome a belief in pain while suffering from it?

It is, by turning the thought resolutely to the source of joy. It is often desirable, however, to avail one's self of a healer's services when pain is acute.

How can we best cultivate a truly spiritual condition?

By always acting in harmony with our deepest conviction of right.

Can the skillful metaphysician ever expect to practice surgery?

Mechanical surgery is a special study, which no one is thoroughly adapted for unless he be in a broad sense a true metaphysician.

Would you allow the use of any material remedies? We know Jesus sometimes used them.

If you carefully read the gospels you will learn that Jesus trusted entirely in the efficacy of Divine Spirit, and in the use of material simples reversed all prevailing beliefs.

Do you consider that metaphysical methods are sufficient to meet every condition and overcome all discomfort?

Decidedly we do, as it would be the height of folly to attribute potency to matter (the lesser) which we denied to mind (the greater).

Are chronic cases more difficult to heal than acute ones?

Not for any other reason than because old fears and prejudices are harder to remove than recent ones.

Are absent treatments as beneficial as others?

Frequently far more so, as mind thereby demonstrates its power more absolutely.

Is there any objection to the term Christian science?

None whatever, save that it is distinctly ecclesiastical, and liable to arouse prejudice.

Can anyone become a healer?

Every one can heal some one, as healing is possible through an immense diversity of methods.

Is there any difference between prayer and faith cures and metaphysical healing?

Metaphysical healing includes the exercise of faith and prayer, but is broader in its definitions.

Do you hold that metaphysics is superior to all other methods, and especially so in insanity?

Unquestionably as all other methods are perforce inferior, and in cases of insanity worthless.

Will disease eventually be overcome and health reign supreme on earth?

Never doubt this and ever work to hasten the day.

How can we overcome materialism and skepticism?

By clearly presenting spiritual truth to honest minds without anxiety.

Is suffering an absolute necessity?

It is necessary as long as you experience it, for you can only outgrow it by interior development.

Shall we in the good time coming die well?

You will leave this earth when you are ready for promotion without sickness.

Is it possible, or desirable to have our lives continued in our earthly bodies beyond a ripe old age?

It is desirable to continue living surrounded by physical limitations until you have ripened spiritually so that you can enjoy a higher state of existence. Physical immortality is a foolish dream, as no one could very long be contented with physical restrictions. Age signifies nothing to spirit, growth is everything. Strive to grow so that you are prepared for a more glorious state of expression, and do not worry yourselves about the destiny of your flesh.

APPENDIX.

In compliance with the expressed wish of many of our subscribers we take great pleasure in here appending a few thoroughly authentic testimonies written by persons of unimpeachable integrity, who gladly publish their grateful acknowledgment of the inestimable boon confered upon themselves through a practical application of the principle of the science to the advocacy and elucidation of which this book is devoted. We have only put before our readers a very few narratives out of hundreds which have been sent to us. Those which we here publish we have carefully selected as being of a character to impress and interest the general reader. Many others were quite as forcible and important, but as our work had already exceeded originally proposed limits, we were compelled to confine ourselves to a few typical instances. In offering these facts to the public we do not desire in any way to detract from the well-earned fame of many noble and honest men and women who conscientiously and effectively practice medicine. What we do contend for is the unanswerable declaration that, without having recourse to any outward appliances, the sovereign power of mind alone is adequate to the accomplishment of all and more than all that medicine can accomplish. Now with reference to medical men and women, magnetic healers and others allow us to state our position clearly; we believe them capable of relieving many sufferers, not alone or chiefly by their art but in consequence of their exercising an influence for good over their patients in ways they often fail to comprehend. In California especially, where we have had many pleasant relations with eminent medical practitioners of the several schools we have found in many instances great breadth and liberality of sentiment and a willingness to investigate this subject.

Druggists, whose business it is to compound prescriptions, and who, therefore, have a special interest in the support of an external medical system, have also in many instances freely testified to their knowledge of the effectiveness of mental therapeutics. One highly accomplished young gentleman in San Francisco, a leading druggist in the city, who attended our classes frequently, was, in our opinion, as thoroughly practical a metaphysician as any who would feel it against their conviction to even administer hot water to a person suffering acute pain who desired relief from so simple and innocent a remedy. Intolerance and prejudice against doctors and apothecaries on the part of mental healers, and the equally unreasoning denunciation of metaphysicians by the advocates of physic, are alike irrational eccentricities of dwarfed and perverted minds. While the spiritual position we have taken for many years we can never relinquish, while we *positively know* and have *abundantly demonstrated* the *absolute sufficiency* of *unassisted mind* to overcome ailments which no medicine can reach, we at the same time fully recognize the necessity and use of duly accommodated truth, and by this we mean an application of healing power to individual necessities in accordance with the understanding and conviction of those working and those worked upon. All over the world the medical profession is coming to represent a truer and broader eclecticism than it ever could represent, until the spiritual awakening of recent years called prominent attention to the spiritual element in therapeutics, and threw down the gauntlet to modern materialism. Mrs. Eddy, of Boston, deserves unstinted praise for opening the door into the light for multitudes, and we who say this by no means endorse all the positions taken by that remarkable woman, whose extreme views necessarily excite an immense amount of controversy. Dr. Evans, that grand whole-souled humanitarian whose many works on divine, spiritual and mental modes of healing are acknowledged text-books of priceless value, has also done more than words can tell, to turn the current of popular opinion in the right direction. Many, many others, writers, teachers, practitioners, have sown good seed abundantly, which is now happily beginning to bear fruit in a happier condition of affairs the world over.

TESTIMONY OF MRS. C. M. LEWIS, 156 WARREN STREET, BOSTON.

A little boy who had catarrh, and had suffered from birth, whose face was continually distorted, and whose nights were disturbed from inability to breathe, was entirely cured. He had been under the care of two medical doctors, without benefit. This child had one hand covered with warts which had refused to yield to every kind of treatment, but with the radiation of truth dissolved into nothingness, they went like dew before the sun, gradually fading away.

This case was healed three years ago, and has stood intact. I mention this as so many claim that mental cures are not lasting. All that I shall mention are cases that have remained cured a year or more.

An old lady who had suffered long with sciatica, and who had lain only on one side for over five years, was entirely cured with one treatment. She can now lie on one side as well as the other with perfect ease; cured two years ago at time of writing.

In a case of eczema that had been under a physician's care, and was being treated with morphine every three hours, the patient after first treatment was left sleeping and slept quietly through the night without morphine or any drug whatever. A complete cure was performed and morphine totally dispensed with. This was more than a year ago. The lady was eighty-six years of age.

I was called to a case where a young man had hemorrhage, and was afflicted with distressing cough. A doctor said he must spend the winter in Colorado if he wished to live, as he would not be responsible if he remained in the East. He responded readily to the truth without traveling, and to-day is strong and well, reflecting truth instead of error. Cured two years ago.

A babe three months old, who had been treated to eight different kinds of food in its short existence, and who was discharging blood all day before coming under treatment came into harmony after first treatment and was healed; is now quite well, two years old. I could give many more instances where truth has dispelled error and where light has proved the nothingness of darkness in equally conclusive ways.

AN INTERESTING CASE.

I was called to a lady very ill of pneumonia. It was feared she was dying the morning I was summoned. I found her, physically speaking, in a very high fever, her lungs so congested that her breathing was like the panting of a dog. The fever soon began to subside, the respiration grew easier and longer, under my "thought," or, at the call of *my* spirit to *hers* to come up out of its physical bondage onto the plane of spirit where pneumonia does not exist. During the treatment I received sudden and strong impression, like a message to "treat the bowels, keep the bowels open," a condition which I believe the regular practitioner seeks to avoid. This surprised me as the point of seeming danger, in the thought of patients and attendants was centered elsewhere, but remembering teh injunction: "quench not the spirit," I obeyed the inner prompting. At my next visit I was told that the patient had passed a tape worm, in two sections, which by actual measurement was seventy-two feet long. The lady's restoration to health was rapid.

Miss Susie C. Clark,
15 Centre St., Cambridgeport, Mass.

Among other cases not generally supposed curable by mental or spiritual methods by those who do not yet realize that the physical is alone the realm of limitation, I would record the cure of some very severe corns and bunions, a case of eczema, one of dyspepsia of twenty-two years' standing, and a case of peritonitis which regular physicians had given up to die. The water had stopped and could not be drawn with instruments, unsuccessful attempts to do so having been made, causing great torture. In fifteen minutes after I entered the room the water passed freely without the patient's consciousness that the stricture and inflammation were removed. Recovery was immediate.

I also treated a lady while two large, double teeth were extracted, she experiencing no pain, or unpleasant sensation.

MISS SUSIE C. CLARK,
15 Centre St., Cambridgeport, Mass.

A TUMOR CURED.

A lady who had an ovarian tumor of nearly eight years, growth was healed in five treatments, although before the fifth treatment she pronounced herself cured, the tumor having gradually subsided until it entirely disappeared. A few months before I studied Spiritual Science, I spent a day or two in her home, during which time she was wonderfully relieved, although she did not then mention it. Does this not show that the spiritual power which heals is a natural out-breathing, rather than the result of mental argument, whether in "silent mind," or in verbal presentation? The Eternal Spirit is always present to heal, if one lives in the conscious realization of this truth.

MISS MARY E. STEINGARDT,
1 Pearl St., Lynn, Mass.

TESTIMONIES FURNISHED BY DR. AND MRS. CONGAR, 247 OGDEN AVE., CHICAGO.

San Antonio, Tex., April 22, 1884.

The case of Miss Anna Phillips had baffled the skill of medical doctors, and she came to us as a last resort. Inheriting as she thought kidney difficulty from her father, who had died from that disease, she had given up all hope of recovery, and constantly feared insanity. She had been unable to walk, or go up and down stairs for over a year. She was healed by seven treatments, entirely mental and spiritual. Miss Phillips proclaimed the glad tidings of health far and near, and was a striking advertisement for truth seen and read by all.

Rosa C. Congar.

San Antonio, Tex., April, 1884.

The case of Mrs. W. N. Coffy, was a combination of uterine difficulties, indigestion, constipation and inaction of liver and kidneys, producing partial blindness and dizziness. One treatment produced a marked change in her condition. She was entirely restored in twenty-four treatments. Few cases can be found more complicated or physically worse than the above.

Rosa C. Congar.

Galveston, Tex., March 1884.

Mrs. Rickey had been unable to work or walk for a year, suffering constant pain resulting from uterine complications, with nervous exhaustion.

Only eight treatments were needed to restore her to health both of body and mind. She reported herself strong and well, six months later, expressing great gratitude for such singular benefit.

Rosa C. Congar.

OAKLAND, CAL., July, 1887.

The case of Mrs. J. S., of New Britain, Conn., who visited California, as a last hope, was one of chronic liver and kidney difficulty, attended with severe cough. She declared that by simply talking with us, she felt better. In twenty treatments she was well. Six months later she told us $1,000 would not pay for all we had done for her. She returned to her home in Connecticut, a strong, healthy woman sixty-five years of age.

ROSA C. CONGAR.

CASE OF CHAS. CLOUGH.

OAKLAND, CAL., July, 1886.

Diagnosis: Rheumatism for over six months; constipation, stomach and liver troubles; had only two weeks to remain before leaving for Mexico. Could he be helped in that time? We gave him strong hope that he could be very much benefited. With four treatments his lameness was entirely removed, and he declared he was in every way woll, and could walk as far as he ever could in his life.

DR. M. E. CONGAR.

CASE OF JOHN MEYERS.

GALVESTON, TEX., March 5, 1884.

Diagnosis: Injured by a fall; kidneys failed to do their work; sunstroke, constipation, rheumatic pains in right shoulder, rupture, etc., etc.; declared he was only fit for the grave; tried mental treatment to please his wife; was healed in twenty-six treatments; volunteered a strong testimonial; a German rationalist, without the least faith to build upon, but looked at the end of one month like a new man.

ROSA C. CONGAR.

SAN ANTONIO, TEX., May, 1884.

Mrs. Mary N—— for seven years had been a victim to periodical attacks of sick-headache; was a physical wreck. Her right lung was diseased, and she suffered from a constant cough and many other unpleasant symptoms. Mrs. N—— was healed in twelve treatments by purely metaphysical methods, and said she felt better than in twenty years previously.

MRS. R. C. CONGAR.

GALVESTON, TEX., February, 1884.

The case of Mr. W. O. Rutledge was one of long standing; said he had taken drugs enough in the past twenty years to stock a drug store; was but a wreck of his former self, the result of a diseased heart, inaction of the digestive organs, and poisoned blood; used tobacco excessively; was perfectly healed in forty-five treatment. He always slept during treatment. He was also enabled to relinquish his tobacco habit. We received many letters from him during the next year, in which he always reported himself strong and fleshy.

ROSA C. CONGAR.

EXPERIENCE OF MRS. LILY D. BOTHWELL, SAN DIEGO, CAL.

In 1874 I had the misfortune to sprain my right knee; slight lameness for six or eight weeks was the result, though I did not at that time realize its serious import. It gave me no permanent trouble. At times I lamed myself for a few weeks, by making some quick movement. One morning in February, 1886, I awoke to find that I could bear no weight on the right foot. Not sensing the actual condition, I gave it no serious thought until the third day when I found that the whole limb was losing power. Two surgeons pronounced the case "fluid around the joint." The limb continued to grow weaker and finally began to shrink. During three months of deep mental and physical depression I was under the care of a most capable surgeon, whose every effort to relieve the trouble seemed futile. The case baffled experience. The weakness of the limb became so excessive that day and night I was obliged to rest it upon a piliow.

A lady asked me one day why I did not try mental cure. I replied that I knew nothing about it. She then spoke of a metaphysician whom she knew to be very successful, and (to use an old phrase) as a last resort I sent for her. She gave me treatments for a week without visible effect on the physical. A fow hours after the seventh treatment, sitting quite alone in my room reading Dr. Evans' Primitive Mind Cure, the chapter on the Art of Forgetting Disease, with crutches beside me, my foot resting on a chair and a pillow under the knee, I became so deeply engrossed in the subject that I was oblivious of self until I realized that I was standing on the opposite side of the room, and that I had walked there of my own free *will*, quite without the aid of the friendly crutches, for there they stood beside my vacant chair. I was greatly excited and continued to walk, cry and laugh alternately for an hour or more. As the different members of my family returned and found what had been done they were in much the same state of mental excitement that I was in.

The following morning the metaphysician came as

usual, and she, too, was quite overcome when she saw the wonderful work that had been accomplished. It was like one of the so-called miracles of old, so marvelous were the results. I shall ever hold this dear lady, Mrs. Shields, of Berkeley, Cal., in grateful and loving remembrance. I consider her work one of the greatest achievements of Spiritual Science. *No weakness was felt in the knee at any time after I began walking.* A course of twenty-one treatments entirely cured me. Some two weeks later Mr. Colville came to Oakland and opened a class in Spiritual Science. Eager for enlightenment I joined it. After the sixth lesson I had the misfortune to slip on the sidewalk and sprain the knee again. It became swollen and useless. Once more I was obliged to resort to crutches. I felt heartbroken that by carelessness I should bring that calamitous condition upon myself. The following morning I attended the class and after the lecture stated the case and asked a class treatment. Mr. Colville said "You have heard the lady's statement, now give her your concentrated thought that she is not lame, that she can walk." The lameness was gone instantly and I arose and walked. My husband carried my crutches home, and from that time I have not used them nor have I been lame.

N. B.—The incident recorded here took place on the campgrounds bordering Lake Merritt, Oakland, Cal., in June, 1886, and was witnessed by fully two hundred persons.

THE EDUCATOR,

CAUSE AND CURE OF ALL DISEASE.

A work of over 650 pages, just issued.

By Rosa Cadman Congar, M.H., and Dr. M. E. Congar.

This work is made up of Twenty-four Chapters, and brief summary.

CHAPTER I.—**Introductory**, by Dr. Congar.

CHAPTER II.—**Causes**: Ignorance and neglect.

CHAPTER III.—**Remedies**: Innumerable and simple; should be as varied in application as are the faces of the human family.

CHAPTER IV.—**Lungs, Stomach and Circulation**: These vital organs and their functions duly considered.

CHAPTER V.—**Heart and Liver.** Their relation and importance considered.

CHAPTER VI.—**Constipation and Piles**: This one chapter is worth the price of the book to every family.

CHAPTER VII.—**Baths, Gymnastics and Ventilation**: The lessons taught in this division are all exceedingly important.

CHAPTER VIII.—**Hygienic Food**: If you desire perfect health, you must make a careful study and live the teachings of this chapter.

CHAPTER IX.—**Physiology of Marriage**: Advice and counsel that parents should not ignore.

CHAPTER X.—**Fevers and Inflammations**: Only signals of distress; friends, and not enemies.

CHAPTER XI.—**Bowels, Kidneys and Bladder**: If diseased, because of bad treatment.

CHAPTER XII.—**Sunshine and Shadow**: Important, *very important* health requisites.

CHAPTER XIII.—**Dress**: The subject dressed as only woman can dress it.

CHAPTER XIV.—**Colds, Catarrh, Consumption, Bronchitis, Asthma and Indigestion**: Causes shown, and simple remedies prescribed which have never failed.

CHAPTER XV.—**Useful Recipes**: Condensed items; necessities in every household.

Published by

Facsimile Publisher
Ashok Vihar, Delhi-110052 (India)
Website: www.facsimilepublisher.com

Distributed by

Gyan Books Pvt. Ltd.
5, Ansari Road, Daryaganj, New Delhi-110002 (India)
E-mail: books@gyanbooks.com, Website: www.gyanbooks.com

2 222000 014612